COUNTDOWN for DECISION

COUNTDOWN

Maj. General John B. Medaris,

with ARTHUR GORDON

for DECISION

U. S. Army, Ret.

G. P. Putnam's Sons   New York

Library of Congress Catalog Card

Number: 60-13671

MANUFACTURED IN THE UNITED STATES OF AMERICA

VAN REES PRESS • NEW YORK

TO those many people in Springfield, Ohio, who contributed to my early preparation for life . . . to those stalwarts of the U. S. Army, particularly Secretary Wilber M. Brucker, who gave me opportunity for accomplishment . . . to those officers, soldiers, and civilians of the Army Ballistic Missile Agency, including Wernher von Braun and his dedicated team of scientists and engineers, all of whom gave me the sum of their effort and faith in time of frustrating trials . . . to my devoted wife, whose patience and humanity have given me strength and purpose . . . and to my children and grandchildren with the prayer that they will find something of lasting value herein that may contribute to their future in a life of freedom . . . this book is gratefully dedicated.

Contents

		PAGE
Prologue		vii

CHAPTER

I.	One Day in Washington	1
II.	The Making of a Missile-Man	10
III.	The Beginnings of the Dream	23
IV.	From G-1 to V-2—and Beyond	32
V.	From Hot War to Cold	48
VI.	Out of the Frying Pan	62
VII.	Who Was Doing What	79
VIII.	Thumbnail Biography of a Guided Missile	86
IX.	I Take Over My New Command	98
X.	The Trial of My Soul—Personal and Official	113
XI.	The Shadow of the Nickerson Affair	129
XII.	Of Men, Monkeys, and Nose Cones	141
XIII.	The Beep That Came to Dinner	151
XIV.	Frantic Days Hath November	165
XV.	The Valley of Indecision	180
XVI.	On the Threshold of Space	192
XVII.	"Goldstone Has the Bird!"	210

CHAPTER		PAGE
XVIII.	The Road Starts Downhill	227
XIX.	Wanted: One Million Pounds of Thrust	237
XX.	The Last Mile	248
XXI.	The Project Snatchers	257
XXII.	A Long Look at the State of the Nation	270
XXIII.	The Summing Up	289
	Epilogue	297

Illustrations will be found following page 114.
These photographs appear through the courtesy
of the U. S. Army and the Huntsville *Times*.

Prologue

In the countdown to the launching of a big missile, the transition from success to failure—from glistening beauty to flaming disaster—can be sudden and complete. But the clock *can* be stopped—disaster *can* be avoided. Hundreds of instruments are monitoring everything related to the missile to catch the slightest indication that all is not perfect. But the instruments can only define the problem—they cannot supply the answer. The key to success is still in the hands of people—constantly watchful, instantly ready to make a *decision*. If a small red light or a single wavering needle on a dial goes undetected, or if the first sign of trouble is not followed immediately by firm decision and instant action, the work of months can be destroyed in seconds.

Finally, in the last few moments before launch, all the actions that will release the pent-up power of flaming thrust are turned over to "automatic." Now, without positive human action the whole process will proceed inevitably to the final result.

But even during those last tense seconds a skilled and experienced hand holds the "cutoff" button. Decisive action will *still* stop the automatic sequence, hold the missile, return the whole complex system to a state of inertia from which a new start can be made.

Throughout the whole process the key to success is *decision*. Knowledge, experience, understanding, and resolute willingness to accept responsibility must stand ready and able to recognize that the clock is ticking—that delay means disaster—that in the blinking of an eyelash the great rocket may be engulfed in roaring flames unless the hand closes, and the decisive commands ring out: "Cutoff!"

So also I believe that decision is the key in the countdown of history toward the survival or destruction of our way of life, and quite possibly toward the survival or destruction of the human race. To a terrifying degree, the pattern of the future depends upon the decisions taken today. There is no escaping this, for the clock of human life—the clock of history—is always running. Unlike the countdown at a missile-launching position, there is no one who can call "Hold" and stop the moving hands of the clock of human destiny.

Positive, affirmative decision is the lifeblood of all organized human activity, and the only process by which progress is made. The absence of decision is in itself a decision—a negative one—and always spells trouble in the future. The U-2 disaster may well be a case in point. Why were we forced to use the vulnerable U-2? Much earlier it should have been replaced by something of greater performance, far less exposed to attack—hopefully, even by a reconnaissance satellite. But there had been no affirmative decision, in time, to provide anything better.

Thirteen months before the first Sputnik shocked and startled the free world, the men of my Command knew they had the ability to launch a satellite. We had built the hardware; we had seen it perform—its upper stages loaded with sand (by directive) instead of the few extra pounds of propellant that would have put its payload into orbit. Even then the techniques required to make possible an effective reconnaissance satellite were well known, and a vigorously supported program could have placed an "eye-in-the-sky" by 1959. For months we begged and pleaded for the chance to put up the first earth satellite, flying the American flag. Could we obtain that permission? Could we get a decision? Only thirteen months and two Sputniks later! And so in May 1960 the U-2 was still flying—and the Russians shot it down.

I repeat, indecision can lead, ultimately, only to disaster.

Basically this book is concerned with the processes of decision

—and indecision. It is first of all the story of my own experiences with missiles and space during those hurried years when the Space Age was born. I shall try—without special pleading, I hope—to use that story as the background against which to outline some of the major difficulties facing our nation.

The truth is that intelligence and the power of decision have become the real "gold standards" of the future. Material resources become relatively unimportant when limitless sources of energy are available to all who have the brains to convert them. Yet brains alone are not enough. Intelligence, high moral courage, and the sense of personal responsibility that will produce timely decisions are the essential ingredients if our treasured liberties are to be preserved.

I believe we are engaged in a countdown for survival—a countdown which desperately demands immediate decision for action. The crisis we face permeates every element of our lives—personal, political, economic, military, and moral. I believe this countdown on the survival of the human race is God's direct challenge to the mankind He created, and to whom He gave the power of choice. Only decisive, courageous, morally guided action can seize the initiative in the struggle for world sanity and lead us away from the appalling choice between slavery and nuclear annihilation.

It is a simple matter to surrender one's liberties in return for physical security. It is, however, a miserable bargain, as all history testifies. Relieving the individual of the burden of decision is the despot's stock in trade, but the price has invariably been slavery.

We have been mockingly described as "the land of the free, and the home of the Committee." If democracy is to survive and to perpetuate the dignity and freedom of the individual, then we must strip for action. Informed and intelligent citizens must demand a vastly greater effectiveness in the decision-making processes of our government.

The countdown continues. It is natural, but can well be fatal, to ignore the insistent ticking of the clock—a persistent reminder that human life is temporal, that our control over our destiny is only partial—but above all, that if we are to influence the future we must hurry.

I do not know whether this countdown has yet gone over to the final automatic sequence, but the ever-increasing tempo of events, the almost compulsive substitution of reckless challenge for thoughtful counsel, and the seemingly irresistible way in which error piles upon error all give rather strong indications that perhaps it has. If so, only a steady hand at the controls and the decisive ability to shout "Cutoff!" can halt the inexorable march toward disaster.

That is why I have called this book *Countdown for Decision*.

COUNTDOWN for DECISION

CHAPTER I

One Day in Washington

Into the life of every man come moments in which, almost instinctively, he finds himself pausing and looking back. Such a moment came to me not long ago in Washington.

It was a cold day in February. I was waiting to be called to testify before a Congressional Committee on Science and Astronautics, a group of legislators intent on reviewing the President's proposal to transfer the von Braun group to NASA. Far from being dismayed by this prospect, I was rather looking forward to it. Congressional Committees were no novelty to me. Besides, it makes a man stand a little taller to think that the lawmakers of his country value his opinion and want him to express it fearlessly.

Outside the Capitol, traffic circled in the wintry sunshine. Inside, like the pulse of some great heartbeat, you could sense the vast governmental machinery turning. After 37 years in uniform, I was feeling a little strange in civilian clothes. My retirement from the Army was so recent that it was hard for me to realize that I was no longer part of the great military establishment that

I had guided for the past four years, first just the big missile and space business of the Army—the Army Ballistic Missile Agency —and then all the Army's missile development and production under the Army Ordnance Missile Command.

For the past four years I had been living, breathing, eating, sleeping, dreaming and planning nothing but rockets and missiles. There had been moments of high triumph and of bitter disappointment. There had been loyalties and disloyalties, brilliant successes and temporary setbacks—fierce competition both at home and abroad, honest opposition and not-so-honest obstruction—a dramatic, colorful, and complicated pattern.

I stared out of the window, remembering it all and weighing once again the advice of friends and associates who had urged me to write a book telling the whole story. I had been somewhat dubious about this. I had no desire to join the ranks of retired generals who wrote books generating more heat than light. On the other hand, I knew that I had been in a unique position to observe the dawn of the space age and the rise of the rocket from a harmless Fourth of July toy to the mightiest missile ever devised by man.

In trying to tell the story, I wondered where I would begin? At the beginning, logically, but where was that? My first remembered experience with a ballistic missile? To record that I would have to go back to a small boy in the little town of Springfield, Ohio, raising an air rifle, drawing a forbidden bead on a milkman's horse, and pulling the trigger "just to see what would happen." Quite a lot did!

I knew that in any attempt to tell my story, I would be up against a staggering problem of identification. In the whole vast missile and rocket area, there were Governmental agencies piled upon other agencies, military commands perched upon and competing with other military commands. Most of these had cumbersome names that were shortened habitually into almost equally confusing sets of initials. There were the code names of various projects, bewildering to the uninitiated. There were the names of the great weapons themselves—ancient gods like Thor and Jupiter rubbing shoulders with fixed stars like Polaris. There were beasts with strange names like Snark and Bomarc. There were whole generations of weapons like the Nike family: Nike Ajax, followed by Nike Hercules, followed by Nike Zeus.

I smiled as an old story crossed my mind, the one about the professor who visited a film studio in Britain where a movie was being made about life in ancient Rome. Along came a disgruntled-looking character in a toga with a laurel wreath around his head. "Are you Appius Claudius?" asked the learned visitor politely. "No," growled the ancient Roman in purest Cockney, "I'm un'appy as 'ell!"

I knew that unless I managed to sort out all the strange nomenclature, and filled in the background fully, my readers would also be "un'appy as 'ell!"

I knew, furthermore, that if I were to record the full story as I had lived and seen it I would have to sketch in some of my own personal background and history. For the story of a man in a job must necessarily include the story of how that man's particular qualities of mind and heart and temperament were fashioned, how they were tempered, how they grew. I would have to outline the mysterious unseen forces that seem to be at work throughout our lives, guiding us through apparently unrelated and meaningless experiences that later turn out to have enormous value for the task at hand. Who would have thought, for example, that my experience in trouble-shooting for a grocery chain three decades earlier would be of notable service to me in the task of putting the first American satellite into space? But it was. Or the year I spent as a brakeman on a railroad. Or the discipline hammered into me by the Marine Corps when I was a kid of sixteen.

Standing there, I thought of the unpredictability and irony of human existence—how, during World War II, for example, I had come uncomfortably close to being on the receiving end of a great German war rocket designed by a man who later was to become my friend and close associate, Wernher von Braun. Outside, a streetcar went by, and I remembered the days when I was a schoolboy conductor in Ohio, trying to earn a few extra pennies in a home broken by divorce. In those days, soon after the turn of the century, the world seemed stable and secure. Now I thought of the state of the nation, and the degree of peril it was facing, and the enormous responsibility borne by those who were charged with making the final decisions affecting the country's safety.

I knew in recent months the public had grown accustomed to an apparently endless parade of witnesses from the Armed Services, each testifying with monotonous consistency to the value of his own Service's role and the burning need for expansion of that role. I knew that consequently every Service witness was suspect; that to many people he stood convicted, before he opened his mouth, of special pleading. But I was determined that, to the best of my ability, my testimony would not be so tainted or my thinking so conditioned.

I was a loyal Army man. Nevertheless I was ready to testify that in my opinion a Navy weapon, the Polaris missile, capable of underwater launching from atomic submarines, represented our greatest offensive potential.

I was also prepared to say that, given all the circumstances, many of which I regretted, the transfer of the von Braun space team from the Army to a civilian agency probably meant that these brilliant ex-Germans would be used to fuller advantage than in the immediate past.

If asked, I would testify that the striking power of the Strategic Air Command represented our major deterrent force in being, and would be a weapon of great value for some time to come.

I was also determined to testify that our best—indeed our only —hope of a defense against missile attack resided in the anti-missile known as Nike-Zeus. This, to be sure, was an Army weapon. But my faith in Nike-Zeus was not based on its Army identity. It was based on my deep conviction that it could be made to work, and was the only weapon system in sight that could possess this capability very soon.

So many grave and urgent questions—and so little time! Standing there, waiting for my summons, I thought of the clashing ideologies and conflicting claims that had so sorely puzzled the nation. Which weapons were best? Which administrative system made most sense? How much defense in terms of dollars could the country afford? How much did it actually need? Was there any answer to the endless problem of inter-Service rivalry? Was another war inevitable? If so, what kind of war?

The question marks were endless, and no one man could pretend to have all the answers. But in some of these areas, at least, I knew my own position very clearly. I believed that in over-all military potential and weapons we were at least equal to the Russians, but that we were still lagging in the space race. I was convinced that the space race was of tremendous, perhaps decisive, importance in the struggle between our two philosophies. The winner of that race would not only be able to command the respect and allegiance of the hesitant, uncommitted peoples of the world—the winner would also have achieved a tremendous military advantage in case global war became a grim reality.

Furthermore, I did not think we would ever close the space and missile gap so long as we persisted in our well-meant but totally illogical efforts to separate military and civilian space capabilities, and continued in our fatal policy of splintering our limited space resources into unco-ordinated and competing fragments. This was the main conviction that I wished to bring to the attention of the Committee.

But there were other things, too, that weighed heavily on my mind and heart. The decline of individualism throughout the nation, the trend toward a passive conformity, the signs of slow erosion of the qualities of discipline and self-sacrifice among our people that had made this country great. The apparent inability of our leaders to seize the initiative in world affairs, and the lack of a clear call upon our people for action to support and preserve the free way of life. The apparent lack of any real sense of urgency in the face of great peril.

I was out of uniform, now—a civilian myself. Even so, I was troubled by the tendency of recent years to pile an ever-increasing civilian bureaucracy on top of the three Armed Services, with the consequent downgrading of the men who wore their country's uniform. I felt that in a republic, the principle of ultimate civilian control of the military was sound and right. But I did not feel that this control should be extended to operating decisions involving strategy or the choice of weapons. True, the military men did not always agree, but was this any reason for letting their voices grow faint to the councils of the nations? I did not think so.

Not all my thoughts as I stood there were gloomy or negative. There was in the nation, I knew, a tremendous reservoir of vitality, energy, skill, potential greatness. The American people had not lost their capacity to rise to emergency, to respond to crisis. They would meet any challenge, if the challenge was clearly indicated and their role in meeting it clearly defined. In their capacity for effort and sacrifice, they were always ahead of what their leaders dared demand of them. They had proved this in war after war. They would prove it again if . . .

There was a footstep behind me. "The Committee is ready for you now, General."

There was the usual interlude in which reporters jostled and flash bulbs flared. Then I found myself seated in the witness chair before the Committee. In the crowded gallery I could see my wife, and I managed a quick smile at her. That smile was based on a little family joke that we were sharing. For this occasion Ginna was wearing a brand-new mink stole. For years she had been dutifully following the unwritten law that forbids an Army wife to wear mink—if her husband has any dealings with civilian industry. She had had a squirrel cape which she always called her "Army mink." But as soon as I retired, she had rushed out and bought herself a piece of real mink. Now with her new stole and a cute little apology for a hat, she was looking extremely attractive—and I was glad to have her there, rooting for me.

In the next hour or so I made statements and gave answers to questions that resulted in a flurry of newspaper headlines that afternoon and the following day.

I tried to make clear to the Committee my conviction that our national policy of trying to keep civilian and military space efforts in separate compartments was a misguided attempt to divide the indivisible, resulting in waste, inefficiency, and duplication of effort.

I called for a unification of the entire space and missile program. To achieve this unification, I recommended that a joint command be created, bringing together the best brains and facilities of all three Services, with the top command rotating between Navy, Air Force, and Army. With all the Services in the act, I said, they would stop fighting among themselves for money or glory, and would concentrate on getting the show on the road. In order to assure adequate attention to the scientific side of space exploration, I urged that the scientific community be represented at command level.

Having made my unification plea as strongly as I could, I then turned to the country's urgent need for an antimissile missile—a "bullet to kill a bullet"—and the promise of such a capability latent in the Nike-Zeus system.

Nike-Zeus is a powerful rocket capable of carrying a nuclear warhead and designed to seek out and destroy an incoming ICBM outside the earth's atmosphere. As the Committee well knew, money had been appropriated for its development, and some for starting it toward production and deployment. But some of this money had never been spent, and there had never been a go-ahead for actual production. The two reasons usually given for the delay were that the complex and very large ground equipments for Zeus would be extremely expensive, and that there was as yet no final proof that the missile would do the job it was supposed to do.

My own conviction, based on personal familiarity with all the problems, was that Zeus *would* do the job it was supposed to do, and that no matter how expensive it was, we could not afford to leave our cities and our citizens defenseless against Russian rockets.

The eighteen members of the Committee listened attentively to my recommendations, and asked some searching questions. And it was during the rapid-fire question-and-answer period that the reason for the writing of this book, and the story to be told, suddenly crystallized in my mind.

I remember the moment very well. I was being queried about the difficulties I had had in obtaining from Washington clear and firm directives on which to base my own decisions in the development and production of big missiles. I was reminded that I once had said that the only thing that would put us back into the race with Russia was the ability to make a decision and then stick with that decision for at least two years.

It was at this point that one of the Congressmen leaned forward. "General," he said, almost plaintively, "is it true that because of all these administrative difficulties and this bureaucracy under which we are living, it is impossible for us to get the positive decisions that will carry us where we want to go?"

That, it seemed to me, was *the* question—the bleak and inescapable question of our times. Could a democracy, with its carefully constructed framework of checks and balances, really compete with the grim, monolithic system of our great adversary? Could we cut through the layers of bureaucracy and red tape that at times seemed on the point of strangling us altogether? Could we somehow streamline our administrative processes, speed up our countdown, make the right decisions and make them in time?

To these questions I had no final answer. But as I left the witness stand that day the thought was strong in my mind that perhaps, if I told the story of my own experiences in the turbulent and complex field of missiles and space work, some of the basic problems might emerge—might even stand out so clearly that in a few areas remedial action might be taken. I knew that the story of the Army's effort, and my own connection with it, could not begin to cover the whole broad spectrum. But perhaps in essence it contained most of the great dilemmas that our Republic was facing in its struggle for survival in a changing and hostile world.

To tell the story adequately, I knew I would have to blend my own life experiences with rocket history and go forward from the point, so to speak, where the two lines crossed.

The remainder of this book, then, represents an effort to do just that.

CHAPTER II

The Making of a Missile-Man

Perhaps it is egotistical to say so, but I cannot avoid the conviction that if an individual is destined to have a place of some importance in the world's scheme of things, nothing happens to him by accident. In my own case, if the events of my career are traced as they took place, it would almost appear to be a life without definite purpose. Yet in the final analysis I believe that everything that ever happened to me contributed to the knowledge and understanding that were required to meet the challenges of the years from 1955 to 1960.

Although there had been little military tradition in any part of my family, I can remember being strangely attracted to all things military very early in my life. As a youngster of about eight, attending grammar school in Springfield, Ohio, and without a father at home to help me with such things (my parents were divorced), I was fascinated by weapons. About a mile from our house, a group of men had a shooting club. On Saturdays I haunted the place and kept pestering them to let me shoot. Finally they loaded up a big old Pope-Smith .303 and put me down on the porch in prone position with the gun resting on a sandbag. I shall never forget that first shot! That little boy slid back about three feet when the gun went off, and the jolt to skinny shoulders was terrific. Far from being discouraged, however, I wanted to do it again right away, particularly since I had managed to hit the target! Thus was begun a love of rifles and shooting irons in general that finally took me from the Infantry to the Ordnance Corps as an expert in small arms.

My family did not have much money, although Mother had developed into one of the earliest of the real women executives. She became Chief Accountant and Treasurer of a manufacturing company in Springfield. In those days, however, women were not paid on the same basis as men, and the income was far from sufficient to raise and educate a boy and support my grandmother.

My grandmother was tall and thin and had every characteristic of the French Basques from whom she was remotely descended. Her principles were strong and absolutely unwavering. To her there was no such thing as expediency and no compromise with what was right. From her I learned all the principles of conduct that have stayed in my mind and governed most of my actions since. I might add that every time they did *not* govern my actions it turned out to be both wrong and disastrous.

In spite of our comparative poverty, we were respected members of the middle class, and it was up to everyone in the family to maintain that position. Thus I began to do productive and profitable work at an early age. I took on a newspaper route in the morning, and before long managed to get another route on the evening paper. As I made my morning and evening rounds, I noticed that one particular lamplighter was covering the same area at about the same time. He was turning on the gas lamps in the evening and turning them off in the morning. I investigated and found that these lamplighter routes were let out on bid, so the next time that particular one came up, I bid on it. Since I already had to cover the route for my newspaper, I was able to cut the price, and sure enough, I got the job. At this point, I was at the ripe old age of eleven!

I grew rapidly, and by the time I entered high school at the age of twelve I was as big as most boys of eighteen. At least I was as tall, although I was quite thin. I was beginning to consider myself too old to be a newsboy, so I began to look around for more profitable ways to occupy my spare time.

I had an uncle who was the local boss for the Big Four Railroad, and he got me a job on the night force in the mailroom. As I remember it, there were about seven trains a night between 6 P.M. and 6 A.M., and I quickly reached the point where the long whistle approaching the first crossing out of town was quite sufficient to arouse me from a sound sleep. That trick of being able to wake up quickly, and the accompanying ability to lie down on a pile of mail sacks and be asleep in fifteen seconds, was to be of great service all through my life and particularly during two wars.

From time to time I talked to the drivers at the only taxi stand in town, which was at the Union Station. I found they were making considerably more money than I was, so I started angling for a taxi job and by midsummer I got one. In the course of driving a night cab in that town of 50,000, I learned a great deal about the essential humanity and goodness of people. The cab drivers of Springfield were a rough and ready lot, but they were very kind to a high school kid.

Actually, it was their kindness that made the job possible, because at the most I could only get a couple of hours sleep in mid-afternoon before I went to work at six o'clock, and when I came off duty at six in the morning I had to get ready and be at school at nine. My rest depended on the snatches I could get between fares. Those snatches would have been few and short had I had to crank up and move my cab every time the man at the front got a fare. Instead of that, the other drivers would push my cab up while I went right on sleeping. When I got to number one position, someone would wake me up. Thus, I managed to get enough rest to make good grades in school.

From taxi driving, I progressed to streetcar conducting. Here I got acquainted with all kinds of people, since I had runs that took me into every part of town from the poorest to the best. My regular run was from 3:30 to 11:30 P.M. This meant that I had to go right from high school to my job, but at least I got some sleep between midnight and dawn.

This covered the winter of 1917–18, and we were at war. May of 1918 brought my sixteenth birthday, and I was to graduate from high school in June. As big, and as old in many ways, as my eighteen-year-old schoolmates, I had the feeling that I must have a part in this excitement. I talked to a number of my buddies in high school, and several of us agreed that we ought to enlist.

My birthday was on May 12th, and on the 20th I presented myself to the Marine Corps recruiting station. The only thing the Marine Corps required was my mother's consent. They were assuming, of course, that I was eighteen years old. Mother knew that I was not, and I suspect that this particular occasion presented her with one of the most difficult problems of her life.

She knew that all she had to do was tell the truth, and I would never go to war. On the other hand, she had the insight to realize that a man must do what he is driven to do by the fact that he is a man. So, with tears in her eyes, and without saying anything to me about the battle that must have gone on in her mind all during the previous night, she answered the telegram, certifying my age and approving my enlistment.

Two days later I reported to Parris Island, South Carolina, for "boot" training. It was a mighty rough experience for a youngster. The tough discipline and the terrific schedule of physical work and exercise in the heat and sand were a trial, but some prior knowledge of drill and of weapons, plus grim determination not to be a baby, carried me through.

I was thirsting for combat, of course, but as things turned out we did not see the front lines at all. The war ended too soon. We did spend some weary hours and days trudging up and down the dusty roads of France.

I finally came back to the States, was discharged, and immediately started to look into the question of a college education. While I was away, my mother had remarried. My stepfather was a hardheaded man of the "rule or ruin" philosophy. He made it clear that if he was to be of any assistance to me, I was to do as he told me without question.

My own father was a lawyer, and I finally swallowed my pride and went to see him. He was willing to help me get a college education, but on the condition that I study law. The law, however, held no attraction for me. All my life I had been devoted to things having to do with mechanics and electricity. As a result, I was convinced that I wanted to be an engineer, but could not make up my mind between mechanical and electrical. In any case, the mere fact that my father was trying to push me into a profession that held no interest for me aroused my Basque stubbornness, and I told him he could keep his money.

Finally, my mother persuaded my stepfather to provide the minimum financing for entry into Ohio State University. I decided to take the 5-year course, which would lead to a degree in both mechanical and electrical engineering. I remember very well how my stepfather accompanied me to Columbus to find me a boardinghouse and buy me some clothes. After my experiences in the Marine Corps I considered myself a grown man, so I was both embarrassed and annoyed by his paternalistic attitude, which included choosing my boardinghouse according to his own ideas. The last straw was when he picked out a suit of clothes of the general cut and color normally worn by men of fifty. I went ahead and registered, but privately I decided that I was going to establish my independence one way or another.

This home situation was to have a very great effect on my life.

My stepfather's attitude had virtually closed me off from any feeling of belonging to my own family. My grandmother was equally upset by the situation, but in her wonderful pride merely held her head a little higher and suffered dependence with quiet dignity. I was neither so old nor so wise.

My Marine training qualified me for the senior ROTC at Ohio State, and thanks to fine Marine training I moved quickly to a position as Cadet Company Commander.

We had a very fine ROTC instructor, and he began talking to me about the Army as a career. Actually, there was no reason why I could not have qualified for West Point. Unfortunately, I knew little or nothing about West Point and had the erroneous idea that one had to have a lot of political influence to get in. So the thought never seriously occurred to me.

With home ties dissolving and a feeling of emotional loneliness, I became seriously interested in a girl. I knew that I would need money to support a wife, so at the end of the school year I got a job. By today's standards it would be considered slavery, but I must say I did not feel imposed upon. I worked 12 hours a day as a draftsman in the maintenance department of a steel foundry in Columbus. Armed with this job, I finally persuaded my girl friend to marry me. By the time college opened in the fall, I had found another job that would let me continue at Ohio State —this time as a brakeman on the Pennsylvania Railroad. My shift operated from 3:30 in the afternoon until 11:30 at night, which for my purposes was ideal, although I cannot say it was as attractive to my wife. In about a year, by talking to everyone who would talk to me, I learned a lot about the problems, difficulties and hazards of railroading.

In my second year at the university, I heard that there would be competitive examinations for regular Army commissions in the spring. Army life still appealed to me strongly, so I made a strenuous effort to meet the requirements (I remember I had to teach myself analytical geometry in 60 days), passed the exams, and in August 1921 reported to Fort Benning as a Lieutenant of Infantry in a mule-drawn machine gun company.

Three years later, in 1924, I was transferred to the 33rd Infantry in Panama. This was supposed to be a very desirable detail, and from the standpoint of living conditions and general surroundings it was. I decided to perfect my Spanish, which I had first studied in high school. I teamed up with a couple of youngsters from a good Panamanian family to work on it. Whenever we got together, they would make me read the local Spanish paper from end to end and then discuss it with them. The result was a good accent and complete fluency in the language.

In those days, my pay was $205 per month, plus quarters, and I found myself having a great deal of difficulty in supporting a wife in the style which she preferred. In an effort to solve this problem, I resorted to many expedients to pick up a little extra cash. I refereed baseball games in the Panama League at constant risk of life and limb. I became a judge at the dog racing track and wound up knowing all the ways those races can be rigged. I left that job thoroughly disgusted and have never attended or bet ten cents on a dog race since.

My hard work on Spanish earned me an assignment to the U. S. Plebiscite Commission in the provinces of Tacna and Arica. The problem was to decide the ownership of these disputed areas as between Chile and Peru. Ten months in the mountains, speaking nothing but Spanish, brought me to a bilingual fluency that has been valuable all my life.

Returning to Panama, I took on an evening chore of writing a column in the *Panama-American,* under the heading of "The Periscope." I did not sign my name to it, but Army Intelligence smoked me out eventually, and I got unshirted hell for some of the things I said that were very much contrary to Army policy.

This brought an end to my writing career and left me in bad shape financially. So when the General Motors Export Corporation observed my fluency in Spanish and offered me a job, I rose to the bait. For many years afterwards, in spite of material success, I regretted my action in resigning from the Army, because I missed the life and associations.

After a year and a half in Columbia, I returned to the United States. It was about this time that I took up flying. In those days, being a pilot was still considered hazardous. I remember saying that I had no intention of being the hottest pilot in the business—I just wanted to be the oldest. Then, as now, I look on flying simply as a means of transportation from here to there in the shortest time and under the safest conditions.

In the fall of 1929, I went fishing in Canada and so was completely out of touch when Black Friday descended on the stock market. I came back to find that only by the grace of God, and through the intervention of a friend of mine who had the nerve to act without authority in my absence, had I avoided being very deeply in debt. My brokerage account had had a paper value of close to $100,000. As things stood, I cashed it for $69.50. I took the money, went into a clothing store and spent it all for a new suit, hat, and a pair of shoes. I walked out broke—but I didn't look it.

The next year was really hectic. Like many people, I literally lived from hand to mouth. I did not go on anyone's payroll, but managed to make enough to live on through short assignments of business evaluation, analysis and recommendations.

One casualty of the depression was my first marriage. The change from relative affluence to near poverty was the straw that broke the camel's back, and my wife and I came to a parting of the ways.

My management consulting work brought me into contact with the Kroger Company, and I spent several good years as a sort of executive trouble shooter for this large grocery chain. It was during this period that I met a young lady (she was playing bridge and I was kibitzing) named Virginia Smith. She didn't seem to mind my peering over her shoulder, so eventually I asked her for a date. I arrived exactly on time, and was most impressed by the fact that she was ready and waiting. We eventually got married, and of course a husband would say (unfairly) that she hasn't been on time for anything since. But it was—and is—a very happy marriage that has survived good fortune and bad.

As the 1930's went by, I was moving up the ladder in the Kroger Company, but I really did not like the chain food business. The higher I rose the more certain I became that I must leave, or stay with it for life. Consequently, when an uncle of mine in Cincinnati offered to set me up in the automobile business, I decided to accept the proposition.

From the standpoint of economic success, this turned out to be one of the worst decisions of my life. My uncle's sudden death, plus the heavy decline in used-car values in 1937 and early 1938, left me with no choice but to throw the company into bankruptcy. In attempting to salvage the venture, I had supported borrowings with my own personal signature, and on the liquidation of the company found myself with debts amounting to some $15,000 hanging around my neck. I can assure you that the Medaris family lived frugally for quite a number of years. It was 1946 before we "burned the mortgage."

In 1938 I was broke, and thrown back again on my varied experience to earn a living. I did enough chores successfully for a number of people to keep the wolf from the door, but my wife and I counted every penny. I remember particularly one Saturday when we went together to do our frugal grocery shopping. Ginna was, and is, one of the finest home managers I know, and can get as much out of a nickel as anyone I have ever seen. We had completed our essential purchases and had fifty-five cents left. We looked at each other and decided a little recreation was essential. We spent ten cents for two cans of Kipper Snacks and took a pitcher to the local beer garden and got forty-five cents worth of beer. We celebrated that Saturday night on crackers, Kipper Snacks and beer.

Throughout all of this I had maintained my military activities in the Reserve. By 1939 Europe was at war, and to many of us American involvement seemed probable. The spring of that year saw the beginning of a build-up in arms production, and provision was made for the call of a few reserve officers to active duty. After discussion with the officer in charge of the Cincinnati Ordnance District, then Major Fred McMahon, I applied for and got the first active duty call in that District. On July 11, 1939, I was back in the Service, as a Captain of Ordnance.

I spent the next twelve months surveying ammunition production and working with industry in Southern Ohio, Southern Indiana, Kentucky and part of Tennessee. All of my previous engineering education, which after leaving Ohio State I had continued on my own, and all of my varied work in the fields of management, became very useful. In July 1940, I was called to Washington to work in the same field on a national scale. In that year and the next I was to extend my knowledge of and my familiarity with industry to the whole of the United States, and was to acquire an understanding of people and resources in industry that would pay off many times in later years.

Soon after Pearl Harbor, by making myself thoroughly obnoxious, I managed to escape from the clutches of Washington and get out in the field to do some real soldiering. By November 1942 I was overseas. Everyone who has fought through a war thinks his own experiences were fascinating, but I realize that this is not the place for mine. I went through the Tunisian and Sicilian campaigns as Ordnance Officer of II Corps, then moved to England to get ready for D-Day, and ended the war as Ordnance Officer of the First Army somewhere in Germany. These responsibilities demanded the best of everything I had learned of management, organization, and leadership. I achieved a maturity and self-confidence that were to stand me in good stead in other pioneering efforts still ahead.

When the war with Japan ended, I found myself in a dilemma

about my future. The question was whether I should apply for integration into the Regular Army and spend the rest of my life in the Service, or go back to civilian life. My family had had a difficult time during the war, and my wife was not sure whether she wanted to go on being an Army wife. For my part, after having been recommended four times during the war for promotion to General Officer without results, I had come to recognize the difficulty of getting ahead in the Technical Service. Promotions to General Officer rank had gone almost exclusively to officers of the line and of the General Staff.

I went so far as to put in for separation and go on leave. While on leave and looking for a stable situation in which to settle down, I had a first-class attack of stomach trouble and reported into an Army Hospital to get it straightened out. It did not take them long to find out it was a pure case of nerves, but a rather severe one. This brought me up short, and made me realize that I was about to walk away again from what was really my first love. Regardless of the apparent disadvantages, we decided that the Army was for us, and I put in for permanent active duty and integration into the Regular Army. I was accepted, and never again questioned my fate.

The next ten years were varied and interesting. This country has always had a tendency to let its armed forces go to pieces at the end of a major war, and this was one of the problems we were up against. The result was a temporary deterioration in the personal and professional quality of the officer corps, and a consequent decline of the esteem in which the civilian community formerly held the officer. I believe this esteem is now coming back, but slowly.

Between 1948 and 1952 I spent three pleasant years as chief of the U.S. Army mission to Argentina. Here, again, my familiarity with Spanish was invaluable. Some of my best friends in the Argentine army were strongly opposed to Perón. It has been interesting since to watch that group take over, and reach positions of prominence and authority. I must also say that during those years in Argentina I was able to observe the arrogance and insensitivity of some of our professional State Department people, the way some of the people in the foreign service lost touch with the American way of life, and the ineffectiveness that results from the selection of unqualified and unsympathetic people as ambassadors.

Returning to the States in the spring of 1952, I soon found myself in the hottest fire I had experienced in a long time—the so-called Korean ammunition problem. Certainly mistakes had been made in the Ordnance Department. However, the major problem had been caused by a completely unrealistic attitude on the part of those controlling the budget. Having to crank up the whole system to provide ammunition for a hot war, under a ground rule that insisted that the war would not last more than another six months, was probably the real source of the difficulty. In any case, the problem did catapult me back into American industry with a vengeance.

In my attempts to help remedy the situation, I was lucky to have the assistance of a young officer named John Zierdt. It was his task to assemble all the information on which my decisions were based, and he did a tremendous job. Four years later, when I was assembling my team for the Army Ballistic Missile Agency, I grabbed him away from the Army War College and hustled him down to Huntsville. He has been equally brilliant there, and I have no hesitation at all in predicting that in the future quite a lot is going to be heard from Col. John Zierdt.

In April 1953 I was put in complete charge of ammunition activities, and in July was promoted to Brigadier General. The guided missile field, then beginning to assume considerable importance, was part of the ammunition responsibility. When I took control of the whole Ammunition Branch, I shifted a good deal of the responsibility for conventional ammunition to experienced assistants and began to interest myself deeply in the problems of Redstone Arsenal, which had been set up in 1950 to be the center for rockets and guided missiles.

Thus I was quietly introduced to the area that was to assume critical importance in my life. It had taken me half a century to reach this point. Rockets themselves had been around quite a lot longer than that.

CHAPTER III

The Beginnings of the Dream

When one stands, as I have often done, as close as safety will permit to the launching of a giant space vehicle or the testing of some great rocket engine with its indescribable scream and hiss and roar, it is easy to feel a fierce pride in the power and purpose thus displayed. Here is man, reaching up to the floor of Heaven, striving to thrust his questioning fingers into the unfathomable spaces between the stars. Here, you say to yourself, is the latest and greatest achievement of our magnificent technology. Here is the ultimate in newness.

But as a matter of fact, there is nothing new about reactive power at all. The lowliest squid that swims in the sea has been using it, practically and efficiently, for millions of years. I don't pretend any great knowledge of marine biology, but I do know that by forcibly ejecting a jet of water the squid manages to go where he wants to go in quite a hurry, and by using exactly the same principle of propulsion that one of these days in the not-too-distant future will land a man on the moon.

23

I must confess, the squid makes a lot less fuss about it!

Man himself has been dimly aware of the reaction principle for thousands of years. Your shaggy caveman, drifting idly on his raft in a placid lake, must have discovered that by tossing stones in one direction he could propel himself, however slowly, in the other. Most of us have observed the same phenomenon, sometimes all too vividly, when stepping out of a canoe.

Later, when man applied fire to water, a few clever souls found that escaping steam could be made to perform odd tricks. Two thousand years before the apple fell on Newton, the inhabitants of southern Italy were astounded by a wooden pigeon built by one Archytas, a philosopher-scientist in Tarentum. Probably suspended from wires, this contraption was apparently able to "fly" for short distances on command. Details are lacking, but it was mentioned by several awe-struck contemporaries, and it seems probable that some sort of steam-reaction device was used.

Some three hundred years later, another tinkerer in Alexandria, Egypt, invented a gadget called an "aeolipile," a metal sphere mounted on an axle that revolved merrily when steam was allowed to escape through two L-shaped tubes. This was the direct ancestor of the modern lawn sprinkler that runs by water pressure. I have always thought it curious that the ingenuity that devised such an oddity failed to harness it to useful work. For a moment there, fifty years before the birth of Christ, one ingenious Egyptian held the key to the Industrial Revolution in his hands. But he did not turn it, and the moment passed, not to come again for eighteen centuries.

The exact origins of the rocket as we know it are lost in the gray mists of antiquity, but most historians credit the Chinese with the invention of gunpowder—and gunpowder was the first crude propellant. By the eleventh century, Chinese historians were describing "fire-arrows," evidently conventional arrows with a primitive rocket lashed to the shaft, not so much to act as a booster as to fill the enemy with alarm and despondency. The military possibilities of these incendiary missiles were so obvious and so attractive that word of the new invention spread rapidly. It moved through India into Arabia, and eventually came to Europe, where Albertus Magnus in Germany and Roger Bacon, the mysterious English monk, gained themselves a somewhat infernal reputation through early experiments with explosives and rockets. Bacon concealed his gunpowder formula in a cryptogram that baffled his biographers for centuries. When it was finally deciphered a few years ago, his ingredients proved to be the same as those mentioned in contemporary Arabic manuscripts.

Nothing seems to stimulate man's inventive genius quite so much as the prospect of slaughtering his neighbors. By the thirteenth century, the Chinese were launching war rockets wholesale from wicker baskets. In 1400, an enterprising Frenchman named Froissart suggested that rockets would be more accurate if fired from tubes, thus establishing himself as the godfather of the bazooka. The Italians were busy experimenting with rocket-propelled battering rams and naval weapons. Even Leonardo da Vinci got in on the act with a self-propelled "wheel of fire" designed to burn and terrify enemy soldiers.

The word "rocket" itself appeared soon afterward. Some authorities think it was derived from an old Teutonic word *rocca*, meaning spindle or distaff, the term arising from the rocket's similar shape.

It was not until the end of the seventeenth century that some of the fundamental principles in rocketry were explained by Sir Isaac Newton. As every schoolboy knows—or should know—his Third Law of Motion stated that action is always accompanied by an equal and opposite reaction. And he added, with staggering foresight, "This is the principle which will enable mankind in later centuries to undertake flight to the stars."

In the decades that followed Newton's pronouncements, the superior accuracy of guns and cannon shouldered rockets aside in the endless race for military supremacy. But rockets had a way of coming back. In 1760, British cavalry in India got a rude shock when a native prince opened up on them with a barrage of vastly improved "fire-arrows," heavy iron-barreled rockets attached to bamboo sticks. When another Indian rockets corps defeated the British again in 1799, Col. William Congreve, a Member of Parliament, began some intensive experiments of his own. The war rockets that he developed were used in 1806 against Napoleon's invasion fleet at Boulogne. They scored an even greater success at Copenhagen in 1807, where Congreve personally supervised the naval launching of some 25,000 rockets that burned the Danish capital to the ground.

Congreve's rockets were also used by the British against the United States in the War of 1812, and were a factor in their capture of Washington. These were the rockets, used against the fort at Baltimore, whose "red glare" is mentioned in our national anthem, and the "bombs bursting in air" were their explosive warheads. Congreve eventually got their range up to some 3,000 yards, and for a while rocket corps were standard in the armies of most of the major powers. A later inventor, William Hale, attempted to give rockets more stability and accuracy by adding curved flanges so that the escaping gases would impart a spin to the missile, and American troops used these against the Mexicans in the war of 1846. But the appearance of rifled cannon again pushed rockets into the background, and although they were used throughout the nineteenth century by coast guard rescue stations, and even by whaling captains who experimented with rocket-propelled harpoons, rockets as a military weapon went into almost total eclipse.

The second half of the nineteenth century saw a great upsurge of interest in astronomy, in the possibility of life on other planets, and consequently the age-old dream of space travel. In 1865, Jules Verne captured the public's imagination with his pseudo-scientific fictional account of a trip to the moon. I remember reading this myself as a small boy in Ohio, in moments snatched from my newspaper routes and other chores. I never dreamed—how could I?—that one day I would be directing a moon-shot myself!

Verne's launching device was an enormous cannon with a barrel 900 feet long. This he imagined as being buried, prophetically enough, in Florida. He calculated the necessary muzzle velocity rather accurately, but ignored such melancholy items as the fact that his passengers would have been flattened into tissue paper by the enormous launching pressure. He made other engineering errors, but his story did impress on people the tremendous amount of energy required if any man-made object was to escape the clutching fingers of terrestrial gravity. It was in September 1956, when our Army Team fired a Jupiter rocket some 3,000 miles, that we knew that we had at last the capability to put a satellite in orbit. This was 91 years after Verne's book was published—and more than a year before the first Sputnik went up.

In the same year that Verne's *From the Earth to the Moon* appeared, an obscure Frenchman named Achille Eyraud published a book called *Voyage to Venus*. It had little success, but was significant because Eyraud's spaceship was powered by a reaction motor, a refinement, he explained, of the familiar gun-recoil principle. Other fanciful novels soon followed, bristling with descriptions of Martians and Venusians who zipped around the solar system in spaceships powered by "anti-gravity" devices. It was the earliest form of science-fiction, and the public loved it. But as the turn of the century approached, the fiction began to fade and science itself took over.

At first the public—and indeed the scientists themselves—found it hard to tell which was science and which was fantasy. The first man clearly to propose the application of the reaction principle to space travel was a crotchety German named Hermann Ganswindt, who as early as 1885 was turning out plans for dirigibles and even helicopters. In 1891 he gave a lecture in which he described an "interplanetary vehicle" to be propelled by a series of dynamite explosions. Nobody took him very seriously, but he had hit upon the right principle. "Calculations have shown," he said, "that such an apparatus, driven by explosives, could function economically only by developing quite an exceptional speed. It would therefore be unsuited to use in the earth's atmosphere, due to the intense air resistance. In a vacuum, on the other hand, there is nothing to prevent the attainment of the speeds of a comet or a meteor. Such speeds are essential for an expedition into space, owing to the vast distances to be covered."

Ganswindt even grasped the concept of a space station, and put forward the theory that the rings around Saturn might be artificial satellites put up by the Saturnians. When people scoffed at his space travel notions, he growled: "These are not Jules Verne fantasies, but part of a plan which I still hope to carry out during my lifetime. The time will come when a voyage into space will be a practical proposition." He went on to father twenty-three children and see at least a partial vindication of his ideas before he died in 1934.

The Russians, with their tendency to claim firsts in every field of endeavor, point to Konstantin E. Tsiolkovsky as the true father of astronautics. He was a self-taught genius, rendered deaf by scarlet fever at the age of ten, whose life span and scientific interests almost exactly paralleled those of Ganswindt.

But Tsiolkovsky's approach to the problems of flight was more thorough and more practical. Working with little encouragement, and almost no money, he designed and built the first wind tunnel in Russia. By 1895 he was drafting plans for dirigibles and even an all-metal airplane. He was the first to see clearly that while rocket propulsion would be necessary for space travel, existing rockets driven by solid propellants were too weak. This led him to propose and ultimately design a liquid-fueled rocket engine. Later he declared that a multistage rocket would be necessary if man was to reach outer space.

Until his death in 1935, Tsiolkovsky continued to carry out experiments and publish detailed analyses of the problems of space flight. His speculative and scientific brilliance gave Russia an interest in space and rockets that has never wavered. There is evidence that the Kremlin chose the 100th aniversary of Tsiolkovsky's birth—September 17, 1957—to launch their first Sputnik. If so, the attempt failed. Sputnik I did not go into orbit until the following month. But the esteem in which the Russians hold the shy, deaf schoolteacher was indicated when, after photographing the far side of the moon, they named one of the most prominent "seas" for him.

The great pioneer of American rocketry was a publicity-hating professor of physics named Robert Hutchins Goddard. As a young scientist, Goddard became interested in marine lifesaving rockets. His studies convinced him that existing exhaust nozzles were very inefficient, and that the shape of the rockets themselves left much to be desired aerodynamically. By 1918 he had designed nozzles of much greater efficiency and had patented what was in effect a two-stage rocket.

During World War I, Goddard was commissioned in the U. S. Navy, where he worked as an experimental physicist and produced an early type of bazooka. At this point, if I may interject a biographical note, I was serving overseas with the U. S. Marines at the ripe old age of seventeen—and nothing was farther from my mind than rockets!

In 1919 Goddard published a paper with the staid title of "A Method of Reaching Extreme Altitudes," describing his experiments and tabulating the exhaust velocities of various types of propellants. He added, almost casually, that with such propellants it was theoretically possible to shoot a rocket to the moon carrying a payload of two pounds. If the payload were made up of some highly inflammable material such as magnesium, Goddard said, and were caused to explode on impact during the dark of the moon, the resulting flash might be visible from the earth through a powerful telescope.

The publicity that resulted from this pronouncement left Goddard so appalled that he retreated into a scientific shell where he remained for the rest of his life. But inside that shell, step by methodical step, the patient, painstaking work went on that in the next few years changed the old, clumsy, fireworks type of rocket into the streamlined, stabilized, fire-breathing "bird" that has revolutionized warfare and given substance to man's ancient dream of reaching the stars.

During the 1920's, behind his self-imposed barrier of isolation, Goddard worked steadily on liquid fuels. After much experimentation, he decided that a mixture of liquid oxygen and gasoline was the most promising and the most practical. The problem then became one of building an engine that would mix these two ingredients in a combustion chamber just before ignition.

Late in 1923 he successfully static-tested such an engine. Three years later, on a cold March day, the first liquid-fueled rocket lurched erratically into the air and flew for two and a half seconds at a speed of about 50 miles per hour before dropping back to the frozen New England turf. Although it attracted little attention, it was an achievement in rocketry comparable to the first flight of the Wright brothers. At this point, I was a young lieutenant on duty in Panama, while in the faraway province of Posen, Germany, a fourteen-year-old schoolboy named Wernher von Braun was acquiring a reputation as an exceptionally brilliant student.

Further tests of his functioning but erratic rockets convinced Goddard that the next problem was one of stability. With some financial backing from the Guggenheim Foundation (a sudden national hero, Charles A. Lindbergh, helped him get it), he moved to Roswell, New Mexico, and gradually built up a rocket experimental station, complete with test stands for static experiments and a launching cradle some sixty feet high.

In December 1930 Goddard launched the first of his "big" liquid-fueled rockets. More than ten feet long, it roared up to a height of 2,000 feet, and Goddard estimated that it reached the then-unheard-of speed of 500 miles per hour. But it still rocked and swerved alarmingly. More intensive work produced a rocket with fins placed in the exhaust stream that greatly increased stability. But now the depression forced Goddard to discontinue his experiments and return to his classroom lecturing.

Later on, the Guggenheim Foundation granted him further

funds, and he went back to New Mexico. By 1935 he was launching rockets that reached altitudes of more than a mile at close to the speed of sound. When World War II broke out, Goddard went back to the Navy and helped develop rockets to assist carrier-plane take-offs. He died in August 1945, having laid virtually all the groundwork for the modern liquid-propellant rocket and having, like Frankenstein, seen his brain child reach a terrifying maturity in the shape of the V-2.

But the work of the Germans—and of the Russians—deserves a separate chapter.

CHAPTER IV

From G-1 to V-2—and Beyond

Except for Goddard's brilliant and solitary efforts, the greatest strides in rocketry during the 1920's and 1930's were made by the Germans. There was an ironic reason for this. By the Treaty of Versailles, the Germans were barred from military aircraft or long-range artillery. Deprived of bombers and big guns, they were ready to consider any substitute—and the long-range rocket offered intriguing possibilities.

The first surge of interest was nonmilitary. Goddard tested the first liquid fuel rocket engine (had he been less modest, he might have called it the G-1) in 1923. That same year a book was published in Germany by an unknown engineer named Hermann Oberth. Little more than a pamphlet, it was called *By Rocket to Interplanetary Space,* and on the very first page proceeded to assert that:

1. In the present state of scientific and technical knowledge it would be possible to build machines capable of passing beyond the limits of the earth's atmosphere;

2. With further progress, these machines could reach such speeds that, moving freely in space, they would not fall back to the earth's surface, but would free themselves from its gravitational pull;

3. Such machines could be so constructed as to allow human beings to travel in them with safety;

4. Under certain conditions, probably attainable within the course of a few decades, the construction of these machines would prove economically justifiable.

The remainder of the book offered a series of mathematical equations as proof of its bold thesis. These were beyond the comprehension of most laymen, but the book sold quite well on the strength of its title. When people made inquiries about the author, they were told that he was a twenty-nine-year-old schoolteacher in the little Transylvanian town of Sighisoara.

Actually, Oberth had been fascinated by the possibilities of space flight ever since, as a youngster, he had discovered the novels of Jules Verne. Later, as a young mathematician, he had gleefully poked large holes in Verne's science-fiction. He calculated, for example, that the "cushion" with which Verne provided his space travelers in the moon gun would have had to be over a thousand miles thick to absorb the shock of the explosion. But he was impressed with Verne's device of using retro-rockets for a soft landing on the moon. Finally, when Oberth submitted his college thesis for his doctorate, he chose the highly unorthodox subject of space travel. This was the manuscript that, after being rejected by some twenty publishers, finally appeared as *By Rocket to Interplanetary Space*.

The public was intrigued by the title of Oberth's book, but his scientific colleagues were less impressed. Some, who should have known better, stated flatly that a rocket would not work in a vacuum. How could it, they asked, with nothing to push against? Others said that the time for investigating such matters had not yet arrived, and probably never would. Oberth tried to find space in the various scientific journals to answer his critics, but was usually turned down on one pretext or another. Finally, disillusioned and discouraged, he went back to Transylvania to resume his teaching.

By this time I had resigned my own Army commission and was selling automobiles, quite successfully, in South America. I still thought of rockets mainly in terms of the Fourth of July, and certainly I had never heard of Hermann Oberth. But some thirty years later I was to have the pleasure of meeting this distinguished pioneer at the arsenal in Huntsville. He and his wife came over from Germany and entered the service of the U. S. Army in the summer of 1955 at the invitation of Wernher von Braun. Later we very much hoped that he would be able to stay permanently, but in 1957 the question of money arose. Obviously, the old gentleman and his wife needed something to live on. He was too old to qualify for a U. S. pension. He had earned a pension in Germany, but had to return to claim it. A United States Senator assured me that a modest stipend could easily be secured from one of the large foundations. But although von Braun and I made many telephone calls, the funds were never forthcoming, and finally the man whom many consider the real father of astronautics was forced to return to Germany.

Despite Oberth's difficulties, throughout the 1920's the idea of space travel was gaining converts in Germany. In 1924 an Austrian war flyer named Max Valier, having read Oberth's book, followed it with one of his own called *The Assault on Cosmic Space*. This, in turn, was read by an eager youngster of nineteen named Willy Ley, who decided that the whole subject needed simpler and livelier presentation. In 1926 Ley's effort appeared, an 83-page pamphlet entitled "Travel in Space." In the meantime a German civil engineer, Dr. Walter Hohmann, published a booklet that gave the exact requirements, in terms of propulsive effort, for flights from the earth to the moon, to Venus, and to Mars.

In 1927 a dozen or so enthusiasts, most of them young, founded the Verein fur Raumschiffahrt (VfR), the Association for Space-

Travel. They had trouble registering the name, since the court authorities insisted, with bureaucratic solemnity, that the German language had no such word as "Raumschiffahrt." I might say, somewhat dryly, that the Germans have no monopoly on this type of governmental reaction. When we finally brought the German rocket experts to this country in 1946, our immigration authorities resolutely refused to recognize the fact that they were here. We finally had to take them down to Mexico and walk them back into the U. S. A. so as to give them official status as immigrants.

The following year in Germany, 1928, saw the first flight of a manned rocket. It was an experimental glider with two powder rockets developing a thrust of 44 pounds each. The glider was launched with an elastic rope, and flew well in the first attempt. But on the second flight one of the rockets blew up, set the machine on fire, and the pilot was lucky to land the glider and himself in one piece.

This was the era of the much-publicized rocket automobiles built by car manufacturer Fritz von Opel. One of these cars, driven by Opel himself, reached a speed of 140 miles per hour. Experiments were also carried out with rocket-propelled sleds and even rocket-propelled human skaters, but the powder rockets were dangerous and difficult to control. Max Valier began experimenting with liquid fuel rocket engines, but in 1930 he was killed when such an engine exploded in his workshop. His death made a deep impression on his contemporaries, including a pale-faced political leader named Adolf Hitler, who knew him slightly. The doubt left in Hitler's mind about the reliability of rocket engines was to be a factor of some importance later on.

In the autumn of 1928, sensing the public interest in rockets and space travel, a film producer named Fritz Lang decided to make a film about a rocket flight to the moon. Reading such literature as was available, he happened upon Oberth's book, and promptly invited the author to leave his schoolteaching in Transylvania and come to Berlin as technical adviser for the movie.

When Oberth agreed to come, Willy Ley proposed that the

movie company set aside funds for the actual construction of a liquid-fueled rocket. It would be a great publicity stunt, he said, to fire such a rocket just before the première of the film—and indeed it would have been if Oberth had been given the time and the facilities to carry out the plan.

As it was, he drove himself almost to a nervous breakdown in an effort to construct such a rocket in three months. At one point, he blew up his laboratory and nearly killed himself. As might have been expected, the rocket was never finished, but the film was a great success.

What happened next was that the Association for Space-Travel took over Oberth's rocket and equipment, and decided to complete the experiment. They had a difficult time raising the necessary funds, but in 1930 Oberth and his helpers (one of whom was an eager eighteen-year-old student named von Braun) managed to demonstrate a liquid-fueled rocket engine that ran for a minute and a half and developed a fairly constant thrust of some 15 pounds. German scientists who viewed the demonstration were impressed, and the VfR was jubilant.

But the day of the independent amateur experimenter in Germany was rapidly coming to an end. By this time the Ordnance Department of the German army was beginning to take an interest in rocket development, and a young officer named Walter Dornberger was given the task of developing solid-propellant rockets. He found so little to work with that the army finally built its own experimental station at Kummersdorf, 18 miles south of Berlin. When the brilliant talents of Wernher von Braun were brought to his attention, Dornberger promptly offered the young man the use of army facilities for experimental work. Shortly thereafter, von Braun became a permanent member of Dornberger's rapidly expanding team.

Soon after Hitler came to power, he issued a directive stating that army ordnance was to have sole responsibility for rocket engineering and development in Germany. This meant that private experimentation amounted to treason. Some of the amateur scientists ceased working, but most were absorbed into the army. Willy Ley, one of the few to see the handwriting on the wall, managed to make his way to the United States.

By December 1932 the German army's first scientifically designed test stand was ready. The first rocket engine tested promptly blew up. It was then decided to design and build a completely new rocket to be known as Aggregate 1, or A-1. This gave way to the A-2, which was tested in December 1934 and reached a height of more than a mile.

The A-3, a 1,500-pound giant twenty feet long, was so large that the German scientists had to have more space for their test firings. Von Braun knew of a remote, almost deserted place on the Baltic coast where his father had often taken him duck hunting. He and his colleagues persuaded the army to buy the Peenemunde area for 750,000 Reichsmarks. By 1937, the great rocket experimental station was in operation.

The successor to the A-3—the A-4—was planned as the most devastating war rocket that the world had ever seen. In World War I, the Germans had shelled Paris with their "Big Bertha" from a range of some 80 miles. With the A-4, they wanted to double that range, and they also wanted to place a ton of high explosives on target. It was with these two requirements in mind that the A-4 was planned and built.

This was the weapon that ultimately came to be known as the V-2, or Hitler's Rocket. Actually, in the early days of World War II, Hitler showed little interest in rocketry. On one occasion in 1939 he came down to Kummersdorf to witness a test firing. Somewhat to the chagrin of Dornberger and von Braun, he simply stared and didn't say a word. A year later, when France had fallen and victory seemed within his grasp, Hitler struck Peenemunde from his priority list. Nobody was able openly to countermand this order, but Field Marshal von Brauchitsch quietly ordered 4,000 "soldiers" to be kept at the Baltic installation. These were actually scientists and technicians, and so despite Hitler's indifference the work continued.

It is strange to think, now, that almost twenty years ago von Braun and his fellow scientists had to face difficulties in rocketry that are still very much with us. The size of the rocket, for example, could not be dictated simply by scientific requirements. There was also the matter of transportation. If it was too long, it could not navigate a sharp curve in road or rail travel. If it was too thick, it might not be able to pass under bridges, or through tunnels. This problem, greatly magnified by the size of modern rockets, confronts us forcibly today.

The first launchings of the A-4 were carried out in August 1942. These were not wholly satisfactory, but on the third firing, in October, the great 12-ton rocket soared to an altitude of 54 miles before crashing into the Baltic over a hundred miles away.

All through the early months of 1943 testing went on. These early V-2s had very little instrumentation, which meant that flaws in performance could not readily be detected. Years later, at Huntsville, von Braun told me how he and Dornberger used to go and sit in the impact area so that they could watch the rocket come down and observe its behavior. In those days, it was probably safer to be on the receiving end of the V-2 than on the firing end. As von Braun said dryly, "Our main objective for a long time was to make it more dangerous to be in the target area than to be with the launch crew."

In the spring of 1943, Hitler's weird fantasies threatened to halt production of the V-2 altogether. In March of that year he dreamed that German rockets would never reach English soil. As a result, Dornberger and von Braun found it almost impossible to obtain the materials and support necessary for the final testing phases. In July they finally managed to obtain an audience with Hitler at his headquarters in East Prussia. They showed him movies of the V-2 in flight, models of the rocket and its means of transportation. In the end, they so impressed the Fuehrer that he decreed that Peenemunde should get the highest available priorities. Now, however, he demanded a 10-ton warhead because he needed "annihilating destruction." Von Braun and Dornberger knew that this was impossible, but promised to do what they could.

The new priorities decreed by Hitler were welcome at Peenemunde, because from the start the rocket project in Germany had been opposed by those who argued that a bomber could carry a heavier load of explosives and place it more accurately. Even after the German air force had virtually been driven from the sky, there were those who felt that the V-1, or Flying Bomb, was a cheaper and more effective weapon.

With this latter conclusion most of us who were in London at the time were somewhat inclined to agree. As a terror weapon, the V-1 was much more effective in disrupting work schedules and affecting people's nerves than the V-2, which arrived with a big bang and no warning at all. People who were genuinely frightened by the ominous sound of an approaching V-1 adopted a completely fatalistic attitude about the V-2, although the physical damage wrought by a V-2 explosion was considerably greater.

The guidance system of the V-2 was quite primitive and no very high degree of accuracy was ever obtained. Between September 1944 and the end of March 1945 the Germans fired at least 1,300 of these alcohol-and-liquid-oxygen-fueled rockets at London. Of these, less than half reached the target area. Of course, if the Germans had developed an atomic warhead, this lack of pinpoint accuracy would have made little difference.

At Peenemunde, the Germans also had a Long Term Planning Group that worked on plans for an A-9 and an A-10 rocket. The design of the A-9 called for supplementary wings that would enable the rocket to glide when the propellant had been exhausted, thereby attaining a range of some 300 miles. The A-10 was to be a giant 87-ton booster rocket that would carry the A-9 above the atmosphere, from which point the A-9 would proceed under its own power for a distance of some 2,500 miles. The target that the Nazis had in mind for the A-10 was New York City, but the huge rocket never got beyond the planning stage.

Von Braun's imagination, of course, soared beyond the A-10

to a three-stage rocket capable of launching a satellite. But in wartime Germany such ideas were dangerous. In March 1944, von Braun and two colleagues were arrested on a charge of sabotage and accused of planning to divert a part of the country's war potential to nonmilitary uses—in other words: space travel. The real reason for the arrest may well have been the fact that von Braun had incurred the enmity of Heinrich Himmler by refusing to support a proposal that the Peenemunde project be taken away from the army and given to Himmler's SS. In the end, Dornberger was able to get his colleagues released by declaring under oath that they were absolutely essential to the V-2 program.

By January 1945 it became evident that the advancing Russian troops sooner or later would overrun the Peenemunde area. Confused and contradictory orders began reaching Dornberger and von Braun. The Commander of the Eastern Army Group wanted to destroy the plant and draft the thousands of employees into the army. The Minister of Munitions wanted the entire establishment transferred to a safer area where it could continue work in the hopes of a last-minute victory.

Von Braun knew that the war was already lost. The conflicting orders gave him, in effect, the choice of surrendering either to the Russians or to the Allies. He called a meeting of his top associates and asked their opinion. He himself had been impressed with the United States as a result of the reports of his brother, who had studied law in this country before the war. His close associates joined him in the decision to move west and surrender to the U. S. Army.

The move began early in April, when the whole of Germany was lapsing into chaos. Von Braun managed to remove some ten thousand men from Peenemunde. Then he and his staff moved westward to meet the oncoming Americans. In the end, these key German scientists, together with 300 boxcars of captured V-2s and spare parts, were sent to America in an operation known as "Paper Clip." There they were assigned the job of instructing

U. S. Army technicians, and the General Electric Corporation, in the development and firing of long-range rockets.

This was known as Project Hermes, and represented the free world's first decisive step toward advanced missilry and space potential.

Meantime, of course, the Russians were not exactly idle. During World War II they had made more extensive use of what might be termed conventional, solid-propellant, short-range free (unguided) rockets than any other of the major combatants. They used multiple-rocket launchers in several sizes as area weapons to provide drenching fire as a preliminary to attack. All of these weapons were fully motorized.

While the United States had available a 4½" solid rocket, also with multiple-tube mounting, the launcher was on a trailer and so somewhat less mobile. In addition, the preoccupation of the American artilleryman with accuracy, and his concern over the flash and dust created by rocket launchers, decidedly limited the use of the American rockets, especially in the European theater.

The Russians' faith in the effectiveness of rocket fire as applied to the drenching of an area led to extensive development of additional free rockets after the war. They were perfectly able, with conventional spin techniques, to achieve a degree of accuracy that was quite sufficient for their purposes. They went on to larger sizes and greater range, and came up to at least a 15-mile capability with the free rocket. All of these used a solid propellant, and were either truck mounted or tracked vehicle mounted, so that the "shoot and scoot" philosophy could be fully implemented.

This development of free rockets was quite apart from the Russians' attention to guided missiles, and represented merely an extension of capabilities demonstrated during World War II.

At the end of that war, most of the factories which were making components for the V-2 fell within the Russian zone. The Russians concentrated on acquiring as many of the German production engineers as possible. Their objective was to get the V-2 back into production on their own behalf. In the succeeding years they fired many V-2s as experimental weapons, just as the United States was doing at White Sands.

In the latter days of the war, Peenemunde was virtually destroyed by air bombardment. It has never figured in any major way in the Russian missile program. There is some indication that a very limited amount of short-range firing has been done in that area, but that is all. This is logical, since Peenemunde is on the perimeter of Russian territory and therefore exposed to free-world intelligence.

The Russians did get a few of the German scientists and creative engineers who were in the missile program, but their handling of them was quite different from our method of absorbing and using the men who came to the United States as a result of Operation Paper Clip. The Germans were never allowed to have a really active part in the Russian missile program, and, in fact, knew relatively little about what the Russians were doing. The German scientists were asked to write reports and summaries of the things they had been working on, and what they had planned to do in the future. In effect, what the Russians did was to drain these Germans of information on the current state of the art, but not utilize them in projects to go on from there. By 1947 they began to release these people and send them back across the border. A few stayed in East Germany, but most returned to West Germany and have since been interrogated by Allied intelligence. By the early 1950's, almost nothing was left in Russia of original German missile talent.

In other words, it is quite obvious that the Russians felt themselves fully competent to carry on a missile-development program, and used the Germans only to be sure that they were familiar with the state of the art as it had been developed in Germany during the war.

Beginning around 1950, a whole new family of free rockets and guided missiles began to appear in the Russian arsenal. Free rockets were brought to an advanced state of effectiveness. By 1957, the arsenal included a heavy 240 millimeter 12-round short-range truck-mounted rocket, a 200 millimeter 4-round truck-mounted weapon with a range of about 20,000 yards and a 280 millimeter 6-round rocket mounted on a tracked vehicle. The largest to appear was over 300 millimeters with a 30,000-yard range and this was mounted as a single rocket on an amphibious vehicle. Finally, by 1957, what is apparently the biggest of the free rockets appeared in the Moscow parade. It is believed to have a range of about 35 miles, still using solid propellant, but now incorporating a large bulbous warhead that would obviously accommodate a nuclear capability.

The development of Russian guided missiles is interesting from several points of view. The first to appear was an upgraded version of the V-2 having a range of about 300 miles. Afterward, they worked backward to a smaller 75-mile missile. There is enough evidence to satisfy me that the Russians took a very early interest in storable liquid propellants. This type of propellant permits the tanks to be kept charged for a considerable period without loss of fuel, thus overcoming one of the principal disadvantages of the conventional liquid-fueled missile, that must be filled at the last minute before firing. It is difficult to be at all certain as to how many of their larger missiles use this storable feature, but I believe that the 75- and 300-mile weapons use that type of fuel-oxidizer combination. I might interpolate here the fact that in my personal opinion the storable liquid missile has virtues beyond either the conventional liquid or the solid propellant missile, where the missile is to be kept mobile but is large enough so that weight could be a penalty, or where it would be difficult to control temperatures in solid propellants under operational conditions. I shall have more to say about solid versus liquid fuels later.

Another very interesting aspect of the postwar Russian missile development is that they have kept all their missiles highly mobile, even up into the bigger sizes. All that have been identified are mounted on a fully mobile, usually tracked, launching platform—until we get to the 300-mile weapon. Even this, which is about the size of our Redstone, is mounted on a trailer pulled behind a tracked vehicle.

Coincidentally with the development of this new arsenal, a new system of air defense based on antiaircraft missiles made its appearance. Initially this system could be fairly well identified from information secured from the returned Germans. This included the so-called "Guideline" missile which was believed to have an altitude capability of 40,000 to 60,000 feet with a slant range of 15 to 30 miles. There is evidence to indicate that a few major Russian centers were heavily defended by this system at a rather early date. Since that time, there is no question but that they have developed one or two new and much advanced air defense missile systems. It may have been one of these weapons that brought down the U-2.

Beyond the points outlined above, security covers most of the available information with respect to short- and medium-range missiles. However, given the direction of development and the time period within which new weapons were appearing, it is quite evident that weapons of ranges between the 300 miles mentioned above, and the IRBM range of the U. S. Thor and Jupiter (1,500 miles), have been developed and fielded. To the Russians, a missile of 11 to 13 hundred miles range is almost an ICBM, since the interior location of Russian and satellite territory permits such a weapon to cover all of Europe and sensitive portions of the Middle East.

By late 1956 there was considerable indication of Russian progress toward an ICBM. There have been many debates over the nature of the motor power used for Russian ICBM's and satellite launchers. It is noteworthy that very early the Russians showed a complete willingness to cluster smaller engines to achieve greater thrusts. Also, the original information received from German returnees indicated the probability that as early as 1950–52 the Russians either had developed, or had in an advanced stage of development, a motor of perhaps 200,000 pounds thrust. I know of no valid indication that a single motor of any greater size has been used in any of the Russian ICBM or space operations to date. Rather, the extension of their normal approach would indicate that heavy thrust has been achieved by clustering. We are currently using the same technique in our big Saturn booster, designed to deliver a million and a half pounds of thrust by clustering eight separate rocket engines.

The Russian space age was inaugurated with Sputnik I on October 4, 1957, and when Sputnik II was launched the following month, it became quite clear that the Russians had an adequate capability for developing an ICBM, if indeed they had not already done so. Their 7,000-mile missile shot into the Pacific Ocean in late 1959 only provided confirmation of this fact.

To me, the most impressive thing about the Russian missile program has been its consistency and steady progress down a straight road. They began with no fear of size, as such, and were quite willing to build big missiles when the state of their nuclear weapons demanded big missiles. Thus was laid the foundation for adequate capability in large, powerful rocket motors. The development of smaller, lighter atomic warheads permitted the exploitation of these big motors in terms of added range for missiles, and heavier weight-carrying abilities in space work. This in turn permitted faster progress, since a margin of power was available to cover minor error. We have never had this margin for error, and we still don't.

The next important characteristic of the Russian program is the tight integration of missile and space work into two basic divisions of effort, with air defense and maneuverable types of missiles in one segment, and ground-to-ground missiles of all ranges, plus extension to the space field, in another group. These divisions are militarily and scientifically logical. From the military standpoint there has been no problem of service conflicts, and the ground-to-ground missiles have been treated throughout as an extension of artillery. From the scientific and technological point of view, it is apparent that there have been no watertight compartments of any kind between military and civilian resources.

The entire program has been treated as a single effort. We may assume that there have been internal differences of opinion, but there has been no indication of changing purpose or basic reorientation to interfere with progress.

From the military standpoint, the Russian ground army is taken as the major point of focus. All important effort with both conventional and nuclear weapons has been centered on direct support of that primary force. The long-range bomber force was never built to great size, and years ago strategic power was focused in the direction of long-range missiles.

When Russia finally moved from the IRBM toward the ICBM, the change represented a steady and reasonable step forward, based on regular progression from the lesser to the greater. Each extension was soundly based on all the accumulated experience to that point. Success was thus made much more certain, and could be demonstrated in less time.

In space operations, I believe Russia has had from the very beginning a clear understanding of the propaganda value of spectacular demonstrations. The progress made has not been marked by any *quantity* of launchings even roughly comparable to our own. Rather, an effort has been repeated only until full success was attained once; then they have moved on to the next problem. Every point of progress seems to mark very clearly a basic concentration on the spectacular, usually with some military overtones. That true scientific progress has to some extent been bypassed by this approach does not in any way offset the undoubted value of the results in terms of impact on world opinion.

I believe, admittedly without clear factual data to support my opinion, that the primary Russian objective in space is to dominate the orbital area right around earth, using as a basic marker of progress the earliest possible establishment of a manned "space station."

Once they have established the capability to loft, man, and maintain such a station, the way is open for whatever devices connected with earth surveillance and domination may seem to them most important at the time. Interplanetary exploration will, in my opinion, be left until later, with full understanding that such efforts will be far easier and more capable of rapid exploitation when based on reliable bases outside the atmosphere. Thus I look for heavy vehicles in lower orbits, to be followed by "man aboard" performance in the same area, and shortly thereafter multiple-manned, reasonably long-life, orbital vehicles. There may be intermittent demonstrations in the farther reaches of space, but if so, each experiment will be carried out only once.

I also anticipate the fairly early use of nuclear propulsion to loft very heavy space vehicles into orbit. But I am getting ahead of my story!

CHAPTER V

From Hot War to Cold

In a manner of speaking, I met Wernher von Braun—or at least was on the receiving end of a message from him—a dozen years before I was introduced to him personally. The incident happened at noon on a day in the early autumn of 1944 at my Ordnance Headquarters in France. I remember it vividly still.

Contrary to my usual habit of maintaining my office, bed, communications and everything on wheels, I had set up shop temporarily inside a partially wrecked building. Also contrary to habit, I had stayed in the headquarters instead of taking off for a day's visit with various units right after the staff meeting in the morning. Most of my Ordnance outfits were in motion that day, and it seemed better to stay by my central communications where I could keep track of them.

It was a warm sunny day. The war was going well. Our front-line units were moving fast—almost too fast, from a supply point of view. Battle losses were low. It was peaceful enough in my little headquarters. But one great paradox of war is that the greatest danger often exists when the whole world seems to be still, quiet, holding its breath.

I was busy scanning the day's reports, covering every conceivable facet of the complicated business that supports a big war: battle losses, equipment recovered and repaired, enemy equipment captured and identified, ammunition moved and used, and so on. I remember there was one depressing item describing how we had just lost a valuable ammunition officer and his jeep driver. Moving forward to find new positions for ammunition supplies, they had driven into a French village supposedly well behind our forward elements, and had been cut down by a small last-ditch group of German SS troops.

I considered myself perfectly safe as I read this grim little document. What I did not know was that screaming toward our headquarters at 3,500 miles per hour was a giant rocket carrying almost a ton of high explosives in its nose.

We knew that such a weapon existed. From our Intelligence sources there had been a steady flow of fragmentary information about Vengeance-weapon No. 2. We already had a pretty fair idea of how big it was. We knew, in general, what it looked like. We knew it was a rocket with a liquid-fueled engine, supersonic velocity, high-explosive payload, and range enough to reach England from territory still in German hands.

Our headquarters was well out of enemy artillery range. But suddenly, sitting there, I was startled by a heavy blast *followed* by a deep rumble that sounded like thunder. Not too close, but close enough to rattle the fragments of broken windowpane and shake down some dust. My first thought was that perhaps an ammunition dump had exploded. But before I could make any inquiries the phone rang.

It was Sam Meyers, our Deputy Chief of Staff. "Bruce," he said, "something big just landed in the ravine alongside the headquarters cook tent. We don't know what it was. The blast took off the ridgepole of the tent and a couple of cooks were injured.

Most of the men were lined up for chow, but fortunately the ravine protected them. Can your people identify this thing?"

"I'll take a look myself," I told him, "but I think I know what it was. That rumble following the explosion means that it was a supersonic missile of some kind. And the V-2 is the only thing the Germans have with supersonic performance."

With a couple of my assistants I drove over to the ravine. Bits of thin metal, a small valve or two, a piece of twisted pipe, a heavy fragment showing a few gear teeth—there was no doubt about it. I had had my first direct contact with Wernher von Braun and his team of liquid rocket experts.

I was quite sure that the missile had not been aimed at us; it had simply fallen short of its intended target. All our intelligence reports had indicated that the Germans intended to use their big rockets as an area weapon for cities, port areas, and so on.

I remember how Sam Meyers shook his head when I gave him my report. "I'm glad they're not aiming at us," he said. "That baby carries quite a wallop, and gives no warning. Maybe the time is coming when it'll be safer up on the battle line than it is back in the civilian areas."

He was half joking, but he was being more prophetic than he knew.

Knowledge that the V-2 was at last operational left us eager to get our hands on as much of the hardware as possible and return it to the States for analysis. I gave my technical intelligence officer his instructions. "Alert all technical intelligence teams working in the forward area. Be sure they know what they are looking for. Give them all the information we have, including our best guesses. Get out a special bulletin to the combat divisions and give them the same information. Tell them that any V-2 hardware they find is to be put under strong guard at once, and this headquarters notified."

With that order, I had done all I could do. But I could not so easily dismiss the V-2 from my mind. We had finally managed a creditable job of defense against the V-1, the buzz-bomb, in any area where radar-directed antiaircraft guns were available in sufficient numbers to achieve the necessary concentration of fire. The V-1s were subsonic, and had limited maneuver capability while en route to the target. Heavy antiaircraft fire, using the new proximity fuses, could and did account for a substantial percentage. But it was obvious that no weapon then available could deal with a supersonic missile of the V-2 type.

Thus, in effect, the V-2 extended the range of heavy artillery to several hundred miles, with the added advantage (for the attacker) that its supersonic speed gave no warning of its approach. Trained soldiers had long ago learned to take shelter, or hit the ground, when warned by the rising wail of an incoming artillery shell. But a supersonic weapon hit first, and the sound followed afterward. Those who heard its blast had already survived; those who were struck never heard the weapon that killed them.

All this was obvious. Even so, on that afternoon in September 1944 I could not foresee even a fraction of the ultimate potential of this new type of weapon. I knew nothing of the atomic bomb, still hidden behind the stone-wall security of the Manhattan Project. I thought only in terms of a battlefield—a large battlefield, to be sure, but still a battlefield.

Did this new type of weapon represent any significant change in warfare as we knew it? What might be the real significance of artillery with a range of two hundred miles or more? In my mind the problem seemed to relate itself to two things—accuracy in hitting the target, and the number of rockets available.

Accuracy, it seemed to me, was the main consideration. Otherwise the cost of such weapons, if they had to be used in large numbers, might well lead the user to what Col. C. G. Patterson, then the comparatively young, imaginative, and forceful Antiaircraft Artillery Officer of the First Army, later called a "technological casualty." As he expressed the idea in 1956, "If a weapon costs more to build, in money, materials, and manpower, than it costs the enemy to repair the damage the weapon causes, the user has suffered a technological casualty. In any long-drawn-out struggle this might be the margin between victory and defeat."

So I speculated, I remember, on that far-off afternoon in 1944. But there was little time in those days for abstract thinking. Germany, I knew, had neither the remaining industrial resources nor the manpower to provide this new weapon in decisive numbers. Big rockets, I told myself, would probably never be a major problem of mine. With that, I dismissed the matter and applied myself to the more tangible and urgent problem of supplying ammunition to our advancing forces.

In the months that followed, the thunderous impacts of the V-2 on London, plus the terrible mushroom cloud over Hiroshima, plainly foreshadowed the shape of things to come. And yet I believe that at first there were few military thinkers who fully grasped the implications of a marriage of these two fearsome weapons.

For one thing, the first atomic bombs were so bulky and heavy that delivering them by rocket seemed hopelessly far-fetched. For another, as the war ended, Americans displayed their historical tendency to act as if war would never occur again. They joyfully began beating their swords into automobiles, and their spears into television sets. The best scientific brains shifted their attention from weaponry to peaceful research.

During the 1930's, while grim necessity was driving the Germans toward the completion of the V-2, little work in rocketry was being done elsewhere. In America, aside from Goddard's experiments, the only serious research was carried on by a handful of scientists under Theodore von Karman at the California Institute of Technology. The original object of the von Karman group was the development of a rocket for high-altitude research and exploration. Toward the end of 1943, they brought their work to the attention of Army Ordnance. In January 1944 a project known as ORDCIT was organized, the name being a reflection of the joint military and civilian effort.

The first test missile produced by ORDCIT was an eight-foot, 500-pound, solid-propellant rocket known as Private A. In December 1944 twenty-four rounds of Private A were fired, with an average range of 18,000 yards. This was a puny effort compared to the mighty V-2 which was already hammering England. But the Private A was destined to have some distinguished successors.

The first was Private F, a winged rocket designed to test the effect of lifting surfaces on a guided missile. Seventeen rounds of Private F were fired successfully in April 1945. Army Ordnance then requested a rocket that would carry a payload of 25 pounds to an altitude of 100,000 feet—or about 19 miles. This led to the development of a liquid-fueled rocket which for some whimsical reason was not given the simple rank of Corporal, but became known as WAC-Corporal. On September 26, 1945, the first WAC-Corporal reached a height of 42 miles above the Army's new testing grounds at White Sands, New Mexico.

By this time the 300 boxcar loads of V-2 components had reached White Sands, and the German team was on its way. They had their troubles fitting the mismated pieces of equipment together, but in the next six years 47 V-2 firings were carried out, the most spectacular being the shot of August 22, 1951, when one of the old Vengeance weapons reached a height of 130 miles.

Two years earlier, however, man had sent his first messenger into empty space. This occurred in February 1949 when a WAC-Corporal mounted on a modified V-2 (the combination was called the Bumper-WAC) soared 250 miles above the earth. This marriage of German and American technology foreshadowed the great day in 1958 when the same combination of skills would put up Explorer I, the first American satellite.

During all this time, the Russians were known to be working on rocket development, but it was fashionable to think of them as retarded folk who depended mainly on a few captured German scientists for their achievements, if any. And since the cream of the German planners had surrendered to the Americans, so the argument ran, there was nothing to worry about.

The main cause for alarm, according to certain experts, was the great long-range bomber fleet that the Russians were said to be building—a miscalculation that was to cost the American tax-payer untold millions of dollars in fighter planes, fighter bases, and detection devices designed to nullify a threat that never be-came a full-scale menace.

The pressure for such expenditure came largely from the Air Force, which was not surprising. It is only human, when you try to assess your enemy's intentions, to assume that he will act as you would act in his place. Air Force Intelligence, therefore, had the Russians feverishly building the equivalent of our Strategic Air Command. Actually, they were concentrating on long-range rockets and laughing at us. But they were careful not to laugh too loud, because our miscalculations suited them just fine.

During the late 1940's, while the engineers in the field and the scientists in the laboratories were struggling with the endless technical problems of rocketry, the men responsible for the or-ganization of our national defense effort were grappling with problems even more complex and confusing.

In 1947, in an effort to achieve greater efficiency and eliminate the ancient bugaboo of inter-Service rivalry, Congress passed the National Security Act, creating a Department of Defense with a civilian Secretary placed above the Service Secretaries, and setting up the Joint Chiefs of Staff as a legal entity. At the same time, the Air Force finally achieved formal independence from the Army. These two changes in the national defense structure had such far-reaching consequences that perhaps a more de-tailed consideration of them is in order here.

In 1947, I was Deputy Ordnance Officer at Fort Monroe in Virginia. The separation of the Air Force did not come as a surprise to anyone. During the war, the different air forces had been given almost complete autonomy, with their own chain of command clear up to the Theatre Commander.

So a separate setup for the Air Force was regarded as more or less inevitable. Still, like many other people, I had my reserva-tions about the advisability of the split.

The first and most basic reservation was that it was fundamentally unwise to set up a whole new branch of the Armed Forces on the basis of an instrument (the manned aircraft) rather than a mission to be acomplished. I felt that this could only lead to confusion and competition in the roles and missions area, with endless arguments as to who should be doing what. It was obvious, even in 1947, that the day of the manned aircraft was past its high noon. Almost from the moment they achieved formal independence, the fliers were facing technological unemployment. Yet, like all human beings, they would fight for survival with any weapon that was handy.

My second reservation had to do with technical support. During the war, the Army Air Corps had depended almost entirely on the Army logistics system and on the support of the Army Technical Services for everything that was not strictly an airplane. Army Ordnance provided the ammunition crews that maintained ammunition and bombs for the Air Corps, and loaded bombs and ammunition aboard the aircraft. It had also provided maintenance for vehicles, and for the weapons carried on aircraft. Ordnance officers had been provided for each of the Air Commanders during the war. The same sort of support came from such services as Signal, Engineers, Medical, and Quartermaster. When I found out the degree of independence that was planned for the Air Force, it seemed to me that they were facing a tremendous problem in trying to develop technical and logistic support for other than aircraft. I thought they were going to have lots of trouble, and wished that they had been more inclined to work out co-operative agreements that would let the Army continue to support them in such areas.

One other point of concern stemmed from experience during the war, where we had found that the separate channels of command for the Air Corps created many problems in terms of combat support. The fighter bombers and fighters available for direct tactical support to the ground troops were controlled by higher Air Corps headquarters, and the Army Commander had to go in and beg for the missions he wanted flown. If the Air Corps people had some deep strategic penetration mission on, the ground Commander was apt to find himself with very little air power available for direct tactical help.

The very co-operative attitude of Gen. Elwood ("Pete") Quesada, boss of the 9th Tactical Air Command supporting the First Army, had made it possible for us to find some satisfactory solutions, but even he did not control his own aircraft. He could be directed by Theatre Air Corps headquarters to support the effort of the 8th Air Force whenever they wanted him to.

Another point of difficulty during the war had been co-ordination between the Air Force interceptors and the antiaircraft troops of the Army. Right from the beginning, the Air Corps had insisted on control of the air and on being able to decide when the antiaircraft guns could take targets under fire. By great effort and negotiation this was partially cleared up and the guns were released more frequently. Before they were released, kills by antiaircraft guns were very few. After the guns were released, and could take targets under fire more promptly, the percentage of kills went up sharply.

Even back in 1947 I felt that the total separation of the Air Force would make these matters of co-ordination more difficult.

As a matter of minor personal history, Pete Quesada suggested to me that I transfer to the Air Force at that time. I discussed with him the question of the lowly status of the nonflying officer. I had been recommended for promotion to General Officer repeatedly during the war, and I was given every indication that if I transferred to the Air Force I might be promoted rather promptly. Nonetheless, I took the position that I did not want to be a second-class citizen in anybody's organization. I was too old to take training as a tactical pilot and get an Air Force rating. Even if I could have done so, this would have taken me away from my technical work. So I declined and said I would stay with the Army. Many other technical officers did likewise, with the result that the new Service was not able to build any solid foundation of in-house technical capability for weapons other than airplanes. Here was laid the foundation for later disputes over the Army's so-called "arsenal" system. The Air Force never had the chance to build such a system, and was, of course, forced to make a virtue of necessity.

I did not at the time foresee the difficulties that would arise from the creation of the Department of Defense. It was obvious to me with three Services, some kind of an umpire was going to be essential. I hoped that the Chairman of the Joint Chiefs of Staff would have enough influence to handle that situation in the military field, leaving the Secretary of Defense to function in the area of civilian policy control.

As I remember, the original act allowed only about 100 people for the Defense and JCS establishments. Most of us in the military thought that the control to be exercised by the Secretary of Defense would be the type of control we had always known. We expected the new department to stick to the business of setting policy and exerting an over-all influence in line with the desires of the Commander-in-Chief, rather than attempting to operate the Services in detail.

The years since have proved that the problems I saw with regard to a separate Air Force were and are far worse than I had imagined. Those years have also proved that many problems would result from the creation of a Department of Defense that I did not foresee at all.

The lack of a sound, experienced, military-technical organization in the Air Force has been responsible for the technical side of that Service becoming almost a slave of the aircraft and associated industries, subject to endless pressure and propaganda. In the area of support to the Army, the situation is also worse than I had envisioned. Operations in Korea very clearly disclosed the inferior capability of the Air Force to provide close tactical air support to the ground Army. This was particularly evident when contrasted to the support provided by Marine Aviation to Marine Corps ground forces. There was some little stir about this at the end of Korea but, as usual, it died down and nothing came of it.

Aside from this problem of tactical air support, there has been nothing but deterioration in the capabilities of the Air Force to provide airlift for either airborne divisions or supporting forces that might have to be moved rapidly into an overseas theatre. The Air Force has been so preoccupied with what they deemed to be their primary mission of strategic air power that the elements responsible for support to the Army have been almost starved. I do not think this situation will be corrected without either the reamalgamation of the Army and Air Force, or the transfer to the Army of the tactical air and troop carrier missions.

At the Joint Chiefs' level, we have probably had the least effective military organization to haunt the United States since the fiascoes of the Civil War. It has not only become a debating society, but the unwillingness or inability of the separate Chiefs to resolve their differences has opened the door to usurpation of actual military direction by the civilian elements of the Department of Defense.

I honestly believe that if the Joint Chiefs, when confronted by an irreconcilable difference among themselves, would lock the door, toss a coin, and agree solidly to support the decision selected by that coin, we would be better off in the area of military guidance than we are at present. Any one of the positions taken by any one member of the Joint Chiefs would, in my opinion, be better than the compromises and directed verdicts that are the result of having to take the whole business to the Secretary of Defense for decision.

My original conception of the Chairman of the Joint Chiefs as an arbiter has not been fulfilled. We have now transferred command control of our joint forces to the Joint Chiefs of Staff, rather than parceling them out among the several services. This means, in effect, that our present military operations are governed by a committee with widely divergent views. There is no example in history of military command being successfully exercised under those circumstances.

The very esssence of military operations is deep-rooted in individual responsibility and authority. Successful military organization has never been achieved, and in my opinion never will be achieved, by any form of so-called democratic forum approach. Military command requires the exercise of unique and dictatorial powers. At the moment we have no one, short of an overburdened President, who can truly exercise the powers and responsibilities demanded as the price of sound military policy.

As of today, lack of forceful military leadership in the form of an authoritative head to the Joint Chiefs has set the stage for the intrusion of the ill-prepared civilian and the nonmilitary scientist into a position of day-to-day control of the military affairs and military operations of the United States. The natural result has been a steady increase in the staff of the Secretary of Defense. The old principle of a few policy-making civilians controlling the operations of the military through direct contact has given way to the creation of an enormous civilian staff of professional Civil Service bureaucrats between the responsible heads of the three Services and the Secretary of Defense.

Nothing that happens today can be correctly interpreted if this critical situation is overlooked. The great majority of facts and opinions digested and presented to the Secretary of Defense and his numerous Assistant Secretaries as a basis for decision are facts and opinions interpreted by this permanent Civil Service staff in accordance with their own ideas. In large measure, the Secretary of Defense is effectively isolated from responsible military opinion. Theoretically he gets that from the Joint Chiefs, but their inability to agree and unwillingness to compromise leave him in the position of making up his own mind. He does so after having had the problem "staffed" by accountants, administrative assistants, and a host of other bureaucrats.

In the last couple of years we have seen the astonishing spectacle of pure scientists moving into the field of military policy and deciding upon the weapons needed by the military. I do not think one must be a professional soldier to question the ultimate wisdom of this.

I sometimes feel the seeds for all this trouble were sown by the refusal of old-line Navy and Army officers to accept the manned aircraft as an effective instrument of war in a period when it actually *was* a powerful and effective weapon. This put the proponents of manned aircraft in a position of martyrdom, and set the stage for a permanent inferiority complex. It is the contrary manifestation of that inferiority complex, the "over-compensation" well recognized by psychologists, that has created the enormous propaganda machine of the Air Force.

Where flying machines were concerned, the Navy faced their internal problem, made certain compromises, and learned to live with it. The result is that today we have one Navy. The Army did not compromise their problem. The Air Force won the ascendancy, and today we have two Armies—one on the ground and one in the air above the ground and based on the ground.

It seems to me now that the Air Force is threatened by the same type of inflexibility that got us into this trouble in the first place. The majority of the rated officers of the Air Force, with some notable exceptions, are clinging to manned aircraft as their outstanding hope for survival—and for their flight pay. This can well lay the groundwork for as disastrous a division within the Air Force itself as was created in the Army earlier by the decline of horse cavalry and the ascendancy of the flying machine and the tank.

In all honesty, I must also add that I do not think the situation has been helped in recent years by having a soldier in the White House. The developments in the fields of military tactics and weapons since World War II have been so far-reaching that anyone whose personal experience ended shortly after that war cannot hope to be abreast of today's military needs in the really professional sense. Yet, having been immensely successful as a theatre commander in a major war, the President is necessarily impressed with his own military knowledge and thus less inclined to listen to the advice of today's military professionals.

We must recognize, however, that our troubles do not stem from individuals, but from basic mistakes made years ago, usually for reasons that looked good at the time. Every effort since has actually resulted in further complication. The result is like putting patch on top of patch on a faulty and leaking roof. We need a new roof!

CHAPTER VI

Out of the Frying Pan

It was during late 1953 and early 1954 that some of us in Army Ordnance got our heads together on the question of acquiring some modern and forward-looking test facilities for bigger guided missiles.

Under the direction of von Braun and his men, the Redstone was being developed at Redstone Arsenal, near Huntsville, Alabama. This was to be the first of the really big missiles. Into it was going all the know-how that these brilliant ex-Germans had acquired in years of working on the V-2, and more years of experiment and hard work at El Paso. Out in California, Jet Propulsion Laboratory had developed the Corporal, and it was going into production as the first American ballistic missile to be put into operation. Redstone was much bigger and had a much longer range. Von Braun knew that if we were to get on with the business of long-range missiles, and particularly if we were to have any foundation for space work, we would have to come up with some really big liquid-propelled engines and some very large missiles.

No such missile can be adequately developed unless test facilities are available, and, as is well known today, these are very expensive. One of the prime necessities is a test tower on which a big missile can be mounted and held down for thorough static testing, before being taken to a firing point. In addition, a modern test facility must have places for testing all kinds of hazardous components, including high-speed turbines and model engines of unique capability.

Gen. H. N. Toftoy, who was in charge of Redstone Arsenal at that time, came up with what for those days was an outrageously ambitious project to build such a complex on the top of a hill at the Arsenal. The Army had no mission beyond the Redstone missile itself, which was well along in development, and there was no possible way that the research people could finance such a test complex because they could find no real excuse for it. Yet if anything significant were to be done in the future, the construction of such a complex would have to start right away. Construction time would be a couple of years at least, and in the meantime nothing bigger, or more advanced, could be undertaken. It was the old story that still haunts the programs of the Army, where you can't get what you need for future work until the work itself is approved, and when that happens it is too late to build what you needed in the first place.

If anything was to be done, it seemed to us that it would have to be accomplished with production money. Now the rules say that production money cannot be used for research and development projects. Yet there was a fair amount of money available in the production budget for building or acquiring facilities, and there was none in the Research and Development budget. Finally we cooked up a plausible story of needing the test tower and other test facilities in order to carry on the required quality control and inspection testing that would be needed when the Redstone missile went into production. On the basis that the facilities were to be used for the testing of items in production, rather than for development tests, we could legally use production money.

I do not think anyone in the Army knew what we were up to, but I watched the campaign carefully and finally wangled it through with approximately 13 million dollars as an initial increment. I very carefully avoided even mentioning any R & D work that might be done on these facilities, because I knew this would prejudice our chances. The people who were responsible for approving these projects were, I am afraid, not too well informed with respect to the guided missile area, and they swallowed our story. It is interesting to note that had not this project been rammed through and approved when it was not really justified by either the ground rules or the needs of the moment, there would have been nothing available to make possible the rapid development of the Jupiter missile or the test work that made the satellites possible.

I was convinced by this time that the future of the Ordnance Corps was in large part in guided missiles. Few were interested in old-fashioned munitions, and getting money to build modern tanks or new rifles or develop new vehicles was very difficult indeed. On the other hand, missiles were beginning to capture the public imagination, and support could be had for additional work and new projects.

In November 1954 when Maj. Gen. E. L. Cummings, who had been the Chief of the Industrial Division, became Chief of Ordnance, he assigned me to his old job. On assuming that task, I took over responsibility for tanks and military vehicles, artillery and small arms, as well as for ammunition and guided missiles. My relationship with industry was close and constant.

I have had cause to remember many times one particular incident that turned out to be rather prophetic.

The whole staff of the Chief of Ordnance was debating the question of what items we should use as the strongest justification for a reasonable budget. There was great pressure to request a lot of money for tanks and some new types of artillery. After listening to the debate for a while, I finally said: "You're fighting a losing game. If you put all your energy and effort into justifying these conventional weapons and ammunition, even though I know we need them, I think you are going to get very little money of any kind. It is far easier to justify a budget with modern items that are popular, and I would strongly recommend that you increase the amount you show in the budget for the production of missiles, limiting yourself on the other items to the modest quantities that you know you can get by with. If you increase your demands for guided missiles, I think there is a fair chance you can get a decent budget. Why don't you accentuate the positive and go with that which is popular, since you cannot get the other stuff anyway?"

As things turned out, I was mighty glad later that I had taken that position.

By the fall of 1955 I was beginning to be bored and frustrated. Life was nothing but a constant battle to push little pieces of paper up through the maze of staff in endless attempts to get a decision. I was never able to discover whether the snail-like techniques that prevailed were designed to hold down expenditures by administrative delay, or whether it was simply that no one could or would make up his mind. I was on very friendly terms with the then Deputy Chief of Staff for Logistics, Lt. Gen. Carter B. Magruder, for whom I have great affection and respect, and with his civilian opposite number in the Secretariat, the Assistant Secretary of the Army for Logistics, then Mr. Frank Higgins. Nonetheless, I don't think I ever got a decision on anything of any importance without trudging to their respective offices many times.

After long argument with lesser staff officers I would finally get to Magruder and obtain military staff approval, but this was only the beginning. Before Mr. Higgins would approve an item for production or approve the provision of new facilities to a producer, he would ask one thousand and one questions. Still worse, the questions did not all appear at one time. I would answer some and leave, thinking I had satisfied the requirement, only to hear the next morning that "Mr. Higgins wants to know this, that or the other about such and such a project," and I would start the rat race all over again.

There are times when I am convinced that the Pentagon itself, as a building, is responsible for many of the problems and inefficiencies in the military services today. There are too many people with too many divergent views too close to each other. No single element of the Services, or of the Staff, or of the Department of Defense can do its work by itself. The rumor factory is always busy, and the one-feather Indians of low rank, both military and civilian, representing all the different echelons of control, run into one another at the coffee bars and the lunch tables, and cook up new harassments for the Commanders.

I believe that if the many segments of the Services that are supposed to have some autonomy of operation were scattered so that it would at least take a little effort and planning to get somebody to come over and see somebody else, there would be more decision and less conversation with attendant frustrations. It is a hard thing to define, but the Pentagon does have a personality and it is not a good one. Only the person who is a true and devoted bureaucrat remains happy in it. To every person of real intelligence and imagination that I have met, it has become a symbol of a frustration. There is more truth than poetry in the rather stale joke that "no enemy in his right mind would ever drop a bomb on the Pentagon, because in its present state it offers him much more assistance than if it were destroyed."

The result of my frustrations was a tentative decision in the early fall of 1955 to retire and go out and see if I could still make money in the world of industry. I finally told the Chief of Ordnance that I thought I would be retiring in March or April, 1956,

By this time, the Air Force project to build the Atlas ICBM (Inter-Continental Ballistic Missile) was well under way, but on a time scale that admittedly would not provide an operational missile until at least 1959 or early 1960. As part of the study, the Air Force had proposed to provide a short-range missile in the 1,500-mile class as a "fall-out" from the ICBM. A committee under Dr. James Killian examined the whole situation, including Russian progress in the development of air defense missiles, and finally came up with the statement that the provision of a 1,500-mile ballistic missile was a *most* urgent requirement of the United States. This requirement was not put ahead of the ICBM, but it was believed that the shorter-range missile could be provided in less time, so it was given equal priority. The theory was that this Intermediate Range Ballistic Missile would be able to strike from existing U. S. bases surrounding the Soviet Union, and thus provide a retaliatory capability that would strongly reinforce our manned bombers.

At about this same time, the initial planning began for a scientific satellite to be used as a United States contribution to the International Geophysical Year (generally referred to by the initials IGY), that would run from July 1957 through December 1958.

Dr. von Braun's organization at Redstone Arsenal made proposals on behalf of the Army in both categories. The satellite proposal was known as Project Orbiter. This plan, put forward by the von Braun group in conjunction with the Naval Research Laboratory and the Jet Propulsion Laboratory operated by Cal Tech, called for the use of the Redstone missile as a booster, with upper stages of clustered solid-fuel rockets, to put up a satellite weighing roughly 20 pounds.

After much debate, committee hassling, and backing and filling, the Vanguard was approved by the Secretary of Defense as the satellite carrier. Vanguard was a new three-stage concept, with little experience and no developed components behind it. However, it was sufficiently dissociated from any weapons system so that it could be an unclassified project, and this was appealing to the civilian scientists. The reasons for the decision were never well understood, and since the record shows that they were based either on poor judgment or bad information, it is doubtful that anyone will ever fully disclose the events that led up to the selection of Vanguard. In any case, the proven talents of the von Braun team were ignored. Originally budgeted at $20,000,000, the Vanguard was to become a $120,000,000 boondoggle that contributed little or nothing to progress in space, future weapons, or the international prestige of the United States. I shall have more to say about this later.

Meanwhile, having lost out on that particular effort, the Army decided to make a vigorous bid for the intermediate-range ballistic missile. The idea of the IRBM as a natural "fall-out" of the ICBM having been rejected by the Department of Defense scientific advisory committee, the Air Force came up with a new design of their own, which was later to become the Thor. Dr. von Braun's group worked hard to come up with a good clean design, using a maximum of components that had been proven in the Redstone, so that the new weapon could be developed on the shortest possible time scale. This became the original proposal for the Jupiter weapons system.

During this period, I was only moderately aware of all of these developments. I talked frequently with Maj. Gen. Les Simon, who was Chief of Research and Development for the Ordnance Corps, and through him and some of his people I kept track of the general pattern. But I was having enough problems of my own in the Industrial Division, particularly in getting the Nike antiaircraft rocket system into full production.

I was catapulted into the middle of the red-hot competition for the IRBM when I found myself Acting Chief of Ordnance due to the temporary absence of General Cummings and General Hinrichs, his Deputy. I got a call from Lieutenant General Magruder, Deputy Chief of Staff for Logistics for the Army, asking me to meet with him and with General O'Meara to discuss a situation that had arisen in connection with the Army's bid for this high-priority project. It had become a very competitive struggle between the Air Force and the Army. Both calculated, apparently quite correctly, that whoever was assigned this particular weapon would automatically take over the intermediate battle area. The Army was taking the position that a 1,500-mile missile was simply an extension of the range of modern artillery, beyond that achieved by the Corporal missile and the oncoming Redstone. The Air Force position was that the IRBM was in no sense a war missile to support troop action, but was in fact a substitute for manned aircraft in the strategic deterrent area.

The Navy had no capability upon which to base a bid for the IRBM but had launched a campaign to convince the Defense Department that a ship-mounted, and eventually a submarine-mounted, missile would provide the best possible strategic deterrent and retaliatory capability. Since the resulting weapon would be in competition with the Air Force, it was obvious that for the Navy to have any part in this development they would have to climb into bed with the Army. The result was that the Jupiter project was transformed into a dual-purpose missile, to be launched from shipboard as a Navy weapon, and also to be mobile and ground based to meet the initial requirements that had been stated by the Killian Committee.

As the report of the Congressional Committee on Government Operations put it four years later, in September 1959:

> The Air Force had long since pre-empted the field of inter-continental-range missiles. The Army had cast a speculative eye in this direction, working outward from the short-range Redstone and the intermediate-range Jupiter. The Air Force started with the Atlas, but temporarily worked inward (in range) to the Thor. The two Services clashed at the IRBM range.

A masterpiece, I might say, of understatement!

Since time was the key consideration, it was obvious that the Defense Department would be influenced by the type of organization proposed and the ability of that organization to move swiftly. The Army was in the midst of writing up their concept in the form of a letter to the Secretary of Defense from the Secretary of the Army. It was this presentation that was under discussion when General Magruder called me in.

The Chief of Ordnance had initially proposed that the IRBM job be given to the Guided Missile Development Division at Redstone Arsenal, which was in fact the von Braun team. He had proposed that this be done within the existing framework of organization. However, it soon became apparent that this was not a good enough bid, and that something more radical and faster-moving would have to be proposed.

Looking far down the road, General Cummings felt that the best bet would be the organization of a new and broader Command in the guided missile area, with a new Agency or subordinate Command as one element. A general officer could be put in command of the new Agency, and that particular group could devote their entire energy to the Redstone and Jupiter for the immediate future.

When I was summoned to talk with Magruder and O'Meara, the draft papers had been up to the Chief of Staff's office and required some changes and modifications to be satisfactory to him and to the Secretary. The papers were very tightly held and not too many people knew about them. The range of the discussion was in itself a clear indication of the problems that would develop in the future.

The Air Force was insisting that their organization at the Ballistic Missile Division of the Air Research and Development Command in Santa Monica had all the required characteristics of independent action and fast response. The organization charts that were drawn indicated all sorts of straight-line access to higher authority, and freedom of action to carry out their work. To those who were familiar with the actual workings of that organization it was quite clear that it was not that simple. It might work very well through the research and development stage, but all sorts of other independent Air Force Commands would have to come into the picture in connection with production and training.

The Air Force had handled this situation by having elements of the Air Training Command and of the Air Material Command stationed with BMD (then commanded by Brigadier General Schriever) at Santa Monica. The Ramo-Wooldridge Corporation —a private engineering management organization—was to be responsible for over-all technical supervision over the Thor, the Air Force entry in the IRBM race. The Air Force would have independent contracts with General Electric and others for nose cones, North American for engines, Douglas Aircraft for the "air frame" of the missile and the AC Spark Plug Division of General Motors for the guidance system.

With much greater experience in both engineering co-ordination and procurement, the Army could not accept that approach as a feasible one, and proposed to follow through on the Army concept of an integrated organization by putting the whole job under one single field commander.

I did the best I could to represent General Cummings in this discussion. The last thing I was thinking of was having any personal stake in the outcome, since I had already decided to retire within a few months. However, in the course of the discussion it became quite obvious that one of the major difficulties was in the selection of a commander. The Ordnance Corps was not too richly endowed with general officers who would have both the command ability and the technical knowledge necessary to spearhead this effort. Several names had been proposed, but none had been found fully acceptable by the Secretary of the Army, nor did he believe that any of them would be acceptable to the Secretary of Defense.

I got in touch with General Cummings right away, and he hurried back to work on the project over the weekend. One of the most amusing situations that sticks in my mind was that Sunday morning in the office of the Chief of Ordnance, with no clerks or junior officers around—just General Cummings and myself pecking away on two separate typewriters trying to spell out the details of our proposal.

Having been in the position of representing General Cummings for the preceding two days, I naturally stayed with the job until it was finished. The final paper took the position that the Army Ballistic Missile Agency should be organized as an independent command at Redstone Arsenal, should take over the people and the facilities of the Guided Missile Development Division of Redstone Arsenal, and should be assigned the job of developing the Jupiter missile system and at the same time taking the Redstone missile from research and development to production and deployment as a weapon. It was necessary that the two be held together, since the same people were doing both jobs, and since many of the components to be used in Jupiter would be derived from the Redstone.

The directive to be issued by the Chief of Staff was to place the highest priority on the work of the Army Ballistic Missile Agency, and was to authorize the Commander to call on any part of the Army for any services or resources that were required to do the job. In other words, he was given the authority of the Chief of Staff to require of the rest of the Army any co-operation, assistance or support needed without the delay that would be imposed by ordinary co-ordination between independent Commanders. This authority was later to prove to be one of the most powerful assets of ABMA in getting its work done.

It was also agreed that the Secretary of the Army would delegate to the Commander of ABMA as much authority as the law allowed to make immediate personal decisions in procurement, the authorization of new facilities, and the execution of negotiated contracts.

This is perhaps the place to note that in four years of using those delegated authorities no serious question was ever raised as to the legality of any action taken, or the judgment and fairness used in the awarding of contracts. If one were to look coldly at these results, it seems to me that it might be reasonable to assume that instead of being the exceptional way to do business, this would be the proper way to handle all of the business of the Army. This would be true decentralization, and would be enormously effective in reducing the administrative delays that are continually costing the taxpayer money. It is also interesting to note that the lesser officials at the Pentagon were never happy with such delegated powers, since it meant that there was no detailed paper work coming in to be shifted around government employees' desks and make work for the bureaucrats. In spite of the fact that there was no criticism of any of the actions taken, the question of withdrawing this delegated authority came up frequently. There was a continuing backstage campaign to persuade the Secretary of the Army that no such authority should be left out in the field in the hands of a mere major general.

In the midst of work over the text of the proposal and directive and the basis for the organization, the question was always cropping up as to who would be selected to command ABMA and develop Jupiter. Finally General Magruder asked me to meet with him on a quiet Saturday morning, and we talked for a couple of hours. He was kind enough to say that he thought if I could take the assignment it would assure the Army of having the opportunity to develop this very important missile. In the meantime my own conscience had been bothering me. I had come to feel that if I went ahead with my plans for retirement I would be running away from a duty. I talked it over with my wife, and we agreed that I could not go about my own business when there was such a demanding task that so badly needed doing. I finally told General Magruder that I would set aside my plans for retirement if the Army believed that I was needed for this particular job. From that minute on, I was completely absorbed in the business of missiles and space.

During all the early negotiations concerned with the Jupiter project, a young colonel by the name of Nickerson had been the legman for the Research and Development Division of the Ordnance Corps and was the custodian of all information as to background, Navy attitude, Air Force competition, the opinions of the several advisory committees that were concerned, and all the back-alley machinations of the junior staff. Since he was by nature an individualist, he was carrying on all this leg work personally, and half of the records were either in his head or existed only in the form of sketchy memoranda that he had written up. Most of these papers were in his possession. Few of them had found their way into the official files. This situation laid the foundation for what was later to become my most bitter experience in connection with ABMA.

On the 8th of November, 1955, approval was finally received from the Department of Defense for the assignment jointly to the Army and Navy of the development of an intermediate-range ballistic missile. Somewhat to our chagrin, numbers were put on the IRBM projects and the project assigned to the Air Force was designated IRBM No. 1. This was a clear indication that insofar as the land-based IRBM was concerned, the Army Jupiter was considered as a "back-up" to the Air Force Thor.

The Department of Defense directive made the situation even more clear by specifying that the development under the supervision of the Secretary of the Army was to provide a *sea-based* IRBM and to serve as a second approach to a land-based missile. This made it quite apparent that the future of the IRBM project for the Army was pretty well tied to the Navy, and that we must assume that our primary reason for existence was to produce a naval weapon. Since this provided much more solid support for the project than did our back-up for the land-based missile, we were quite satisfied to close ranks solidly with the Navy.

Upon receipt of this directive by the Army, I was named "Commanding General Designate" of ABMA, and Army orders were issued for the formation of the Army Ballistic Missile Agency as a separate command, effective February 1, 1956.

I had been given the broadest kind of authority and therefore, from the official standpoint, was able to impose my desires on virtually anyone in the Army short of the top Army Staff. However, authority is one thing—intelligent use of that authority is something quite different. While I could legally order all sorts of installation Commanders and even the Chiefs of other Services outside Ordnance to do anything we needed, it was quite obvious that injudicious use of such authority could easily create a "bull-in-the china-shop" situation. From the beginning, therefore, I resolved that I would make every possible attempt to get what was needed by respecting the responsibilities of others, and requesting co-operation rather than issuing orders. This policy was to pay off in many ways.

I was not scheduled to move to Huntsville until February 1st, but from my post in Washington I assumed official responsibility for the prosecution of the Redstone missile program and the development of the new IRBM. The interim was filled with just about the fastest action in which I had ever had a part. The first requirement was to secure enough of the right kind of people to provide top-quality staff. The selection of these people, and getting them in motion from all over the world toward Huntsville, was a first order of business.

It was here that the unusual authorities given me were of great value, because I was able to hand-pick my team very quickly. Insofar as I could, I selected people that I already knew, and who had worked with me previously. Thus I could be certain of loyalty as well as ability.

As Assistant Chief of Ordnance for the Industrial Division, I had had a young administrative assistant—Lt. Horace Tousley, nicknamed Whitey. I really don't know how we could have managed in those first difficult months in ABMA without Whitey's high order of intelligence, quick and discerning mind and eye, and ability to follow up a thousand tasks without letting anything get away. He became, in truth, "aide de camp," with his notebook being the only official record of many of our early actions.

Due to its relatively isolated location, one of the major problems of the new Command was communications. I have learned from long and bitter experience that the ability to control is only as good as the ability to communicate. Also I may add that I have never learned how to handle any far-flung operation sitting at a desk on the seat of my pants. Personal contact is an absolute essential if all the strings of a complex project are to be kept in hand. At that time Huntsville had very poor transportation communications with other areas, and only mediocre wire and radio access. I set about correcting this immediately. Fortunately there was a good airstrip at Redstone Arsenal that had been built during World War II. The supporting facilities were almost nonexistent, but the strip itself provided something to build on. Consequently I set about organizing an Army Air Section to provide our much needed transportation.

I had been using the Army Air Section based at Davisson Field, Fort Belvoir, for much of my own travel around the United States, and had gotten well acquainted with one of their pilots, Capt. William H. Ballard. I had Bill Ballard and one airplane assigned to me immediately, and I virtually lived in that airplane for the next few months. More than once we landed at Huntsville in the middle of the night, with no communication to the civil air lanes except the radio on our own airplane, and with nothing on the field but an open shed and one telephone. In addition to moving me around the country, Bill Ballard set about getting the assignment of additional planes and pilots as fast as possible.

During my first official contacts with von Braun and his group of top-level scientists and engineers, we came to understand each other very quickly. He had about 1,700 people in the Guided Missile Development Division, all of them scientists, engineers or good technicians. The top rank of ex-Germans were remarkable men in many ways. I was struck from the start by their self-discipline and persistence, and by the remarkable way in which they could blend imaginative theory with a practical approach to things. They also had no fear or hesitancy about admitting mistakes—a sure sign of good leadership and high morale.

It was obvious to me that if von Braun was to be able to take full advantage of the capabilities of his group, I had to build around them a supporting organization which would keep the scientific and technical people from wasting their time on anything other than really technical work. This purpose became the central theme of the organization of ABMA. We took over the development group intact, and then moved with all possible speed to build up an organization that could provide them with their supplies, handle all purchasing and procurement from contractors, deal with other elements of the Army and with the Navy, supervise the training that would be our responsibility in connection with turning the Redstone into an effective weapon system, and provide complete administrative, fiscal and logistic support.

I could get only a few of the people I needed from Washington. I was able to pick up Col. Milton H. Clark as Executive Officer, and latched on to Maj. Leonard S. Frankenstein out of my own Industrial Division. Here again young Nickerson entered the picture. He had been in Washington four years. The rules required that he get out of the Pentagon on February 1st, which coincided with the organization date for ABMA. I didn't particularly like Nickerson's method of operation, and a careful scrutiny of his record showed clearly that he had exhibited only mediocre capability. He was intelligent, but undisciplined in his methods of handling official affairs, and had given ample indication that he was personally arrogant with respect to his own opinions as to how things should be done. In spite of all this, his familiarity with the background of the Jupiter Project, plus the fact that he had to be transferred out of Washington, made his assignment to ABMA seem logical.

I discussed the situation with General Cummings, and I can remember finally saying to him, "Okay, I'll take Nickerson. I guess I can handle one wild horse in the barn."

As it turned out, I was wrong. I couldn't handle that particular one.

CHAPTER VII

Who Was Doing What

I think it is important—essential, really—before plunging into the complexities of my assignment at Huntsville to give the reader some idea of what the missile picture was in all three Armed Services at the time, and also a brief indication of the immense amount of labor, experience, and technological skill that goes into the conception and development of a giant rocket.

When I went to Huntsville, at the beginning of 1956, the United States missile program was beginning to be quite active. It was also becoming steadily more confused. Each of the three Services was busily engaged in developing missiles to aid in accomplishing its own particular mission. There was nothing inherently wrong with this. I think that each Service should be allowed to develop the tools to do its assigned job. The trouble was, the assignments were not always clear. We were beginning to pay the price of the fundamentally ridiculous decision to determine military missions on the basis of the tools to be employed, rather than stating the task to be done and letting each choose the tools he needed.

The old rule of thumb that "anything with wings is Air Force, anything without wings is artillery," had long since broken down. Generally speaking, at this point the Air Force and the Navy were permitted to develop, produce, and employ air-to-air and air-to-surface guided-missile systems required by their assigned functions. All three Services were permitted to develop, produce, and employ surface-to-surface missiles, except that the Army was limited to missiles against tactical targets in combat zones, and the Air Force was given authority over missiles of intercontinental range. In air defense, all three Services were permitted to develop, produce, and employ surface-to-air missiles. The Army was supposed to work on missiles with a restricted range for defense of specific areas or cities, whereas the Air Force would defend wider areas, using missiles to supplement manned interceptors.

As you can imagine, this added up to a lot of missiles!

The Navy, understandably, was primarily concerned with air defense of their carriers and other naval craft, and had concentrated most of their rocket work in the field of ship-to-air missile systems. There had been the Tartar, followed by the Terrier, and by 1956 the longer-range, higher-altitude, but decidedly complicated Talos system was being brought to the point of final test. Although this system was devised for use aboard ships, where all the accessory systems and power supplies of the vessel itself could support the system, arrangements were under way for building a complete system on land at the White Sands Proving Ground. This was to be the basis for a test by the Air Force as to the suitability of Talos for use in the defense of air bases. Even this early, it was obvious that the Air Force did not want to see the Army develop the strong position in land-based air defense that was historically the outgrowth of antiaircraft artillery.

Extensive paper studies had been made by the Air Force in an effort to support a weapon known as "Wizard" in competition with the Army's oncoming advanced Nike systems. This conflict was settled, at least temporarily, in 1957 when the Army was assigned the task of evaluating Talos, and the Nike-Hercules was confirmed for deployment, and Nike-Zeus for development. The "Wizard" studies were reluctantly canceled.

Both the Navy and Air Force, naturally, were interested in air-to-air missiles for combat between manned aircraft. Navy came up with the Sidewinder, which was a spectacularly effective weapon of very low cost. It was good enough to take precedence for both Navy and Air Force over the Navy's Sparrow and the Air Force Falcon.

By 1956, the Navy and the Air Force were also showing interest in more sophisticated air-to-ground missiles, which had had their beginning with the German-developed glide bomb of World War II. The purpose was to achieve the capability of letting the aircraft stand off further from the target, and free of danger from local antiaircraft defenses. The Navy started with the Corvus, and the Air Force developed the Rascal. Both of these projects eventually died and gave way to the Navy Bull Pup, which is now being used by both services. It is interesting perhaps to note that these weapons are so big that they themselves are vulnerable to attack by modern antiaircraft missile defenses.

All of the early surface-to-surface efforts of both Air Force and Navy were concentrated on what might properly be called "pilotless aircraft." Navy came up with the first Regulus, a ship-based subsonic surface-to-surface winged missile. The Air Force developed the Matador, which was highly touted as a mobile land-based missile for support to troops in the field. It was subsonic, low altitude, with limited maneuver capability, and highly vulnerable to enemy countermeasures. Matador was later followed by Mace which, although much faster and more reliable than Matador, is still a big and relatively easy low-altitude target for enemy antiaircraft fire.

The first bid for a very long-range missile was the Air Force Snark. This is nothing but a simple pilotless bomber, subsonic, that can actually be pursued and shot down by our own manned fighter planes, or anybody else's. Snark was just about getting into business in 1956, and it is hard to understand why it is still hanging around when practically everyone admits that it is obsolete.

The Navajo was a major Air Force bid for a long-range high-performance surface-to-surface pilotless aircraft capability. Its development began very early and it was supposed to have been operational long before it was finally canceled after having consumed over 750 million dollars. If Navajo had come out in accordance with its original time scale, it would have been an effective weapon. However, it is my opinion that the development program was ill conceived and as a result, Navajo's major difficulties did not appear until late in the test program, when there was insufficient time to straighten out the problem.

The Navajo program made one contribution to the Army's efforts. The rocket engines for the Navajo booster represented North American Aviation's first real effort to improve on the old V-2 rocket engine. This effort was later switched insofar as Navajo was concerned, but the early Navajo engine became the basis for the liquid-fuel rocket motor used in the Army's Redstone.

The record of winged missiles would not be complete without a mention of Bomarc. When the Bomarc project was first started by the Air Force, it was simply an effort to develop an unmanned interceptor. It was supposed to be operational by 1956, but at that point it was already far behind schedule and beset with difficulties. The first version had already been outperformed by manned interceptors and, in fact, by surface-to-air missiles. It was based on an extremely complex control system and was entirely unsuccessful in achieving its purpose. Bomarc B, with higher performance and longer range, was already coming on the horizon, although in my opinion winged missiles were beginning to be outdated by the onrushing space age.

By 1956, the Army had come up with the liquid-fueled

Corporal, which was our first surface-to-surface ballistic guided missile. Its ground handling equipment was heavy and complex. Nonetheless, it was an effective surface-to-surface missile and has been a strong element of our field forces in Europe right up to today. It will be replaced by the smaller, lighter, more mobile, and much faster-reacting solid-propellant Sergeant. Corporal was under 100 miles at maximum range.

Redstone, of course, was the Army's bid for a longer-range ballistic missile. The Redstone program had undergone at least two stops, starts, or reorientations, but one of my missions was to get it out into the field as soon as possible.

The ICBM history as related to the long-range ballistic missile was curious indeed. Since a weapon of intercontinental range is clearly a strategic weapon, the ICBM was from the start an Air Force project. Initial effort leading to an ICBM was started as early as 1948. In 1950 the ICBM project was canceled as being impractical at that time. From then until the project was reinstated about 1953 it was kept alive by Convair, who spent their own money to keep on studying and working at the problem. In 1953 Atlas—as our first ICBM was called—was given a more firm base, and by the time I went to Huntsville it had been joined by the Titan—a back-up program designed to provide even longer range.

There was some very interesting correspondence between Maj. General Leslie Simon, then Asst. Chief of Ordnance for Research and Development, and the Air Force, dated in 1954 and '55. Les Simon had offered the assistance of the Army and its people at Redstone in any way possible to help the Air Force on the ICBM project. He met virtually a stone wall of silence.

When I arrived at Huntsville, in addition to the work being done on the Redstone the Arsenal was busy with many other Army missiles. Some were being produced almost entirely in-house, but most were being developed or manufactured by industry under the technical supervision of Arsenal personnel.

The Nike air-defense missile family was handled from its inception by an industry team under Western Electric as prime contractor. Bell Laboratories had done all the development work on guidance equipment, both ground-based and missile-borne, and Douglas Aircraft built the missiles themselves. Nike-Ajax had been defending American cities for some time, and Nike-Hercules, the big brother, was nearing deployment. Development of Nike-Zeus, the antimissile missile, was just getting under way on a small scale.

Hawk, a highly mobile homing missile for defense against low-flying aircraft, was well along, with Ratheon as prime contractor. Early tests had demonstrated its potential effectiveness.

LaCrosse was under way—a very special, very accurate, battlefield missile that could be brought home on fairly short-range targets with deadly effect. This weapon was being brought up through advanced concept by Cornell Aeronautical Laboratory. Follow-on hardware, final development, and production were assigned to the Martin Company.

The free rockets, Honest John and its younger brother Little John, were to some degree in-house products. Shortly before going to Huntsville, I had been engaged in a hassle with Douglas over who owned the Honest John design. Douglas lost this argument, and Honest John was being bought competitively from Douglas and Emerson Electric.

Little John was being brought along as a smaller, faster, battlefield rocket for easy airborne transport and use. Most of the technical work was being done by the Ordnance Missile Laboratories at Redstone Arsenal. Work was also under way at OML to improve the basic accuracy of these free rockets.

Dart was being developed by a subsidiary of Curtiss-Wright as a wire-guided antitank weapon. It was having its troubles, and would later be canceled in favor of an antitank weapon developed by the French.

By this time Corporal was out in the field, but the Arsenal continued to have responsibility for logistic support, parts supply, distribution, and maintenance back-up. Corporal was the outgrowth of experimental design at the Jet Propulsion Laboratory, and had been transferred to Firestone and Gilfillan for production. Since JPL was a nonprofit organization operated wholly for the benefit of the Army, this could be said to have been in-house developed and then transferred to industry for production. The same procedure was to be followed with the big Army missiles, Redstone and Jupiter.

Sergeant, the fast, solid-propellant successor to Corporal, was being developed by the same JPL, and would go to Sperry for production. It was in initial test stage at that time, and would eventually replace the liquid-fueled Corporal.

Many smaller developmental efforts were being carried out or controlled by Redstone Arsenal. Improvement of solid propellants, better accuracy for free rockets, cheap guidance systems, and feasibility studies related to badly needed new weapons were under continuous study.

The most dramatic projects, of course, were the Redstone and Jupiter missiles. Both, in a sense, were descendants of the V-2—giant, liquid-fueled rockets. The Redstone was actually longer than the Jupiter, but its diameter was considerably smaller and its range was only some 200 miles. Jupiter, with twice the thrust of Redstone, was to have a 1,500-mile capability.

But to give my readers some idea of the complexity of these big birds, another chapter is necessary.

CHAPTER VIII

Thumbnail Biography of a Guided Missile

A guided missile, someone has said, is nothing but a rocket with a brain. This implies that there is something essentially simple about such a missile. Nothing, I assure you, could be farther from the truth.

No one who has not been personally involved in this complicated field of activity can be expected to comprehend the almost incredible complexity involved in the creation and evaluation, on paper, of a new design for a big missile or multistage space vehicle. The task could not be done at all, and we would not have any missiles, if it were not for the tremendous advances that have been made in electronic computers—the high-speed mathematical "brains" that reduce years of computation to minutes.

Every step of design is subjected to the cold mathematical scrutiny of these fantastic machines. Stresses, strengths, structural vibration, weights, balance, heating from the friction of the atmosphere, bending forces, the demands that will result on the guidance system, the forces that will be required to control the vehicle—all these things and many more, too complex to describe in nontechnical language, are calculated and recalculated, combined together and calculated again, with relatively few high-grade mathematicians, theoretical scientists, and engineers working as a team.

Finally the whole vehicle may be reduced to what is known as a mathematical model—a statement in numerical terms understandable only to a big computer, of all the parts and structures still to be fabricated. Then the scientists store away in the computer a series of problems that represent all the conditions of atmospheric pressure, temperature, winds aloft, acceleration and deceleration, and any other condition that may be encountered by the vehicle in its anticipated flight. The "electronic model" can then be "flown" by the computer against a whole series of varying combinations of conditions and environment, and the answers tell how the missile and its parts will respond. Where a choice of design is offered, each of the several possibilities may be substituted in the mathematical model, to see which gives the best results.

In spite of all these modern resources and methods, however, there is still no substitute for experience both in design and in development and test. Without a sound approach to design in the first place, the process would be even longer and more costly— unless some of the key steps were omitted with increased risk of failure after the hardware had been produced. Without flight experience, the computers could not be told of *all* the strange and varied phenomena that could have a greater or lesser effect on the vehicle in flight, nor of the many possible reactions within the complex gear aboard the missile which, if not understood and evaluated ahead of time, could bring millions of dollars down in a flaming wreck.

This is why the initial test results in the missile and space programs of the nation vary almost uniformly from very good to very bad, depending upon the experience of the designers and builders. It is also why the bulk of the work in advanced space systems will (or certainly should) stay in the hands or under the control of stable teams of scientists and engineers for whom the high price of gaining the experience has already been paid. We at ABMA were fortunate that Hitler's Germany had paid the price of endless "trial and error" through which many of our top scientists and engineers had gained their knowledge.

The major characteristic of a ballistic missile (as distinguished from air-defense or cruise-type weapons that are guided all the way to the target) is that the purpose of guidance is to constrain the missile to a predetermined course until it reaches an exact required velocity, and at the same time is pointed in a precise direction in space. The result, without any further effort or guidance, will necessarily bring it to earth on its predetermined target.

It is somewhat like aiming a large artillery piece, where the combination of the speed contributed by the powder charge and the direction given by the cannon barrel sets the missile on a course that is bound to take it to the target. The major difference is that for a large guided missile the "rifle barrel" may be 100 miles long. The purpose of guidance, then, is to keep it inside the rifle barrel and not allow any erratic behavior.

The course of a ballistic missile cannot be substantially changed after it is launched. Once it has passed the point where the motor is cut off, the only way to keep it from getting to its destination is to blow it apart, and even then the fragments will come down not too many miles short of the original target. The difference will lie only in the fact that the fragments will be slowed down faster and follow a more erratic course *after* re-entering the atmosphere than would the original warhead, with its carefully calculated ballistic shape and heat protection covering.

The process of developing such a missile is pretty much the same in all cases, although opinions differ as to how many missiles have to be fired to accomplish development.

First there is the careful process of calculation and engineering design. The selected shape is put through many tests in wind tunnels to be sure that it will behave in flight as it is expected to. These tests also determine the amount of power and size of control surfaces that will be required to overcome any variances in motor thrust, or outside disturbances such as wind gusts, and keep the missile on its required track.

When actual flight tests are begun, the first requirement is to prove out the propulsion unit, and make sure that it will deliver the required power in a dependable fashion. The motor has already been subjected to many tests tied down to a static test stand, but the final answers can be had only by actual travel up through the atmosphere and out into space.

The first missiles in a test program are only given the amount of guidance that is required to keep the missile in a reasonably straight path and not let it tumble. This can be done with the type of rudimentary inertial autopilot that was used years ago as the sole guidance system for the V-2. However, if it is a liquid-propelled missile, the tanks, pumping system, and the control actuators that direct the thrust to correct instability must be pretty much as they will be in the final missile. The over-all shape and the distribution of weight in the test missile are also in final form, or very close to it, so that when the propulsion system proves satisfactory it will not be necessary to make a lot of external changes that would require again going through wind tunnel experiments and flight tests for stability. When something goes wrong with a test flight, careful corrections are made and another missile is flown, preferably without adding anything more than was on the previous one, so that new unknown factors are not introduced.

After these initial propulsion tests, we begin to add the various parts of the refined guidance system that will be required to give the missile accuracy. Usually these are first flown just as "passengers," with instruments on board that are sending back to the ground, by telemetering, full information as to what would have happened had these new guidance elements been in control. Then, one at a time, the guidance components are hooked up and given a share in controlling the missile. Each flight that is successful permits going to another step with the next flight, providing there has been enough time allowed in the original schedule for making any corrections after the results of the last previous flight are known.

Next, and sometimes at the same time that guidance is introduced, the procedures that will separate the warhead and guidance compartment from the booster, when that booster has finished its job and is no longer needed, are tested in flight. It's quite a trick to make a clean separation between the parts of a missile in flight through space, without injecting the slightest disturbance that would send it off its path.

During the original tests of guidance, on-board accessories such as power supplies and electrical networks with all of their important bits and pieces are also checked. It is not unusual at this stage in the tests of a big missile to have as many as 150 separate pieces of information being sent back to the ground from the missile in flight, so that the behavior of all elements can be carefully followed, and so that if anything goes wrong, it is possible to determine not only what went wrong but exactly when.

Next must be put in all of the controls that will make the warhead perform its mission and explode when, and only when, it is supposed to. This in itself is a complicated process, since it not only must assure that if everything goes as it should the warhead will go off at exactly the right altitude for maximum effect, but also the system must make absolutely certain that if anything at all goes wrong aboard the missile the warhead will *not* detonate, and the missile will fall to earth and destroy itself as a dud without doing damage where it was not intended.

Once these basic steps have been gone through, including tests of the heat protection for the head to assure that it will survive and protect its contents in coming back down through the atmosphere at high speed, the balance of the program is devoted to refinement and to assurance of reliability. At the same time all the necessary, and sometimes complicated, ground-support equipment that will have to accompany the missile when it is used under operational conditions must be developed and tested.

Our method here was to start by developing as much as possible of the ground equipment right with the missile-development tests at the missile range, in a form that could be readily converted to use in the field. This not only saves time but also adds reliability, since the equipment thus has more tests than it could get if we waited until later in the program. The Army procedure was to do all static testing of missiles at Redstone Arsenal before sending them to the Cape. We did not then have to provide at Canaveral the complex and heavy devices required to hold the missile down while it is statically tested, and we could start right in using the simpler type of launch platform that would accompany the missile into operation.

Most missile-development programs are set up to have almost all the test firing done at something considerably less than the expected maximum range of the final weapon. This is done so that the missile can handle the weight of all the additional fact-finding instrumentation that assures that no accident will have to be classified as a "random failure." (This usually means that nobody is sure just what did happen.) Somewhere toward the latter part of the development program a missile will be trimmed to the exact weight of the tactical version and will be fired for full range, just to be sure that the calculated distance can be obtained.

Another reason for firing at less than full range is to give the cutoff mechanism, which is set up to shut off the engine at exactly the desired velocity, a chance to operate and prove its accuracy. At full range there is little opportunity for this mechanism to work, since every ounce of available power is wrung out to fling the missile as far as possible.

If early test firings are scheduled at too rapid a rate, it will mean that some errors will be repeated more than once, since there will be no opportunity to make a correction before the next firing. This is an expensive and wasteful process. On the other hand, if firings are scheduled too far apart, irreplaceable time is lost. At just precisely the correct time, the frequency of tests must begin to accelerate. At this time major errors are behind us, and repetitive testing for reliability becomes a major factor.

This necessarily brief biography of a big missile would not be complete without some discussion of the different types of propulsion now in use or on the horizon. As almost everyone knows, all our very large missiles so far (Jupiter, Thor, Atlas, and Titan) have been liquid-fueled rockets, and all our space work has been based on boosters of this type. However, the upcoming Minute Man ICBM will be a solid-propellant rocket. The Navy's submarine-launched Polaris is a solid-propellant weapon. The Army is using solid propellants in most of the battlefield rockets. And so the trend, on the surface, seems to be toward solid propellants.

But this current fad for solid propellants tends to ignore the basic advantages and disadvantages that are inherent in both liquid rocket engines and solid propellants.

The assumed disadvantages of liquid propellants include the time required for fueling the missile, the equipment required for fueling, the expensive and bulky manufacturing equipment, and the fact that the fuel, particularly the oxidizers, boils off rather rapidly under ordinary conditions.

On the other hand, the thrust of a liquid-propellant engine can be controlled much as one would throttle an automobile. In certain applications, particularly space work, a high-acceleration factor is very undesirable. There is, of course, a limit to the acceleration that can be withstood by a human, but aside from that, the higher the acceleration that must be accepted, the more costly it is to build all the delicate guidance mechanisms so that they withstand the force.

A solid-propellant grain (cross-section) can be designed to almost any acceleration, but the design is thereafter fixed. On the contrary, it is possible to make continuous changes in the thrust of a liquid engine by any standard programing device. Thus the flight of a missile using liquid propellants can be controlled to apply the most efficient thrust throughout the flight without exceeding any established maximum "G" factor.

When the exact required velocity is attained, the cutoff process for liquid engines is simple and precise. Obviously, merely terminating the flow of fuel is sufficient. On the other hand, although devices have been invented and proven successful for terminating the thrust of a solid-propellant rocket, they are much more complicated. Also, since it is impractical to "swivel" a whole heavy solid-propellant motor, the control over the direction of thrust requires that some type of mechanism (jet vanes, jetavators, or the like) be introduced directly into the jet stream. The temperatures and shock values are very high, and there is a constant problem of finding materials that will withstand this usage. In addition, introducing anything into the stream has the effect of reducing the efficiency to some extent.

Surrounding temperatures have a very considerable effect on the thrust generated by a solid propellant. This would not be too much of a problem if it were possible to know exactly the temperature at all parts of the grain at a given time, and to develop a satisfactory chart for predicting the results. This can be done with small grains, but when you get into the very large ones there is no accurate method for knowing exactly how far heat or cold may have penetrated. The resultant inexactness throws an additional and difficult load on the guidance mechanism. The earliest method for controlling this factor (and still about the only practical one) is to base performance on fairly high temperatures and provide some kind of heating blanket for maintaining a uniform temperature in the grain.

This is what makes the use of solid propellants for submarine-launched missiles practical. It is not difficult to control the environment, since the missile is always enclosed within the submarine. The same would be true for Minute Man so long as it is used in a closed silo where temperature control is not difficult. This matter of temperature becomes significant, however, the minute it is desired to have a large missile that is quite mobile.

This matter of mobility affects the choice of propellant in still another way. In handling a large liquid-propellant missile, the weight to be moved and erected is small compared to the total missile. The real weight is not added until fuel is poured in. For example, the complete Jupiter IRBM, ready to fire, weighs over 100,000 pounds. However, for handling purposes the empty weight is only about 15,000 pounds, and that is divided into three sections. This matter of handling is not a problem on board ship or at a permanent site, but obviously is a major factor if mobility is desired. Actually then, this important logistic factor alone puts a practical limitation on the size and range of a solid-propellant missile that is to be truly mobile.

There are several additional, although perhaps less important, factors affecting this choice. Solid propellants are more expensive than the commonly used liquid propellants and oxidizers. Any time a solid-propellant missile is statically tested, only the motor case is salvaged. Usually even the jet vanes have to be replaced. Thus the development tests involved in coming up with a good solid-propellant missile are, in general, more expensive.

It is interesting to note that not too much has been done in this country about storable liquid propellants, and yet in my opinion they offer the best possibility for combining the virtues of solids and liquids. I believe that the Russians have done more than we have in applying storables to practical missiles. I have been urging the virtue of storables for about four years, with little success. I note a recent announcement that Titan II may use this type of liquid propellant.

Many people claim that the use of solid propellants is preferable because, with the missile always fully loaded and ready, the reaction time will be significantly less. This is only partly true. Very fast fueling methods have been developed which permit fueling a large liquid missile in 15 minutes. Actually it is fueled in less time than that, but the total reaction time has been reduced to 15 minutes. The fact is that the guidance mechanism for a large missile requires at least ten minutes of warm-up time before it will function correctly. Thus, unless the guidance system is kept continually warmed-up and stabilized, only five minutes has been gained by the application of solid propellants. If a truly instantaneous reaction is demanded, and the guidance system is kept warmed-up, the frequent replacement of the gyroscopes will be extremely costly. As a matter of fact, to keep a substantial force of ICBM's fully ready for instant reaction would come close to the cost of maintaining the bombers of the Strategic Air Command in a state of constant alert.

All I am trying to say is that the choice is not clear-cut, and actually demands careful objective engineering analysis of both operational and technical requirements with respect to any given mission if the best possible propellant system is to be accepted. The tendency in our country to decide that because a thing is new and good for something, it is good for everything, has made it difficult for our planners to achieve such an objective approach.

While the chemical rocket engine, either liquid or solid fueled, is the only presently available propulsion system, three other types have been suggested for space vehicles. The most obvious is the nuclear reactor to provide the basic heat energy for accelerating an exhaust gas. In the present state of development, it would not be economical for use in vehicles of less than several hundred tons —much larger and heavier than anything constructed to date. But engineering may improve this method faster than most people think possible.

In another type of propulsion system, the propellant mass

would be converted to ions accelerated by an electric field. Much higher exhaust velocities could be realized. The potential ratio of fuel weight to vehicle weight increases the attractiveness of this type of system. For the purpose of comparison, a chemical rocket capable of a trip to Mars would require a fuel load about 25 times the weight of the useful portion of the vehicle. On the other hand, an ionic ship outlined by Dr. Ernst Stuhlinger, one of the members of my Army space team, would require a fuel mass only about equal to that of the vehicle itself.

There is an inherent characteristic of ionic propulsion, however, which limits its area of usefulness. The very low order of thrust could not overcome the forces of gravity and air friction at Earth's surface. Consequently the system would be useful only in the outer space vacuum—perhaps in a spaceship taking off from a manned satellite station. An experimental ionic-propulsion engine is now being built.

The most fantastic of the conceivable propulsion systems, and the only one beyond presently known techniques, involves the production of thrust by the emission of photons—that is, by the emission of light energy. The photons would be created by direct, total and controlled conversion of matter into radiant energy according to the Einstein equation. The process has been observed in the laboratory, but has not been demonstrated on an engineering scale. If it can be applied, it would make possible space travel beyond the reach of all other systems. For instance, a photon-powered spaceship should reach the moon in three and a half hours, and the nearer planets in two days, and would require only 3½ tons of fuel for the latter journey.

More significant masses must be reckoned with for trips outside the solar system. To reach the nearest star, Alpha Centauri, would require a fuel mass twice the weight of the ship. For a round trip of the present-known Universe, the total fuel mass required would just about equal the mass of the earth. Within our present knowledge of the basic laws of physics, we can therefore perceive definite limits to the extent of space travel, wholly apart from engineering limitations.

But these glittering prospects are for the missile-men of the future. Let us now return to the more prosaic problems that confronted me upon my arrival at Redstone Arsenal in February 1956.

CHAPTER IX

I Take Over My New Command

Redstone Arsenal, destined to be my base of operations for the next four years, presented a weird picture on that first day of February, 1956, when I arrived to constitute officially the new Command. The custodian of 40,000 acres in North Alabama, just inside the bend of the Tennessee River, the Arsenal was the kind of hodgepodge of the new and the old that too often results from the changing needs of the government being lashed to land already owned.

The Arsenal had originally come into military usage during World War II as a production plant for chemical munitions, and the safety requirements imposed by that hazardous work had dictated the dispersion of groups of buildings into widely separated small centers of activity. Since 1950 the whole had been converted to the many different kinds of activity connected with the Army's responsibilities for missiles and rockets. Still, however, the stark skeletons of highly specialized and now abandoned chemical manufacturing buildings, and the occasional fenced area posted with a skull and crossbones as "contaminated," stood as mute testimony to the fact that the installation had not been built for its present purpose.

The Arsenal, as an operating unit under the command of General Toftoy, had several different missions. First, as the commander of the installation, Toftoy was the "housekeeper" for the whole—land, buildings, miles of roads and railroad track, power lines, steam plants, water system—all the appurtenances of an industrial city.

The principal mission, however, was the technical one having to do with research, development, production, supply, and maintenance for Army missile systems. In accordance with the long-standing and proven policies of Army Ordnance, this mission required that the Arsenal have the competence among its own people, military and civilian, to control, direct, and technically supervise all the work for which it was responsible. With the very large majority of this work being done by industrial contractors, this required a standard of capability that would demand the respect of those contractors and assure quality results. Such engineering competence can hardly be maintained in a vacuum. Engineers who perform no actual engineering work have great difficulty in retaining up-to-date competence. So the Army sees to it that there is enough real research and development work, as well as maintenance and sometimes pilot production, done by its own people to insure that the Army can control its contractors, rather than being technically at their mercy. This is the so-called "arsenal system" that has been the subject of so much misinformation to the public, and that has been the constant target of industry that is accustomed to working for the Air Force.

Since the Air Force never has developed an in-house research, engineering, or production capability, staffed with its own government employees, it deals much differently with its contractors. Lacking demonstrated capability, it is difficult to challenge or verify the contractors' technical recommendations, and so naturally greater latitude is allowed to those Air Force contractors. The aircraft industry particularly is devoted to that position of strength, and has always seen the Army's system as a potential challenge to their technical control. Here again, we see an area of conflict that had the effect of placing the von Braun team, for example, in the position of being a constant threat to aircraft industry's freedom of action.

In addition to these principal tasks, the Arsenal also had a depot storage and issue mission that was there simply because of the availability of ammunition storage igloos, and warehouses for other products.

Last, but far from least, were three other activities in the Arsenal—one Army, and two industry. Under separate command, located in the northeast corner of the reservation, was the Ordnance Guided Missile School. Here were being trained the military technicians responsible for maintaining the missiles and ground support equipment in the field. Here, too, were being trained the first contingents of technicians from the military forces of other NATO nations, who would later teach their own people to support and maintain missile systems being made available to our allies.

A small, but very modern and efficient laboratory, doing advanced research on modern solid propellants, was operated by the Rohm and Haas Corporation, on a nonprofit basis, as an essential support to the Army's future tactical missile needs. Lastly, the Thiokol Corporation had an area set aside for the development of solid propellant motors for missiles.

The total working population of the Arsenal was about 13,000 including almost 2,000 military. This was to grow to 25,000 in the next four years. A quick understanding of the housing problem can be gained with the knowledge that there were only 144 sets of family quarters for military on the arsenal, and the town of Huntsville numbered only about 16,000 inside the city limits. Military and civilian were scattered all over northern Alabama and southern Tennessee, with many driving 50 miles to work.

In this beehive of activity, government employees were doing research and engineering, letting large contracts to industry and supervising their execution, engineering the maintenance methods and procedures required to keep our weapons ready in the field, purchasing spare parts and components, testing small missiles and rocket motors, and providing all the complex elements of management, inventory control, and distribution that would assure the continued effective usefulness of Army rockets, ballistic missiles, and air-defense missile systems in the hands of our troops.

A group of about 350 military and 1,700 civilians made up the Guided Missile Development Division of Redstone Arsenal. GMDD was doing the actual development of the Redstone Missile, and would pass their work to the Chrysler Corporation for production of the finished missile. This was the group under von Braun that was to form the nucleus for the new Army Ballistic Missile Agency—my new command. Over 200 of the military were actually graduate engineers, doing compulsory military service and being used in the field for which they had been educated. This to the benefit of both themselves and the Army.

Around this center of top scientific and technical capability I had to build a fully rounded and capable organization, provide the physical resources for its expanded tasks, add engineers, scientists, and capable officers to meet the growing need, find or provide housing to meet the fast-growing and desperate requirement, nourish morale and a sense of purpose and dedication, push back the frontiers of missile knowledge and experience, and so control and manage the whole as to stay within quite modest budgetary limits—all without letting this fast-running group skip one single stride in the process.

There were several novel factors about the ABMA organization which cut across traditional Army lines. Although ABMA was to be an Ordnance Command, the responsibility extended into all sorts of places outside the Ordnance Corps. Had I confined myself to traditional methods of co-ordination with the Signal Corps, the Corps of Engineers, Transportation Corps and the Continental Army Command at Fort Monroe, there would have been many delays and frustrations. Instead, I decided that the interests and responsibilities represented by these major organizations should be incorporated directly into ABMA. I talked to the Chief Signal Officer, the Chief of Engineers and Chief of Transportation and asked that each of them select and assign to me an officer in whom they had complete confidence. He would become the head of a group at ABMA that would be charged with all of the responsibilities of the particular Service that he represented, and would be able to work directly with his own Corps to get the needed support.

In the case of the Continental Army Command, I called on General Wyman and made the same request. Col. C. G. Patterson was then at CONARC. He was an old associate of mine, since he had been the Anti-Aircraft officer of the First Army throughout the European campaign. I knew he was competent, aggressive, and a progressive thinker who would not be tied to the old traditional artillery methods. We were to produce and field radically different weapons, and tradition could become a handicap. General Wyman had great confidence in Patterson. It was agreed that Patterson should come with me, and head up a unique group which would be composed entirely of officers from the combat arms. He would be responsible for assuring me that whatever we did with our development work, the product would meet the needs of the soldier in the field.

Perhaps this is the place to make a few observations about Army organization. The organization of the United States Army into three combat arms and a half-dozen technical services, with officers spending their entire career inside of one of those arms or services, is the result of the long period of Army development when it represented the entire land-based capability of our defense forces. All of these arms and services had their roots deep in tradition, and until the passage of the Defense Organization Act in 1947 the services (Ordnance, Engineers, Signal Corps, etc.) had been independent bureaus handling their own funds and preparing their own budgets.

It is my opinion that this watertight compartmentation has made the Army its own worst enemy in its dealings with the other two Services. In any attempt to harmonize the requirements of the several Services it is not at all unusual to encounter an Air Force position and a Navy position, with three, four, or half a dozen Army positions. The Chief of Staff of the Army finally takes a position for the Army, but the individuals who participate in the conferences and studies leading up to his decision are frequently in disagreement among themselves, and often accept that decision reluctantly. "A man convinced against his will is of the same opinion still." I have often observed in private conversations that if I had the privilege of taking one single action with respect to the Army that I love so much, I would remove every Branch Insignia from every officer overnight.

Just as the Air Force has suffered from the evil of having only rated flying officers considered as first-class citizens, so the Army has developed its own second-class citizenry in the technical and administrative services. It appears to be beneath the dignity of an officer of the combat arms to subordinate himself to any activities of a technical service. While I was, and am, as proud of the Army Ordnance Corps as any other Ordnance Officer, I felt that our important task at ABMA could not be accomplished with the simplicity that comes from harmony unless we could make everyone feel that ABMA was in fact an *Army* Command rather than an *Ordnance* Command. I was to have many discussions on this point with the Chiefs of Ordnance over the next four years. It was difficult for them to understand that in taking this position I was not being a traitor to Ordnance. I am still convinced, however, that the way this was handled was the only approach that could have brought about the continuing high morale and eagerly harmonious effort that we achieved.

By the middle of January, I had had key people moving toward Redstone in reasonable numbers, and a few were already on the ground. I had managed the recall from overseas of an outstanding officer, Lt. Col. Glenn Crane, and he was on his way to Los Angeles to take on the thorny job of representing me at General Schriever's Headquarters at the Air Force Ballistic Missile Division. He had one of the most difficult of all our assignments, since he was almost in the position of an ambassador to an unfriendly nation. Fortunately, his tact, personality and intelligence were equal to the task.

During this same period I had been traveling frequently to Redstone. Although it was responsible for the missile programs of the Ordnance Corps, the Redstone Arsenal had not achieved a great reputation at that point. General Toftoy and his people had had to struggle for everything they got. The creation on their home station of a new and independent organization with all the glamour of high priority and apparently unlimited resources naturally gave rise to a certain amount of jealousy. As I said before, the possession of broad and overriding authority carries with it great and difficult responsibility. Although I was devoted to the idea of creating harmonious relations wherever possible, I was also faced with the fact that, when the chips were down, if I did *not* make use of my authorities, and the program suffered as a result, I would be derelict in my duty. In weighing the actions that had to be taken at Redstone to provide the people and the facilities necessary to carry on our work, I was continually faced with the dilemma: "Do I compromise with the Redstone Arsenal people and possibly prejudice our results, or must I risk the creation of further hostility and jealousy by arbitrarily seizing personnel or facilities?"

It was in this area that the wisdom of General Cummings original recommendation to create an over-all missile command, with ABMA as a subordinate entity, was continually apparent. The existence of two completely independent organizations on the same installation, with no common Commander short of the Chief of Staff of the Army (since in this case I was directed to report directly to him on the priority programs), was a constant source of friction, and was to remain so until the Army Ordnance Missile Command was finally established in March of 1958.

At this point, the town of Huntsville together with the surrounding area numbered perhaps 40,000 souls. The creation of ABMA would obviously provide work for many more civilian employees. As a result of the publicity on this organization and its mission, Huntsville began to experience all the headaches that go with a boom town.

From my standpoint, the problem of housing was acute. There were very few quarters available for military personnel on the Arsenal, and rental housing in town was nonexistent. In the early days it took a major effort just to get a roof over the heads of the officers being ordered in for the new project. We had to set up housing priorities on the post and this, of course, did not exactly diminish the jealousy between the organizations. For many months my senior officers were to live under conditions that could not even be considered adequate. Junior officers were parked all over the countryside. At the same time we were having trouble recruiting good civilian employees, and I lost many simply because they could find no place to live.

Fortunately the Huntsville authorities were understanding and highly co-operative, and I will never cease to be grateful to Mayor Searcy and his City Council, as well as the other influential citizens of Huntsville, for their wise and vigorous approach to the solution of our problems. The Governor of Alabama held the State Legislature in session to pass a special Act to expand the city limits of Huntsville. If this had not been done promptly, the city would not have been able to meet the demands for expansion of utilities, sewer system, and roads which were essential to the construction of housing for the expanding civilian population.

I made an early "peace treaty" with the city authorities that formed a solid basis for our relationship throughout the next four years. We agreed that the expanding civilian employment at the Arsenal was a problem for the city. These people were coming as permanent citizens of the community, and were expected to pay community taxes. It was, therefore, the community's responsibility to look after them. I, on the other hand, agreed to be responsible for the growing military population.

One of our problems was where to put Very Important Visitors. At the beginning, such VIPs were accommodated at a hotel in Huntsville, 10 miles away. It required a great deal of government transportation and time to shuttle them to and fro, and I felt sure that they could not get a very good idea of our operations if they constantly had to be herded back and forth.

I talked the problem over with General Toftoy and the Post Engineers at Redstone to see what solution we might find. It turned out that there was an old farmhouse on the reservation which was probably 100 years old. It was so far out that it could not possibly be used for quarters, because the cost of taking power and water to it would be excessive. On the other hand, being built throughout of hardwood, it could stand moving. The Post Engineer made a quick budget and decided that it could be economically moved to a spot right across from the headquarters of the Arsenal, placed on a new foundation, and remodeled inside to provide decent VIP accommodations at reasonable cost. Using my new authorities, I directed him to go ahead on an urgent basis and try to have it ready for use by early February.

This became the famous "Wheel House," so christened by some soldier who figured that the "big wheels" would be staying there. It was later officially named "The Goddard House."

It was completed on schedule with much effort and ingenuity and furnished largely with furniture and equipment available to the Quartermaster for issue. I was very proud of the result, particularly since by that time I had been informed that a very high-powered group was coming to visit us shortly.

This group was the first to go into the Goddard House. The list of dignitaries included Charles E. Wilson, Secretary of Defense; Daniel Thomas, Secretary of the Navy; Wilber M. Brucker, Secretary of the Army; James H. Smith, Assistant Secretary of the Navy for Air; Lt. Gen. James Gavin, Chief of Research and

Development, U. S. Army; and Dr. William H. Martin, Army Director of R & D.

When this distinguished group arrived, I conducted them to their quarters. All seemed to be pleased, and notice was taken of the fact that we had put this guest house together in record time. Only Charlie Wilson made no comment, and kept looking around in critical fashion. We went on about our work, but when we got back that evening Mr. Wilson asked some very odd questions.

The old farmhouse had had a fireplace in every room, and we had left the one in the No. 1 guest suite. There was some nice cedar on the reservation, and a few cedar logs had been carefully cut in a long wedge so that they showed the typical and beautiful pattern of heart of cedar with the very light-colored outer rings. Mr. Wilson asked rather ominously what it cost to paint those logs so that they would look so pretty. He then began asking all sorts of questions about the cost of the quarters, how much money we had put into them, and so on.

I explained the situation to him and added that it would be a profitable investment for the government, considering only the amount that would be saved in hotel bills, since it would always be occupied. I also noted that the saving in transportation would be very substantial. He was unimpressed.

No sooner had the party returned to Washington than I began to get critical questions through Comptroller channels as to this particular expenditure. I finally prepared and sent to Washington a complete cost tabulation, but added my own figures to show the return from occupancy and the conclusion that at almost minimum utilization, the return to the government would be at least 9 per cent. The furor finally died down, but I never recovered from the shock of encountering such a negative reaction to what was an infinitesimal expenditure of money compared to the program as a whole, particularly when I had felt we had done something really constructive. I found later this was to be the first of many such shocks.

The first days of ABMA were one long succession of rapid-fire decisions. I was glad that I had long ago reached my own conclusions about the importance of decisiveness, and had schooled myself to accept the responsibility for coming up with answers when they were needed, without worrying if every answer was exactly correct.

It seems to me that one of the things that must go with authority is the responsibility to give the people under you definite answers so that they can go ahead with their work. Certainly my experience has shown that loss of momentum due to vacillation is a great deal more costly and serious than the small amount of error that may come from making up your mind quickly.

Those who have worked with me for a long time have heard me go through the drill to myself out loud in difficult cases. It starts like this: "Now is there anything you can think of that might have a real bearing on this decision—anything about which you do not already have all the available facts?" Of course, if the answer is "yes," you immediately send someone to get the facts. Surprisingly enough, however, if you honestly want to come up with a decision, you will find that a good many of the pieces of information you might ask for don't really have a bearing on the outcome. Chances are you will ask for them only out of curiosity or, more frequently, from a subconscious desire to delay the necessity for giving a decision. My soliloquy always ended like this: "All right, you've got all the pertinent facts, now make up your alleged mind!"

I stuck strictly to my self-imposed rules in this respect. Often I needed a decision myself from higher authority, and all too frequently could not get one without long delays. I would not allow that to weaken my conviction that it was my job to give my people answers on which they could proceed.

Everyone came to understand this, and the result was that very seldom indeed was there any loss of momentum at the working level through not knowing what to do. Looking back today, I think that was one of the most significant elements in the speed with which we accomplished our tasks.

The next most important thing was the basic question of having definite objectives for everybody and being able to measure progress against those objectives. Knowing the importance of this, I had included within the organization of ABMA a different sort of staff office known as the Control Office. The Control Office did not exert any real command authority. It had, however, the responsibility for having all the knowledge about our progress and our schedules, and for alerting me the minute anything looked as if it might go wrong.

Right at the beginning, I charged this organization with the duty of providing what I called "yellow lights." I put it this way. "If you don't know something is wrong until it boils to the top by itself, it will be too late to do anything about it, and we will come to a screeching halt. I have tremendous resources that I can call upon to help us out, but they are no good unless I know when I must call on them. Your job, then, is to dig down far enough in all the things that are happening to find the first sign of something being delayed or going wrong. In other words, I want to see a yellow light far enough down the road so that I can get it changed to green before the main stream of traffic hits it, and not have a red light flashed in our face when we are going fast."

Because of the priority that had been assigned to the program and the conclusions of the Killian Committee as to the importance of the IRBM operation, *time* was our critical factor. We therefore set up our whole system on the measurement of time, rather than simply on the commitment of resources or money to the job. The original schedule that we had filed with our proposal for Jupiter was taken as the basis for all our calculations. Every day that had been set up on the schedule for the firing of a test missile, and for the readiness of the next developed step in the orderly processes of testing a complete missile, was registered in permanent form, never to be changed. It is very easy to say, "We are on schedule," if the schedule you refer to is a new one that you just made the day before because you could not keep up with the one you had made a month ago. When anybody says happily, "We are on schedule," I think the proper response should be, "What schedule?"

By registering permanently the original schedule and measuring all our progress against that, we were able to achieve throughout the organization a feeling that time was the most important thing, and that the schedule itself was almost holy. One might think that for a Commander to say, "You cannot change any firing date without coming to me, personally, and getting my approval," would be as futile as King Canute's gesture toward holding back the waves of the ocean. But this is not true. The mere fact that the responsible individuals would have to come up to me personally, and justify in detail every action and every failure that appeared to demand a delay, made everyone so conscious of the importance of promptness that each would exert Herculean effort to avoid a delay. Before bringing themselves to face my grim examination, they would exhaust every possible resource. The result was that we were not only on but ahead of our original schedule throughout the entire Jupiter Project. In addition, we achieved a reputation for promptness in our firings at Cape Canaveral that resulted in our being given full priority on the range on the dates we originally set for each shoot.

Getting thoroughly and personally acquainted with Wernher von Braun's group of top-grade scientists and engineers was one of the most pleasant and fascinating duties of those early days. Practically all of the senior group had worked together since the days of the German V-2 and the experiments at Peenemunde. They knew each other's thoughts and reactions before they were expressed, and I knew that I must have the same feeling if I were to be able to control my operation. I participated in their technical meetings and joined with them on many informal occasions. I visited each in his own working laboratory and fortunately was able to arrive at a degree of intimacy that enabled them to confide in me. Thus, I came to know the capabilities and weaknesses, the ambitions and the heart's desires, and many of the family problems and joys of most of the group.

It may perhaps appear strange that top-grade scientists will accept operating and technical decisions from a man who could not possibly achieve himself any of the results of their scientific and technical work. But there is an element of fundamental psychology at work here.

The best scientists disagree when dealing with highly advanced ideas and theories. There are few problems connected with advanced developments that cannot be successfully solved in more than one way. Every good scientist necessarily is immersed in his work and believes that his own approach to a solution is the best. He holds his head high among his brother scientists, and even in the most friendly groups maintains a certain feeling of being in competition with the rest of the scientific world.

It goes hard with such people to set aside their own pet method in favor of the approach proposed by another scientist. And if that approach is adopted, there is always the very human feeling that its inventor has been influenced by *his* own pet ideas more than by the opinions and judgments of his associates.

With that sort of background, it is easier to understand that if there is an impartial authority who can understand their language, and what they propose to do, but is not himself in competition as the inventor or creator of a solution, they will accept the decisions of that authority. It was thus that I became the arbiter in many areas in which, as an individual, I could not claim any degree of personal expertness.

Differences of opinion were many, and I quickly arrived at the solution which I used throughout the period. I would ask Dr. von Braun to bring before me all the people who had an opinion to offer. I would listen and occasionally ask a question while they debated vehemently among themselves. Finally, I would reach a conclusion and simply say, in effect, "Gentlemen, I know we could come out all right if we followed any one of your suggestions. For practical reasons we are going to do thus and so and I will take the full responsibility for the outcome." Invariably they would all fall to and go in the direction I had approved, always with outstanding results.

It seems to me that in this relationship between the manager of a Research and Development activity and his top scientists and engineers, the manager must, of course, understand their language and be able to recognize what they are trying to do and the general nature of what each proposes. He must not himself be in competition as a working scientist or engineer. He must be able to stimulate and encourage the broadest use of their imaginations while at the same time resisting their tendency to pursue inviting side roads. Only this way can he keep creative activity within the bounds of practicability and cost.

Above all, the manager must be willing to take full and final responsibility for his decisions, good or bad. There must be on his desk an invisible sign that says, "The buck stops here."

It is of these capabilities, when all is said and done, that good managers are made.

CHAPTER X

The Trial of My Soul—
Personal and Official

April 1956, with things rolling extremely well, was to bring me personally a shock, the shadow of tragedy, and the ultimate conviction that the Lord still had work for me to do or my life would not have been spared.

I had been taking some antihistamines as an aid in controlling a sinus condition that plagued me at times. I was running out of this medicine, and so I called the doctor at the Redstone Army Hospital to ask if I might send a messenger over to get more. I was fortunate. The man on duty when I called was a young doctor of Lithuanian origin, who was serving in the Army for the time being. His name was Salna. In his gentle voice and with a trace of accent, Dr. Salna said, "Of course you can send for the medicine. On the other hand, you are going to be around here for a while and it is my job to see that you stay healthy. I haven't even seen you. Don't you think perhaps you should come over and let me see what my job for the next couple of years looks like?"

I recognized the reasonableness of his request and in spite of the fact that time was so precious, agreed to see him the following day. I had had a complete physical examination the previous October, including the usual prostatic check-up. This was only six months later, and my next physical examination was not normally due until the following October.

Feeling that it was merely a concession to Salna's professional standards, I went to the hospital and let him put me through a regular physical. At the very end, when it came down to the prostate examination, this young fellow shook his head. "I don't like it," he said. "There is something. I don't know what it is, but it shouldn't be there."

Some may believe this and some may not, but the moment he said that to me I was filled with the absolute conviction that I had prostatic cancer. No panic—just a tug at the heart and a feeling of "Let's don't just stand here. Let's be about it."

"It could be just an infection," Dr. Salna was saying. "On the other hand, it could be something quite serious. The only thing I can suggest is that you go over to Ft. Benning where there is a specialist in urology who can tell you more about what you have."

Because of the conviction I had felt, I did not hesitate to agree, even though hour by hour, schedules were becoming more demanding. Within a very few days I flew to Benning and was examined again. Within minutes after my return to my headquarters I had a call from Colonel (about to become General) Jack Schwartz, who was then head of the Urological Clinic at Walter Reed in Washington. I was never talked to so roughly in my life. Jack Schwartz said: "For a man with your responsibilities to be playing around with this thing is inexcusable. The place for you is here in Walter Reed, and I don't mean a week from now, I mean tomorrow. Now you get yourself in here just as quick as the good Lord will let you, understand?"

In two days I was there, and in less than a week I was operated

Tactical type Jupiter missile on model site used for training Air Force personnel at Redstone Arsenal. The "orange peel" shelter around the base of the missile is used for protection against the weather and peels back automatically at the beginning of the firing sequence.

A replica of the Jupiter C rocket with the Explorer I earth satellite is placed in position for permanent exhibit at the Smithsonian Institution.

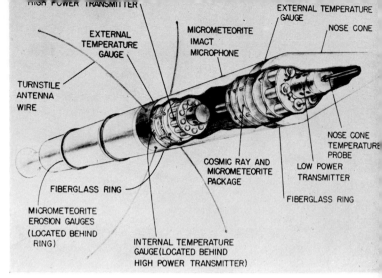

HIGH POWER TRANSMITTER

EXTERNAL TEMPERATURE GAUGE

NOSE CONE

Schematic drawing of Explorer I

EXTERNAL TEMPERATURE GAUGE

MICROMETEORITE IMACT MICROPHONE

TURNSTILE ANTENNA WIRE

NOSE CONE TEMPERATURE PROBE

LOW POWER TRANSMITTER

FIBERGLASS RING

COSMIC RAY AND MICROMETEORITE PACKAGE

FIBERGLASS RING

MICROMETEORITE EROSION GAUGES (LOCATED BEHIND RING)

INTERNAL TEMPERATURE GAUGE (LOCATED BEHIND HIGH POWER TRANSMITTER)

The firing of Jupiter C Missile 29 from Cape Canaveral, Florida, January 31, 1958, at 10:48 P.M. EST, launching Explorer I, the free world's first satellite, into orbit. *U. S. Army Photograph.*

Above, The final weather conference at Canaveral before the firing of the rocket bearing the first American satellite. The firing had already been twice postponed. This time General Medaris made the decision to go ahead. Left to right about the table: Dr. Hausermann, Director of the Guidance and Control Laboratory; Dr. Homer Jo Stewart of JPL; General Medaris; Dr. Jack Froehlich of JPL; and (holding cigarette) Dr. Kurt Debus, Chief of the Missile Firing Laboratory at Canaveral. Behind Dr. Debus is his deputy, Dr. Greune.

Right, The biggest "extra" in Huntsville since the War Between the States.

SATELLITE EXTRA ★ ★ ★ ★ ★

The Huntsville Times

SATELLITE EXTRA ★ ★ ★ ★

VOL. 47, NO. 271 | CHICAGO DAILY NEWS SERVICE | HUNTSVILLE, ALABAMA, SATURDAY, FEB. 1, 1958 | ASSOCIATED PRESS — WIREPHOTO | 5c PER CO

Jupiter-C Puts Up Moon

Eisenhower Officially Announces Huntsville Satellite Circles Globe

Wail Of Sirens Brings In Era On Space Here

Thousands Gather On The Square For Noisy Success Demonstration

By ALEX THOMAS
Of The Times Staff

The wail of sirens, blasting horns and the fiery trails of re-bought rockets ushered in the country's first step towarc conquest of space at Huntsville last night.

Less than an hour after a Jupiter-C missile built at Hunts- hurled America's first satellite into an orbit around the th's surface, the ear-splitting whine of dozens of sirens told l people of the Army Ballistic Missile Agency's success.

uccess was sweet, but it came r several years of frustration, acks and delays before the y and its Redstone Arsenal tists were allowed to prove nselves.

s thousands of people gath- d on the Courthouse Square, one generally held respon- e for much of the Army's bles—former secretary of ense Charles E. Wilson— burned in effigy, while sands cheered and waved erican and Confederate s.

din grew louder on the e as word spread of the ite's success. People crowd- the center of town from ng areas and distant towns. acards proclaiming "Move Sputnik," "Our Missiles Miss," and "We Dood It" red in the crowd and waved the mass of people. The of sirens and tooting horns punctuated by the streak of ckets and exploding fire- ers.

e South did rise again," shouted above the racket. hant was taken up and through the crowd be- ssipating into "War Eagle" .

ke to have the concession charging all these batter- wag shouted aloud to as the roar of horns rose Square.

n all crowds, there were who wondered what the on was about. "What's n here?" a puzzled visitor man waving a placard." satellite's up," he was he man shook his head lked away.

thinks a satellite is some- farmer hangs from his saddle," another voice

0 & R's fire engine raced e Square with tooting transporting dozens of They shouted and waved ngine pulled out to circle k.

ville representatives at s annual Chamber of ce banquet left in a rush ded back to Huntsville by a sizeable convoy ir residents. Other cars e Square bore license om Limestone, Marshall gan counties.

ation's press took im- notice of the celebration in the streets of Hunts- Times reporter spent an hour on a tele- s a restaurant on the relaying details of the n to The Associated nited Press and Inter- News Service.

entatives of Life maga- gled with the crowds h newsmen from area rs.

night, the wire service he news that official on announcements re- at the Explorer, the first satellite, was cir- earth.

es had no effect here, s reliably known that te was in orbit before . B. Searcy ordered sirens into action at

g to unofficial reports, ls and scientists were return here early this from Cape Canaveral,

ly, a more formal re- of the Jupiter-C's suc- aps a parade—is being metime Monday. After this is being written, d decision has been about the continued .

9 Labs Here Aided Project Of Launching

It Took Every One To Successfully Put Up 'Moon' Vehicle

The concerted efforts of all laboratory facilities of the Army Ballistic Missile Agency, lie behind the Army's successful launching of a scientific earth satellite.

Each of the agency's nine labs, which comprise the Development Operations Division, had a share in the integrated teamwork that led to the development and firing of the rocket. Dr. Wernher von Braun is director of Development Operations.

The satellite project, assigned to the Army, was a joint undertaking of the Army Ballistic Missile Agency and the Jet Propulsion Laboratory. ABMA supplied the main stage of the rocket (a modification of the Jupiter C), and JPL furnished the upper stages assembly, plus the satellite vehicle.

Responsibility for the preliminary design and the later detailed structural, propulsion and mechanical design of the vehicle, was assigned to the ABMA Structures and Mechanics Laboratory. This included, among other things, increasing the size of the thrust unit while reducing tank skin thickness; modifying the thrust unit to accommodate the use of a special fuel; and development of a system to accomplish separation of the thrust unit and instrument compartment. The lab also designed and developed the spin launchers for the JPL upper stages. Spinning the upper stages by means of electrical motors provided a stabilization similar to that of a rifle bullet.

Structures and Mechanics, in addition, was responsible for technical coordination with JPL, and was the project engineering unit within Development Operations.

The Aeroballistics Lab had charge of the flight performance and aerodynamic problems. In particular, this lab and JPL studied the feasibility of the project in its beginning. Aeroballistics Lab planned the ascending trajectory and established the exact flight data for the firing, including the possible pattern of expected largest deviations. The Lab's duties also included responsibility for the aerodynamic behavior of

Turn To Page 2, Column 7

Satellite Gets Official Name; It's 'Explorer'

WASHINGTON, Jan. 31 (AP)—The American earth satellite shot into the heavens at Cape Canaveral, Fla., tonight was christened Explorer by the Defense Department.

The name was announced by officials at the Pentagon shortly after the launching of the Jupiter-C rocket carrying the satellite.

In announcing the name, officials emphasized they did not yet know whether the satellite had actually gone into orbit.

Shortly after the launching, Secretary of the Army Brucker sent word to President Eisenhower at Augusta, Ga., of the successful firing.

JUPITER-C IN TAKEOFF—The Jupiter-C rocket is shown at the moment of takeoff from Cape Canaveral, Fla. At the left is the missile service tower. (AP Wirephoto).

Here Are The Basic Facts

Weight of satellite proper—18.13 pounds.
Weight of final stage—12.67 (after burnout).
Total weight orbiting—30.80 pounds.

The Army satellite was launched by direction of the Department of Defense as a part of America's contribution to the International Geophysical Year scientific research program. Within the Army, the project was undertaken jointly by the Army Ballistic Missile Agency and the Jet Propulsion Laboratory. The satellite was launched by the modified Jupiter-C missile, which is an Army vehicle developed for nose cone re-entry tests.

Instrumentation and telemetry in the satellite is gathering and transmitting four types of information.

These are: skin temperature (i.e., surface of the projectile), internal temperature, cosmic dust erosion and cosmic ray data. The main part of the package is a cosmic radiation experiment designed by Dr. James A. Van Allen of the State University of Iowa. The major element of this experiment is a Geiger counter.

The data gathered by the instruments is continuously dispatched by two transmitters.

The most powerful transmitter operates on 108.03 megacycles, transmitting with 60 milliwatts, or six hundredths of a watt. This signal can be readily received by ham radio operators. It is expected that this transmitter, the more powerful one, will operate for a period of two to three weeks.

Second of the transmitters is operating on 108.00

Turn To Page 2, Column 3

THOUSANDS THRONG THE SQUARE—Here are some of the thousands of persons who crowded into the Square in downtown Huntsville about 11 o'clock last night after word was received that the Army missile team from Huntsville had orbited the nation's first earth satellite. Screeching sirens, whistles and horns proclaimed the news.

Weather Change Sped Launching

AUGUSTA, Ga., Feb. 1 (AP)—President Eisenho announced early today America's first satellite is ir bit around the earth.

The President's dramatic announcement was iss at his vacation headquarters a few minutes befor a.m. EST by White House press secretary James Hagerty.

The satellite was launched at Cape Canaveral, at 10:48 p.m., EST, last night.

The baby moon was ram into space by an Army Jupi rocket.

With thousands of other A cans all over the country, E hower waited about two h after the launching for word satellite was in orbit.

* * *

The text of the Preside statement:

"Dr. J. Wallace Joyce, hea the International Geophys Year office of National Scie Foundation, has just informed that the United States has cessfully placed a scientific e satellite in orbit around the ea

The satellite was orbited b modified Jupiter-C rocket.

This launching is part of country's participation in the ternational Geophysical Year. information received from satellite promptly will be m available to the scientific c munity of the world."

The three paragraphs co tuted the President's official nouncement.

Eisenhower was kept clo posted regarding the launch preparations and the actual fi from late yesterday afternoon il word of the orbiting was ceived here.

* * *

Eisenhower flew here fr Washington this afternoon fo weekend of golf and relaxation was his first time on a golf cou since he suffered a stroke N 25. He played 18 holes and rep ed he enjoyed it very much.

As a former five-star gene and an Army man for 40 yea Eisenhower was even more dee interested in the satellite laun ing than otherwise would ha been the case.

The Navy a few days ago had give up temporarily in its effo to launch a Vanguard test sat lite. Its first effort Dec. 6 failed

At the Augusta National G Club, the President's weeke headquarters, the chief executi was kept informed regarding ste leading to the Jupiter launching.

* * *

Word when he left Washingt had been the Army probab would not make another launchi attempt until early next wee But weather and wind conditio at Cape Canaveral improved u expectedly and Eisenhower w advised late yesterday afterno that there might be a launchi during the night after all.

When the launching did com at 10:48 p.m., EST Eisenhowe personally got on the telephone Washington — on a line which ha been open and manned by Hage ty for some time — and receive reports on the flight progress the Jupiter-C.

A word picture of that progre into space was relayed to th President from Cape Canaver by way of the White House an the Pentagon.

Those reports were made ever 20 to 25 seconds during the firs few minutes of the flight. Eise hower was on the phone for sligh ly more than 10 minutes.

* * *

Here is Hagerty's version o how the word came to the Presi dent:

At 5:20 p.m. EST yesterday Brig. Gen. Andrew J. Goodpaster White House staff secretary an liaison man with the Pentagon phoned from Washington and re ported the weather at Canavera was improving. He said it looke then as though the Jupiter-C rock et could be fired during the eve ning. The firing target time a that point was 10:34 p.m.

That message was relayed t Eisenhower who had just come off the golf course and had settled

* * *

Army Reveals Second Moon Is Scheduled

70-Foot Carrier Roars Into Starry Night At Cape Canaveral

CAPE CANAVERAL, Fla. (AP)—The United States' first man-made satellite whirled around the earth today and the Army disclosed it is preparing to hurl another into orbit.

It was the Army's Jupiter-C missile that fired a 30.8-pound moon aloft last night, recovering some of the U.S. prestige lost wh Russia boosted her two Sputniks into space last fall.

Eisenhower exclaimed when news of the Army's success reached him at Augusta, Ga., where he had gone for a weekend of relaxation.

With a huge burst of flame and a thunderous rorar that could be heard for miles along Florida's east coast, the Jupiter-C blasted off from this top-secret firing base at 10:48 p.m. (EST) yesterday.

About an hour and three-quarters later, its satellite had completed its first journey around the world and tracking stations were receiving its radio signals.

It was so well established in orbit, said Maj. Gen. John B. Medaris, head of the Army's missile test program, that it will remain aloft from 2 to 10 years.

It is unlikely the Army's satellite will be visible to the naked eye. In an announcement, the Army said: "It will appear in its orbit with about the brilliance of a one-fifth to one-sixth magnitude star, and a star of this brightness can barely be seen without some magnification."

There was confusion in early reports about the altitude of the satellite. Medaris said the distance from the earth in its eliptical orbit would range between 185 and 1,230 miles. Dr. Wernher von Braun, designed of the rocket, said it would swing as high as 2,000 miles and as low as 230.

Von Braun said the 6-foot-long

Turn To Page 2, Column 8

Launching Hits ABMA Birth Eve

The successful launching of ABMA's Jupiter-C and its now orbiting Explorer satellite came appropriately on the eve of the second birthday of the missile agency.

Although the previously planned anniversary program began yesterday at 4 p.m., the Army moon carrier and its passenger satellite certainly will now be the highlight event.

Established on Feb. 1, 1956, ABMA will open its birthday program this morning at 9 a.m. with a parade.

Maj. Gen. J. B. Medaris, ABMA commanding general, will arrive at the Redstone Arsenal airstrip at 8:30 a.m. today and proceed directly to the birthday parade, despite his strenuous evening yesterday.

Included in the overall program will be exhibits of missile guidance equipment, communications equipment, models of missiles and demonstrations of

Some 1,500 miles from Canaveral in the Atlantic Ocean, Navy frogmen place the nose cone of a Jupiter fired from Canaveral on July 17, 1958, in a special container aboard the destroyer escort USS *Escape*. It was this recovery that proved the final solution of the reentry problem by use of an ablation covering.

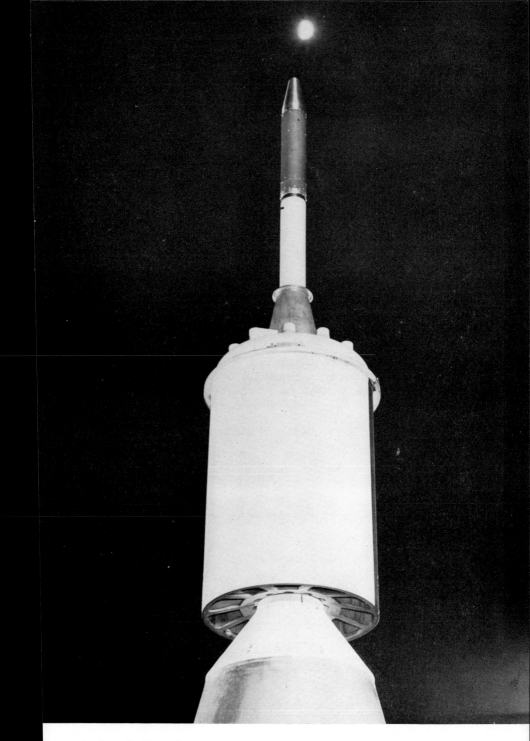

The launch tub and upper stages of Explorer III with the satellite on top.

Jupiter Missile 101, delivered to the U. S. Air Force at Redstone Arsenal in August 1958. 101 was the first tactical Jupiter. It was delivered on time, according to a schedule laid down more than two years earlier, when not a single piece of Jupiter's components existed.

Professor Herman Oberth, the brilliant and persistent pioneer of rocketry.

The Jupiter IRBM which, in modified form, served as the first or booster stage of the Army-NASA Juno II space probe, is shown here in the final stages of fabrication on the assembly line at Redstone Arsenal. The rear portion of the booster was corrugated to increase its strength. Although Redstone's prime responsibility was research and development, pressure of time required that some assembly operations be carried out at Huntsville. In time this "manufacturing" threatened to impede the arsenal's basic R & D function. *U. S. Army Photograph.*

Lifting the shroud over the upper stages of Pioneer IV, the successful moon probe which is now a satellite of the sun, at Canaveral in March 1959.

Dr. Wernher von Braun at a downtown Huntsville celebration honoring the firing of the first successful U. S. lunar probe, Pioneer IV, launched March 3, 1959.

Pioneer IV, the first successful U. S. deep space probe, rises from the launching pad at Cape Canaveral at 12:11 A.M. EST on March 3, 1959. *U. S. Army Photograph.*

Dr. Keith Glennan, Director of the National Aeronautics and Space Administration, General Medaris, Dr. von Braun, and Brigadier General Jack Barclay, Deputy Commander of the Army Ordnance Missile Command, discussing the Saturn program around a model of a full three-stage Saturn. Another topic of discussion was the impending transfer of von Braun's brilliant group to NASA. *U. S. Army Photograph.*

The test stand at Redstone as it looked in April 1959, in the midst of the long and major task of being modified to accommodate Saturn.

An early test model of the Army's Nike-Zeus antiballistic missile of the type that was successfully test-fired at the White Sands Missile Range in December of 1959. *U. S. Army Photograph.*

General Medaris and Dr. Wernher von Braun before the static test stand at Redstone shortly before the General's retirement. The model in his hands is a Nike-Zeus antiballistic missile, while grouped in the background are the missiles with major significance which were part of the General's responsibility during his four years at Huntsville. Standing behind the pair are, left to right, Jupiter, Juno II and Redstone, while another Jupiter is in the test stand, and Nike-Hercules slants before the three larger missiles. The tail of Hawk appears to the left of the General's shoulder, Lacrosse is visible between the General and Dr. von Braun, while Sergeant is visible to Dr. von Braun's right. Nike-Ajax is present but blocked from view by the General's head. *U. S. Army Photograph.*

Bob Mosher, chief of the countdown crew at Canaveral, in conference with General Medaris during a countdown.

Pershing, the Army's latest medium-range ballistic missile, was first fired in February 1960 at Canaveral. A mobile, solid-propellant missile, the Pershing is relatively lightweight and can be fired at almost a moment's notice.

Full power static test of Saturn on the test stand at Redstone Arsenal in the spring of 1960. On the other side of the platform stands a Jupiter IRBM.

on. My surgeon was Lt. Col. Van Buskirk. Van Buskirk is a very fine surgeon, but beyond that he has a wonderful philosophy of life. I asked him, one time, why he was in the Army Medical Service when a man with his skill and reputation could command almost any kind of money in civilian life.

Van's answer went something like this: "After World War II, I did practice in civilian life, and was doing very well financially. But I got to the point where I simply could not stand looking into a man's pocketbook before I could tell him how much I could help him. In civilian life I was always having to decide whether the man's economic position would allow me to order one X-ray or twenty, and in the end I couldn't stand this. I came back into the Army, and I am very glad I did. No matter who walks in my door, from a private to a 4-star general, I can order for him the kind of treatment and the kind of attention that I know he needs, and I don't have to ask any questions before I do."

I think I was most fortunate to get into Van's hands. He told me afterward that my particular cancer was growing so rapidly that if it had not been caught by young Dr. Salna, I would shortly have reached the point where the best surgery in the world could not have saved me. As it was, they caught it in time. I have had special tests every six months since, and there is no evidence of its recurrence. The Lord was good to me, because there was no reason on earth why I should have gone in for a physical examination at that time.

In the hospital, in between getting myself adjusted to the idea that I had had cancer and to the peculiar psychological problems that go with a radical prostatectomy, I had people come to see me who could brief me further on the advanced phases of missile technology. Ten days later I was back in Huntsville. I was supposed to take a 30-day convalescent leave, but there was too much work to do. I did cut my office hours a bit short and, of course, during the next two or three weeks I could do no traveling.

By this time we were moving fast with both Redstone and Jupiter. There were, of course, a few clouds on the horizon. Redstone was an all-Army weapon, but even so some Army men were jealous of it. The ballistic missile represented a threat to conventional artillery and to tanks as well. Consequently, we were never able to get a clean program in numbers of missiles to be deployed or numbers of units that would handle them in the field.

My own feeling was that Redstone was capable of more uses than were being planned for it. It was a big missile and could carry a big payload. I tried to look down the road to the point where ballistic missiles might be used as cargo carriers, or even troop carriers. By designing alternate types of warheads, some important experiments could have been carried out even with the Redstone. But when it came to interesting the people in the Pentagon, I failed dismally.

One of the internal problems I faced was how to keep Jupiter from competing with Redstone. There was a natural tendency for our scientists to be more interested in the newer and more dramatic project. To a large extent we were drawing on the same resources for the development of both missiles, and it took a lot of time and attention to keep the program in balance.

The problem of public relations became steadily more acute. I was well aware of the importance of getting out accurate information within the bounds of security. Not only did the public have the right to know what their tax dollars were being spent for, but it was also essential that the people in Washington who directed the flow of these dollars be aware of what we were doing and have confidence in us as a team.

One of the problems we had in handling the press was in the area of security. The newsmen, by and large, realized that we could not give out classified information, but we were frequently being asked our opinion as to what the Russians were doing or might conceivably do in the field of missiles and space. I finally ordered my people not to answer such questions. The reason was simple. Those who knew anything worth knowing about the Russian activities got their information from intelligence sources that were highly classified. Those who did not have access to such sources could not discuss the topic accurately or intelligently. In the field of classified information we certainly did not want the Russians to know how much we knew. Any careless revelation on our part might jeopardize the sources of our information. Consequently, my orders were that questions in this area were to be answered with two words: "No comment."

There was one other problem that was very real. This took the form of subtle and sporadic, but nevertheless persistent, criticism of the German scientists who were such an important part of our team. The fact that they had fought against us and had sent the V-2 against England was still remembered by some people rather bitterly. These men were now all American citizens, or in the process of becoming so. Most had children born in America. They were well accepted in Huntsville, where they were good citizens and made many worth-while contributions to the town. Nevertheless, the sniping continued.

I was afraid that if it went on, the morale of these men might be affected, or their right to work on advanced or secret projects challenged. So we set about trying to correct the situation. We never referred to them as German scientists if we could help it. We called them "first-generation Americans," or "former German scientists who are now American citizens." These men were understandably sensitive on the subject; they liked to point out that they had become Americans by choice, of their own free will, when they could have remained Germans—or even joined the Russians. Gradually, I think, our campaign produced results and the sniping diminished, although it has never vanished altogether.

These were relatively minor problems. Of much greater concern, as the weeks went by, were the rumors that began reaching me indicating that the Navy was beginning to back away from using the Jupiter as a ship-based missile. In retrospect, it is easy to see the forces that were at work. Some were practical. Refitting the ships as rocket launchers was expensive. Liquid-fuel rockets were a safety hazard on shipboard, and a solid-fuel rocket seemed more suitable for submarine use. Some reasons were psychological. No Service likes to be asked to employ a weapon which it has not developed itself. In any case, the rumors were disturbing because if the Navy did pull out, it would leave Jupiter with no alternative but to compete with Thor for its very existence.

In such a competition, I knew we would be facing grave disadvantages. It was true that we had a decided edge in experience and know-how, thanks mainly to the Redstone. But the Thor had been designated IRBM No. 1. The implied priority encouraged the Air Force to approve more money and larger quantities of missiles, and if it came down to canceling one missile or the other, I knew that there would be those who would advocate canceling Jupiter simply on the grounds that it represented the smaller investment.

One of the biggest controversies in those early months at ABMA raged around the procurement of engines for Jupiter. The Thor was using the same engine, built for the Air Force by North American. The Air Force took the position that we should buy our engines from them, not directly from the manufacturer. I knew that we would have to make many engineering changes in our engines, and to do this we would have to deal with the manufacturer direct.

We finally won this battle, but we practically had to carry the case to the Supreme Court to do it. We also had to fight continuously to get the money for additional facilities at Redstone Arsenal and elsewhere that were essential if we were to get on with the job.

It was my function to handle these problems without allowing them to interfere with the efficiency of our technical staff. I did the best I could to shield von Braun and his people, telling them —somewhat optimistically, I fear—that if they just worked hard and produced the best missile, everything would turn out all right. They had their hands more than full trying to design a weapon that could be used on shipboard as well as on land. Actually, they found the technical problems of ship-based launching and guidance so fascinating that I had to remind them frequently of the fact that there was a national priority on the demonstration of a land-based missile.

Since such a missile was to be mainly a deterrent, I felt that it was quite important for our potential enemy to know we had one. The sooner we could fire to IRBM range, therefore, the better. With this in mind, we were concentrating every effort on our plan to fire Missile 27 to maximum range in September. We felt that in the field of international diplomacy, such a demonstration might be very useful, even though we also knew that the payload to be fired was quite small.

This Missile 27 was an elongated Redstone with solid-fuel upper stages known as Jupiter C. We had been authorized to fire twelve of these as part of the Jupiter's nose cone re-entry development program. The problem of designing a nose cone to withstand the terrific heat generated as a missile re-enters the earth's atmosphere was one that had occupied the attention of our best scientists for many months. Missile 27 was not to carry such a nose cone. We merely wanted to test the Jupiter C vehicle itself.

I must confess here that the nomenclature of these different missiles was—and is—confusing, but there was a reason for it. In testing components for Jupiter, we were constantly using the Redstone missile as a vehicle. But Jupiter had a much higher priority than Redstone on firing dates at the Cape, and in other ways. We therefore decided to label these Redstones used for testing Jupiter components, "Jupiter A." They were not Jupiters, of course, but the label identified them properly with the program, and gave them the necessary priority.

Similarly, when we put together a composite vehicle for testing nose cones, we called it "Jupiter C." The first true Jupiter missile was not fired until May 1957.

Actually, for this first long-range shot, we were readying two identical missiles, No. 27 and No. 29. We wanted to have a spare in case the first shot failed. These two missiles looked—and in fact were—exactly like the satellite carrier that we were to use over a year later, except that for this test shot we were using a dummy fourth stage. If we had put a solid propellant into the fourth stage instead of the inert material we were using to get it to the right weight, we could have fired that particular missile into orbit as a satellite. We didn't do this for the simple reason that we were forbidden to do so. We had no mission for putting up a satellite—Vanguard had that assignment. And nobody had any intention of giving us that mission. So we put sand aboard the fourth stage instead of powder.

The latter part of September was a thrilling period for all of us. The missile itself was on the pad at Cape Canaveral for over six weeks undergoing tests of every kind. Finally, on the night of September 20, we fired Missile 27.

The firing itself was uneventful. Countdown proceeded on time, and the signals coming from the payload were strong and clear. It was quite a sight to watch this missile, much longer than the Jupiter A's we had been firing, rise majestically from its pad and take off into the darkness.

In this case it didn't take very long to find out that our shot had been successful. The payload went straight down the Atlantic Missile Range for a little better than 3,000 miles. In the course of its flight it attained an altitude of 600 miles. Both of these distances surpassed anything that had been achieved by an American missile at this time.

Feeling as I did that half of the value of this demonstration lay in its psychological impact on both our friends and our enemies, I had made every effort to get a press release approved that would announce in very careful terms what we had achieved in terms of range and altitude without going into classified detail as to the nature of the project or the nature of the missile itself. However, we were absolutely forbidden to make such an announcement and were told that no information was to be given to anyone.

Having worked so hard, our people were very disappointed by this decision. So was I. I remember telling Wernher that the whole thing reminded me of the old story about the minister who preached violently against playing golf on Sunday, but was an ardent golfer himself.

This preacher's house was right on a golf course. One beautiful Sunday morning, very early, the fairway looked so inviting that the Devil tempted him to go out and sneak a shot—just one. Temptation prevailed, and the preacher crept out to the nearest tee.

At this point, St. Peter looked down from Heaven and saw him. "Look at that hypocritical preacher," he said to the Boss.

"Never mind," said the Boss. "He'll get what's coming to him."

The preacher swung, the ball soared two hundred yards, right into the cup.

"Hey," said St. Peter indignantly, "look what he did. He made a hole in one!"

"I know," said the Boss gently. "But who's he going to tell about it?"

This was the position we were in after the firing of Missile 27. Who were we going to tell? As a matter of fact, the story did leak out. This was the first but by no means the last time that the magazine *Missiles and Rockets* was to have a profound effect on our people. To this day I do not know where they got the story. In the light of later events, it could well have been Colonel Nickerson who leaked the information, although I have no evidence of this. In any case, *Missiles and Rockets* proceeded to publish some pretty straight dope on the kind of missile we had fired and what it had accomplished. There was a great uproar in Washington, and a sizable investigation, but it turned up nothing and the furor finally died down.

Some weeks later, without mentioning any figures, the President announced that the United States had sent an artificial comet to a fantastic distance and altitude. This at least gave an element of veracity to the magazine story. I am still convinced that if the proper kind of controlled announcement had been made, there would have been less leakage of security information and a greater impact in the international field.

In any case, our first long shot had succeeded beyond our best hopes. We now knew not only that we had an outstanding vehicle with which to test our nose cone, but that without a shadow of a doubt we also had a satellite carrier. We had not needed Missile No. 29, so we put it back on the shelf with hope in our hearts that some day we might be able to use it as a satellite. This was twelve months and two weeks before the Soviet satellite known as Sputnik I was launched.

The first shot of the Jupiter as a missile was scheduled for the first of March. In the meantime we resumed what had become routine testing of Jupiter components on Redstone missiles. We had five of these Jupiter A flight tests scheduled between the firing of Missile 27 in September and the first of March.

The second of this series went haywire and put us in the position of having to take a lot of teasing from our associates in the missile business. At this time there was much construction going on at the Cape. A little way down the beach from our launch pad an enormous installation designed to handle the Thor program was being built. It was very large and complex because Thor was to be statically tested at Cape Canaveral, as well as test-fired from there. We only needed rather simple launch facilities for Jupiter because all our static testing was done back at the Arsenal in Alabama. The completion of the Thor launch complex was extremely important to the Thor program, and they could not possibly get under way even nearly on schedule if anything happened to it.

On the night of October 30 we fired a routine Jupiter A—a Redstone missile with Jupiter experiments aboard. But in this case somebody goofed. We found out later exactly what happened, and as a matter of fact I had it made the basis for a training movie to impress on our people the importance of doing every small thing exactly right. The movie was designed to teach each technician that a fifty-cent mistake could easily destroy a million-dollar missile.

In this case, two connections which should have been thoroughly soldered down were not well fastened. Just after the missile lifted from the launch pad, the vibration of the tremendous engine separated these two small wires from their connections. As a result, the missile went completely out of control. At about 200 or 300 feet in the air it flattened out and started right down the Cape in the direction of the Thor launch pad.

Of course, as soon as the missile turned over and started in that direction, the Range Safety Officer blew it up, and it dropped with a resounding crash in the middle of an empty field. There was a tremendous fire, but the only person injured was a fireman who was standing on the firehouse and was so excited by the disaster that he stepped backward without looking and went down far enough to break an ankle.

You can imagine what a ribbing we took. We were accused of having a very inaccurate missile since we had found it impossible, even at that short range, to hit the Thor launch pad. The teasing, of course, was based on the fact that if the Thor complex had been hit by our missile, our rival would have been out of business for several months. This particular failure became known as the IPM—the Inter-Pad Missile.

Since this was only the second failure out of a string of some seventeen Redstone firings at that time, we were not too concerned, and the series was resumed successfully. But now some of the clouds that had been gathering on the horizon were blowing up into a real storm.

Early in November I began hearing rumors that shortly one of the two IRBM programs was to be canceled, and that the system marked for elimination was the Jupiter. It seemed incredible to me that the weapon being developed by proven men who had an average of fifteen to twenty years' successful experience in the large ballistic missile field could be crowded out by the claims of a group of people who so far had demonstrated no missile capability whatever. But at this point neither missile was yet ready for its first firing test, and as a result there was no way to show anyone not familiar with the programs in detail that Jupiter was in fact running ahead of Thor. There is always an unofficial exchange of information among missile-men, and we at ABMA knew that the highly optimistic firing schedules laid down for Thor could not be maintained, but I suppose they sounded perfectly logical to anyone who did not have our experience.

However, the spectacular success of Missile 27 and our record of high reliability with the Redstone were points in our favor. On November 9, I went to Washington for a "coats-off" session with a number of high-level civilians in the Department of Defense and the Department of the Army. I argued our case so vehemently that at one point Mr. Reuben Robinson, Deputy Secretary of Defense, wanted to know if I could document my statements. I said that I could, and shortly thereafter drew up a comprehensive report which became known—possibly because it was so pointed—as the "Dagger Report."

As few people as possible were in on the preparation of the "Dagger" document, and careful record was kept of everyone who had access to it. Of course Colonel Nickerson was included, since he was the Chief of the Office whose primary duty it was to keep in touch with all other missile programs. As it turned out, the combination of Nickerson and "Dagger" almost put us out of business.

"Dagger" was a forthright document that pulled no punches and did not take into account anyone's feelings or friendship. It compared and documented in detail the history of the missile programs of all three Services, and showed clearly that only the Army had had consistent success with almost every program attempted. It set forth very bluntly the fact that neither the contractor involved in the Thor program nor any Air Force contractors had so far demonstrated any success with ballistic missiles and contrasted this fact with the long missile history of the Army, the successful record of the Corporal, the proven success of Redstone, and the achievement of the Jupiter C. The document also went into the question of the history and background of the use of missiles as artillery, the necessity for mobility as against the fixed-base concept, and the reasons why the Army should be the user of land-based missiles regardless of range.

During the same period the Navy was waging a campaign to substitute a smaller solid-propellant missile for Jupiter, basing the case on the advantages of the smaller weapon for submarine use. It would take longer by several years, and would have to carry a smaller nuclear payload. Nevertheless, that's the way they wanted it. Finally, the Navy requested permission from the Defense Department to withdraw from the Jupiter program and go ahead with this missile of their own, which later became known as Polaris. This news, with its attendant withdrawal of Navy support for Jupiter, pushed the morale of our people even lower. The Secretary of Defense did not actually approve the withdrawal of the Navy from the Jupiter program until December, but in many ways the uncertainty was more nerve-wracking than the final actuality.

The famous Wilson memorandum assigning new responsibilities for roles and missions to the different Services was published on November 26, and represented a crushing victory for the Air Force. The net effect was to prevent the Army from having any operational responsibility in the long-range missile field. The maximum range for an Army missile was set at 200 miles. Everything beyond that became Air Force responsibility. This meant, insofar as Jupiter was concerned, that we were now producing a weapon that was not really wanted by the people who would hold responsibility for its use. The psychological impact at Huntsville was devastating, not only at the Arsenal but in the town, and morale reached an all-time low.

As soon as Mr. Wilson's decision was made public I called a staff conference and gave our top people an outline of the situation as I saw it. As I recall, I said something like this:

"You all remember that when the Jupiter Project was first laid down, there was no decision as to which Service was to employ the IRBM. That was specifically held back. Since the Jupiter job was given to the Army without consideration of who would fire the missile, it is completely illogical to assume that assignment or operational responsibility to the Air Force makes any drastic change in the program for development. Neither IRBM has proved itself yet, and chances are there will be no change in the programs until one missile or the other has demonstrated some success.

"This has been a tough decision for Mr. Wilson to make, and I am sure that he has been pulled and hauled in all directions while he was making up his mind. That very fact, however, tells me very clearly that there is one thing that we must not do under any circumstances, and that is to attack the decision itself. The very last time to harass a man is just after he has made a tough decision. Any such attack, direct or indirect, will make him furious and could easily get us thrown out of the picture.

"Our problem now is solely the question of who can do the best job of providing the earliest IRBM capability for the nation. Army Ordnance has a long history of having made weapons for other Services, and we can use that fact to reinforce our right to be considered on an even basis with any other contractor in this case. But I repeat that under no circumstances are any of you, publicly or privately, to attack the roles and missions decision."

Everybody accepted my reasoning except Nickerson. Later, I had another meeting in my office with Nickerson and Lt. Col. Glen Crane from the West Coast, and we went over the same ground. Nickerson tried hard to convince me that we should make an all-out attack on the decision itself. I repeated my conclusions and was most emphatic in stating that under no circumstances should this be done. I said that although I wanted to be sure that everyone who might be interested in helping us had the facts about our technical ability and our right—in fairness to the country—to continue the project, we were to keep our hands clean and stay away from the roles and missions decision.

Nickerson made a trip to Washington, ostensibly on his proper duties of maintaining contact with the Army Staff and the Ballistic Missile Committee. On his return he stuck his head in my office, this time alone. His face was red and he was obviously agitated. Again he tried to talk me into changing my mind. This time I told him flatly that the surest way to get the Jupiter Project canceled would be to allow either the Air Force or the Department of Defense to become convinced that our major purpose in staying with Jupiter was to keep the Army's foot in the door with the eventual intention of trying to get the roles and missions decision overturned. I was a little angry myself, and I finally told Nickerson, "Now if you allow anybody to hear you say that this roles and missions decision must be overturned, or if you do anything to indicate that that is our purpose, you can ruin us. Under no circumstances are you to do or say anything that will give anybody that indication. Now get out, and don't come back on this one, and stick to what I have told all of you."

I heard nothing further from Nickerson on that subject. Certain of our friends in Congress and particularly in the Alabama Congressional delegation were interested in knowing what the situation was and what they could do to help, and, of course, it was perfectly proper to inform them. I maintained close contact with the Secretary of the Army, and he supported us fully.

From where I sat, by the end of December, the situation was easing somewhat. This being the case, what happened next was unexpected and highly upsetting.

It was the afternoon of the 31st of December. Everybody was set for New Year's Eve and a good party had been planned on the post. Mrs. Medaris and I were going for a very brief period, since our attention was centered on the traditional official New Year's Day reception the following afternoon.

Unexpectedly, I got a phone call from General Cummings, the Chief of Ordnance in Washington. His voice and manner were as cold as ice. He informed me that the Inspector General of the Army, Lt. General Ogden, would arrive at Redstone Arsenal on the following day and that he expected to see me immediately on arrival. General Cummings would give me no indication of the purpose of General Ogden's visit, but merely said, "He will tell you when he gets there."

Now, I had been around the Army for quite a spell. It was obvious to me that the Inspector General of the Army was not going to come out on New Year's Day to investigate some ordinary breach of regulations involving a junior officer. I could only deduce that this had something to do with a General Officer and that in view of General Cummings' attitude, this matter must be directly related to me. Yet scour my brain as best I could, I could think of absolutely nothing that I had done or failed to do which would make me a target for the Inspector General.

I called in General Barclay, my Deputy, as well as my Aides and most trusted Staff Assistants. We searched our minds and our consciences for something that would make sense. None of us was able to come up with anything.

I went through the next 24 hours with my head up, but more upset and worried than I had ever been in my life. I carried out my role as host at the reception as best I could, and immediately afterwards went to meet General Ogden at the Goddard House. What he handed me there left me both dismayed and angry, and facing what was to be the most unpleasant period in my life.

CHAPTER XI

The Shadow of the Nickerson Affair

The document General Ogden showed me at the Goddard House on the night of January 1, 1957, bore the innocent-sounding title: "Considerations on the Wilson Memorandum." It was the bombshell that exploded the "Nickerson Case."

The document had been delivered in Washington to Jack Anderson, who was handling Drew Pearson's column during Pearson's absence, by one of Nickerson's assistants. Of course, at the time, we did not know how it had gotten to Anderson. Anderson took it straight to the Air Force to "check it for accuracy and get further information." If he wanted an uproar, he certainly got it.

The paper contained a bitter attack on the Air Force and the assignment to that Service of operational responsibility for the IRBM. I am sure that when it got to the Secretary of Defense, he blew up. Mr. Wilson put the Secretary of the Army on the spot at once, and Secretary Brucker directed the Inspector General to launch a full-scale investigation to determine who was responsible for the distribution of such a document to "certain members of the press."

When I examined the document that night I was thoroughly shocked. The contents showed that it had been prepared by someone who had full access to highly classified military information. Such information was sprinkled all through the paper. There were such ultrasensitive items as projected dates of availability and deployment of some of the Nation's newest weapons. Threaded all through the paper was a consistent and denunciatory attack on the good faith, capability, and record of performance of the U. S. Air Force. Even aside from the classified information, such an apparently authoritative assembly of broad indictments on one of our Armed Forces could not fail to bring aid and comfort to any actual or prospective enemy. I knew as I read it that the paper completely dynamited my carefully considered policy about not taking issue with the roles and missions decision, and my campaign to establish the capability of ABMA to perform loyal and constructive service for any element of our Armed Forces.

General Ogden's first question to me was, "Have you ever seen this paper before?" I had no hesitation in assuring him, both personally and officially, that I had not. Yet the contents of the paper indicated most strongly that it had originated from some source within or very close to my Command, and I was informed that it had been prepared on a kind of typewriter of which there were very few around. One of them was in my own office!

Actually, there were very few people known to me who held so strongly the views expressed in that paper, and Nickerson's stubborn opposition to my policy and violent feelings on the subject crossed my mind at once. I told Ogden about the background of Nick's private war. I also gave him everything I knew about the kind of duplicating facilities at Redstone that had been used to print the paper. It was all too clear to me, from the way the investigation had been launched, that someone had felt there was at least a possibility that I had had a hand in the affair myself. I therefore placed every resource at the Inspector General's disposal to help his investigation so that the whole matter could be cleared up as quickly as possible.

It didn't take long to get to the bottom of the case. The trail to the local printing plant was clear and definite. Within 24 hours the essential facts were known, and responsibility had been placed squarely on Nickerson. His security clearance was lifted, and the way was prepared for the start of the long legal procedure of investigation, trial preparation, and court-martial that would drag out for a total of six months.

A thorough check turned up the fact that other classified papers were missing. I ordered my security officer to head up a full investigation to locate everything possible, tighten our whole security system, and assess the damage that had been done.

Meantime the Inspector General of the Army had finished his work and reported to the Secretary of the Army. My conscience was clear, but I still had a duty to perform. I asked the IG to advise the Secretary that, although I had had nothing to do with the affair, I would retire from my post if the Secretary felt that my usefulness to him or his confidence in me had been impaired. I did not want to leave the command I had come to love so much and that I knew was capable of great things. On the other hand I would be a hindrance rather than a help to the progress of ABMA if there remained the slightest vestige of feeling that I had been derelict in my duty, or had condoned in any way such a breach of security and of good judgment. My regard for the Secretary hit a new high when the word came down promptly that the Secretary had complete faith in my leadership and integrity.

I had asked that the further conduct of the case be taken out of my hands so that there might be no question of prejudice involved. By the 7th of January, I was advised that the Commanding General of the Third Army, Lt. General Hickey, had been given full responsibility.

In spite of the transfer of responsibility, Nickerson was to continue to be a source of a great deal of trouble to me throughout the next six months. He asked to see me, and I have a record of the interview on January 12, at which my aide was present. If I had known at the time, as I discovered soon after, that Nickerson was soliciting sympathy and financial support for his cause from the people of Huntsville on the basis of a campaign of innuendo indicating that he was taking the rap for me, I would have been sorely tempted to make the text of that interview public then. From a legal standpoint I am sure that it was much better that I did not.

On entering my office, Nick said, "I guess I pulled a boner, and I'm sorry for all the trouble I've caused you."

My reply: "Yes, you certainly did, and you know that you went directly contrary to my policy and my instructions to you."

His answer: "Yes, you are right."

In closing the interview I told him the same thing I was to say directly and officially to my whole staff a few days later. I said, "You know that I will support and defend anyone who makes an honest mistake in trying to carry out my policies or my instructions. But I cannot support *or* defend anyone who, with full knowledge of my policies and my wishes, acts in direct opposition to those policies as you have done."

The ensuing period was extremely trying. I found out about the whispering campaign, but in view of my official position in the case, and the possible legal effects, I could do nothing about it. It was not the sort of thing with which I could take issue openly, and I had no choice but to keep quiet and trust to the future to make the situation clear. Meantime some newspapers were making a martyr of Nickerson, and both the community and the garrison suffered from some division of loyalties.

From the standpoint of the accomplishment of our mission, this was a period of red-hot activity, and we could ill afford any bedeviling distraction. My greatest fear was that the Nickerson paper would make Secretary Wilson so angry that he would direct the summary cancellation of the Jupiter program. This did not happen. I remain grateful to Secretary Wilson for his forbearance, and to my people at ABMA for their loyalty.

It is impossible to make clear the problems resulting from the Nickerson case without a brief recital of the important events and decisions that were to be at stake during the next critical months. The withdrawal of the Navy from the Jupiter Project had left us with only one customer—the Air Force. But the customer was in no hurry to buy our wares. This reluctance became painfully evident when we tried to get from the Air Force the specifications for the Ground Control Equipment that would be needed to fire the Jupiter operationally. We made request after request; the Air Force could not or would not answer our queries. This left us more or less in the position of a tailor who has the finest cloth and the best cutters but cannot persuade the customer to give his measurements. In this case, the reason was all too plain—the customer was busy cutting his own cloth, and was not interested in other labels.

On the 14th of January the Scientific and Advisory Committee of the Defense Department, headed by Dr. Millikan, had a full-scale hearing on a comparison of the Jupiter and Thor programs, making a technical evaluation and assessing the probability of success on the shortest time scale. In the halls of the Pentagon, word was going around that Jupiter was as good as dead. But we would not lie down to be buried, and the final decision directed that both programs go ahead until at least one had demonstrated successful flight testing as a complete missile.

Nonetheless, this action touched off a new series of "re-evaluations." The budget boys impounded almost seven million dollars of Jupiter funds that were urgently needed for the development of ground support equipment to make possible the eventual firing of Jupiter from operational sites. This was a bitter blow, and when finally the chips were down for rapid deployment, it almost knocked us out of the race. Preparation for production was held back, quantities of Jupiter were limited to about half the number allowed to Thor, and finally we were put under rigid restriction on the use of paid overtime on the pretext that "you won't even need half of what you have by the end of the year."

The Pentagon termites also took advantage of the situation to make a new attack on my delegated authorities. If the attack had succeeded, we would have been slowed down to the point where we could have been canceled out with ample reason. Fortunately, they didn't.

February saw a very bad flood at Redstone that virtually cut the post in two. We had helicopters on stand-by to assure access to the post hospital. The new quarters were ready for some of the senior officers, and after seeing them all occupied, the Medarises moved into their new house in driving rain and with red mud up to their ankles. Every carport had a line-up of boots and galoshes for the kids. One couple with a small dog met their pet at the back door after each outing, and hoisting her on high, took her straight to the sink for a foot wash. Everybody was so glad to get something decent to live in, however, that it was all taken with a cheerful smile.

After much detailed negotiation, ABMA got the award for the missile carriers for the Hardtack experiments that were to take place in the late spring of 1958. For these high-altitude nuclear test shots in the Pacific, the bombs were to be carried aloft by the good old dependable Redstone, loaded down with special instrumentation. To accomplish this with our limited personnel took some very close and complicated scheduling of people and hardware, which I am glad to say came out right on time, and with the finest results.

At this time we began requesting permission to enter the space race. It was obvious to our people that Vanguard was in trouble and would not be able to meet its time schedule, if indeed it ever managed to do the job. Designed from the ground up as a brand-new missile, using no proven components, Vanguard was in fact a full-scale development program for an operational missile, insofar as cost, time, and test requirements were concerned. Focused strictly on the very small satellites to be used for the

IGY experiments, it was purposely designed to be as small as possible and still do the job. There was no latitude for error or for minor mistakes, nor for added weight to provide assurance. With no objectives beyond the IGY, and little growth potential, Vanguard had become a very expensive toy. Already the national purse was paying heavily for the very first decision designed to separate civilian space exploration from military missile development. In the end, Vanguard cost over $110,000,000, and five out of its first six launchings were failures. This was to be only the first down payment on this costly and ridiculous division of the indivisible.

I must confess, to a military man—even in those days—an earth satellite had much more than peaceful scientific interest. To a soldier, the promise of trouble-free communication to all parts of the planet—to say nothing of keeping the enemy under constant surveillance—made pre-eminence in the space field absolutely essential. It was perfectly clear to me—and had been clear to von Braun for years—that the first nation to establish a permanent, manned space station would have taken a giant step toward domination of the whole planet. And a satellite—any satellite—was the first step toward such a station.

As for possible combat in space, we knew that wherever man has gone, on land or in the air or under the sea, sooner or later he's managed to get into a fight. We saw no reason to suppose that space would be any different. Suppose in a brush-fire war one side put up a satellite and tried to use it for battle communications. One of the first things you do in a scrap is try to blind your enemy. So the other side would go right up there and try to knock the satellite down. The first combatant would try to stop this, and there they'd be . . . fighting in space.

In any case, we had known ever since the success of Missile 27 that we could orbit a satellite. So we felt the time might be right to make our first bid. I cautioned our people that in offering to launch a scientific satellite we must refrain from attacking Vanguard, since there was too much pride and too much money committed to its support. We checked our available hardware, skinned costs to the bone without any margin for error, and came up with a bargain-basement bid to make six satellite launchings for eighteen million dollars, pleading the desirability, at those low prices, of providing back-up assurance to the nation's prestige that was riding precariously on the Vanguard. For the first of many times we were told to go back and mind our own business.

Again, looking to the space field, I got grudging permission from the Department of the Army to provide minimum essential support to an RCA effort on miniaturized flying TV. We had ambitious plans, and hoped this could become the basis for a successful "eye-in-the-sky" satellite in the future. We had no mission to put up satellites and no money for them. The RCA project was therefore justified under the heading of a "damage assessment" device, to be carried aboard a missile like the Redstone, and to take a picture of the nuclear burst over the target and send it back immediately to home base. We never got the chance to get into the reconnaissance satellite business, but we did in fact complete the development of the damage assessment package, and it has been successfully flown on Redstone at White Sands Missile Range. Takes good pictures, too.

We also made a full-scale feasibility study on a longer-range MRBM, somewhere in the 500-mile category. This could be achieved either with a wholly new solid-propellant missile, or by reducing the warhead weight and upgrading the power on the Redstone. The first would be more efficient and more mobile. The latter could be done much faster and would cost much less. We got approval for neither, but the effort was to result in the solid-propellant Pershing a year later.

Our manpower was limited, yet we made many proposals for both space and missile projects. We were driven to this by the necessity for providing a hedge against the possibility of having the Jupiter terminated. If that happened, we would have enough work for a short time, but would desperately need something new coming along. I remember one day at a staff meeting a worried officer suggested that we ought to prepare an emergency plan for pulling in some of our outside contracts and adjusting our situation if the Jupiter should be canceled suddenly. Eberhard Reese, von Braun's deputy, replied with a perfectly straight face, "Much vorse ve need an emergency plan in case ve should be told to go ahead vith more than half of the bids ve have made." Everybody laughed, and we didn't make either plan. We were taking a calculated risk and playing the percentages, and it worked.

Jupiter made its formal bow on March 1st with the test firing of Missile 1-A. Our scheduled firing date was not until May, but we decided to pull two Jupiters ahead of schedule, labeling them 1-A and 1-B, in order that any mistakes could be corrected before launching Missile 1. This turned out to be a wise move. In both cases we had something go wrong, but we did not permit either mistake to happen twice.

Missile 1-A. As the missile gained speed and rose into thinner air, the flame from the engine ballooned out into a much wider and more shallow pattern. The tail of the missile was hollow, with the engine recessed inside. That hollow created a vacuum of its own, and promptly sucked the jet flame up inside the tail. The temperature rose, critical wires were burned in two, the missile went out of control, and broke up. Solution: apply a flexible, heat-resistant, fiber-glass shield around the engine partially to prevent the formation of a vacuum, and shield wiring and piping from the flame. No more tail heating.

Missile 1-B. Off the pad beautifully and rising steadily. As it started to tilt over toward its distant target, as it was programed to do, the large diameter took its toll. Fuel and liquid oxygen set up a spiral-sloshing action inside, as will water in a pail if it is rapidly tilted from side to side. This "sloshing" of large quantities of liquid exerted tremendous and uneven forces on the sides of the missile. The control system did its best to correct the trouble, but the requirement was beyond its design limits and it finally gave up. The missile went out of control, and again broke up with a spectacular fire in the sky. Problem: how to control "sloshing" in a big tub, and to do it quickly?

This time some special experiments were needed, and they were conducted night and day. Time was at a premium. We wanted two solutions, one that would do for the moment and get our missiles in the air, and another that would be sound and practical for the final design. We could take our time about the second one, but the first one had to come quickly if we were to stay on schedule and fire No. 1 in the month of May.

The answer was found, and we got plenty of joshing from other missileers about it. Certainly it was crude, but it kept us on schedule and let us get on with the job. We made a whole bunch of big "beer cans" out of heavy wire mesh, put floats inside so they would stay on top, and filled the whole top surface of each tank with them. This had the effect of breaking the great big tank into lots of little tanks insofar as the effect on the surface of the fuel was concerned. Result: no sloshing. Missile No. 1 made its schedule on the last day of May, and went for the distance— some 1,400 miles. Jupiter was in business.

The speed with which we solved the sloshing problem was, I think, a good example of the advantages of centralized organization with all the key personnel physically located at the same place. This was the great and unique value of ABMA. Within forty-eight hours after the flight failure the problem had been analyzed and identified and it was determined that an entirely new test rig was necessary for the ABMA test site. This gear consisted of a set of full-scale tanks from the Jupiter missile mounted on a full-scale railway truck and a set of railway tracks. It was to be rigged in such a fashion that it could be driven back and forth at various speeds by a large electric motor through a set of gears. The idea was to drive the full-scale Jupiter tanks, loaded with thousands of pounds of propellants, at various speeds in such a fashion as to re-enact the sloshing that had occurred during the actual flight. The rig proved highly successful and quickly led us to a solution.

The way we put this rig together may be of interest. All of the basic structural members used were taken from scrap material or were purchased from various secondhand sources. As soon as preliminary sketches had been drawn, action was under way to find the needed hardware. Within eight hours an old electric motor of sufficient size was located in a railroad yard 100 miles away. This was purchased and overhauled for $750. A cast-off gear case, used in oil field operations, was found in a St. Louis disposal yard and also purchased for $750. To generate current for the motor a locally available welding machine was utilized. While hardly an approved method for normal operation, the last item required for the test rig, an old railroad rail itself, was procured by that effective, though unorthodox, old Army improvization—a moonlight requisition on the local railroad yard. The total cost of the rig was less than $42,000. It was completed and in operation in three and a half weeks. It is certain that a comparable *contract* effort would have cost about $70,000 and would have taken four months to complete.

Two weeks before we fired Jupiter No. 1, we shot the first Jupiter C with a reduced size protected nose cone. Although the missile went where it was supposed to go, we never recovered the nose cone. We had some reason to believe later that the sharks beat us to it. On one of the later full-sized nose cones that we lost, we found evidence that sharks had opened a leak in the balloon that kept it afloat. After that we doubled the quantity of shark repellant.

The Nickerson affair ended with his trial in midsummer. As I said in one of my official reports, the incident was regrettably typical of what too often happens when the enthusiasm of intelligent men is thwarted by unintelligent circumstances.

As part of the relatively light sentence that Nickerson received, General Hickey administered a written reprimand. The text was a classic, and has remained with me as a clear statement of the damage that can be done when a trusted officer violates his superior's confidence and defies his guidance. I read the reprimand, and with a prayer that Nickerson would seek and find some measure of humility and self-discipline, I "closed the book" on the whole episode.

CHAPTER XII

Of Men, Monkeys, and Nose Cones

One of the great weaknesses of our civilian-military administrative system (and I must confess I do not see any simple remedy) is that, as you get closer to the summit of the pyramid where decisions are supposed to be made, the individuals who are supposed to make those decisions simply do not have time to absorb all the pertinent information on which the decisions should be based.

As a result, such information as they get is always digested, condensed, and capsulated to the point where it is almost unrecognizable. What's worse, differences of opinion are eliminated, or made to appear very slight, when they are, in fact, highly important.

In a field as complex as missilry, oversimplification can be disastrous. And yet it happens all the time. Suppose a report is prepared by the people in the field, at the operating level. They know more about the hardware, and about their own problems, than anyone else. But they can only forward that report to the echelon above them. That echelon knocks out two thirds of the significant elements and leaves one third. The next higher echelon takes out half of that. Finally the man who is permitted to talk to the Secretary of Defense boils it all down to one page when the time comes to brief the man who actually makes the decision —and by that time everyone might as well have stayed in bed.

Of course, a lot depends on the man who is handed the final capsule. If he has a sharp and penetrating mind, and has acquired the habit of not being satisfied with surface appearances only, he can pry out a lot of real information very fast. But it is hard to do this unless you have at least a rudimentary knowledge of the subject in the first place, which some people in high places don't.

I remember being very forcibly struck by this flaw in our system during both of my appearances before the National Security Council. On both occasions, what I was permitted to say was very carefully screened and controlled, and I imagine this is standard procedure. This means that if the National Security Council calls for a presentation on a given subject, that presentation is prepared, dry-run, emasculated, and sand-papered, re-prepared, re-dry-run, re-emasculated and so on at least four times before it gets to them.

It seems to me that if the National Security Council would call in the most responsible and knowledgeable person in whatever field, and would let him talk freely for twenty minutes without interference, or pre-session "guidance," they would save time, get better information, and have a more realistic foundation on which to base policy and decisions.

The decision problem was very much in evidence during those days in 1956 and 1957 when the Army and the Air Force were pursuing two completely different methods of protecting missile nose cones from the terrific heat generated by re-entry into the earth's atmosphere. The Air Force favored the heat-sink method, in which—roughly speaking—you use great slabs of metal to absorb the heat. They favored this to the extent of sinking about

$100,000,000 annually into their research and development program. So the heat-sink method was also a money-sink method.

Our people, on the other hand, had been experimenting for years with all sorts of materials, exposing them to the blasts from rocket motors on their own test stands, and had come to the conclusion that the most effective approach was the one known as the ablation method, in which a heat-resistant material peels off the nose cone and is left behind as the rocket rushes through the atmosphere.

This method has some outstanding advantages, one of which is that you can build a much more accurate missile. In this ablation approach, all that happens at higher velocity is that a little more material peels off in the process of re-entry. This means that whatever velocity one desires can be achieved simply at the expense of slightly thicker material. Another advantage is that the temperature inside of any kind of container, like a nose cone, that has been covered on the outside with this material will be much lower than will result from the use of any other kind of material. This is because the materials used in the ablation process are in themselves insulators against heat rather than absorbers of heat, as is the case with the heat-sink method.

This, in turn, means that the nose cone can be made longer and slimmer. It will then come down through the atmosphere much faster. This is desirable from the military standpoint, because sometimes the very high-speed wind currents in the upper air can drift a nose cone quite a distance. These winds may be a major cause of inaccuracy, particularly since you cannot decide at the launch site what kind of wind will be encountered over the target.

The slimmer and sharper the re-entry body is, then, the faster it will come down. The faster it comes down, the less it will be affected by these wind currents. On the other hand, in the heat-sink approach, the metal can only absorb so much heat, and it becomes necessary to make the nose cone much more blunt so that it will not fall so fast. Falling more slowly, the blunt nose cone is more susceptible to drift, and therefore you have a less accurate missile.

There are other advantages to the ablation method. It is very flexible. It can be put over corners and around edges—anywhere you need a protective covering. All these things convinced me that the ablation method was the one we wanted to use. In the end (years later) even the Air Force was converted, and all IRBM's and ICBM's now use the ablation method.

Final proof was lacking, of course, until we were able to fire such a nose cone, recover it, and demonstrate that it had suffered no damage and that the temperatures inside had been very moderate. We passed this milestone on August 8 when our second attempt, Jupiter C, Missile No. 40, was fired with a scale model nose cone which we were able to recover. This was our second attempt at recovery; the first one was a failure.

This business of recovering nose cones is a lot more complicated than most people suppose. It is utterly impossible to use a parachute for slowing down a re-entry body when it has first come into the atmosphere. Any kind of parachute, metal or fabric, would be burned away in a fraction of a second. If a body is to be recovered, therefore, it must either be slowed down by retro-rockets before entering the atmosphere, or else it must be allowed to come through the highest heat area and descend to an altitude where it has begun to cool off again before a parachute can be deployed. A properly designed re-entry body decelerates sharply as it comes down through the atmosphere. This means that at an altitude of ten or twelve thousand feet, the use of a parachute becomes possible.

The mechanism required to do this is very complicated. Inside the object to be recovered there must be a device that will sense the deceleration when the body enters the atmosphere and begins to slow down. Sensing the deceleration, this device will trigger a very complex and extremely accurate timing mechanism that will first put out a small pilot parachute to initiate the slow-down and follow it with a bigger chute to achieve a reasonable rate of descent.

Furthermore, the object must be able to float, and if it has been built with sufficient strength and protection to withstand the extremely high temperatures of re-entry, it will be much too heavy to float by itself. This means that there must be a balloon to keep it afloat. In addition, if you want to find it, there must be some type of locating device aboard. The resulting combination of equipment that has to be put into a fairly small space is extremely complex and has to be built very precisely. I can tell you that we were all very happy when Missile 40 finally proved that the ablation method worked and that recovery was possible after all. It was in such a vehicle, now at full-scale size, that we later gave a space ride to the two famous monkeys, Able and Baker. They survived the experience very well, although later one of them died.

I was unable to go to Patrick Air Base on Cape Canaveral the night we fired Missile 40, but followed the action from the Comcenter at ABMA. The missile was fired very early in the morning. It was planned that way so that there might be darkness overhead during the flight, and the big cameras down the range could catch the pyrotechnic flares that helped trace the trajectory. It would be daylight, barely, at the eastern end of the trajectory, and the recovery vessels could go into action promptly without the added handicap of complete darkness.

Everything went exactly as planned. Each step of the complex operation in the nose cone was precisely on time. The recovery ships were able to see the red comet of the re-entry body as it came down through the atmosphere, and were on the way to the approximate spot even before the subsurface explosions of the small depth bombs, ejected during the last moments before the nose cone hit the surface, were picked up by the underwater sonar net and a far more precise position reported. Aircraft, homing on the tiny radio beacon atop the flotation balloon, were circling the cone within minutes, and had the brilliant yellow balloon in sight from then until the recovery vessel came alongside. It was only a little over an hour until the signal was flashed: CONE ON BOARD. APPARENTLY UNDAMAGED. We were jubilant.

Two days later, a Saturday, I was working at home in my study when a phone call asked if I would receive Kurt Debus, Chief of the Firing Laboratory at Canaveral, who had an important item to show me. Within a few minutes Kurt showed up with the look on his face of the cat that had eaten the canary. He was carrying a small packet wrapped in waterproof plastic, which he opened in front of me. Inside was a letter, stamped and postmarked at Canaveral, addressed to me by "rocket mail." The letter was in perfect condition, and he presented it to me with pride.

The letter had been written and signed by Kurt before Missile 40 was launched, and postmarked by connivance with the postmaster without disclosure of the purpose. Sealed in its small waterproof envelope, it was strapped inside the nose cone for the long ride down the range. The condition of the packet and of the letter itself was dramatic proof of the effectiveness of the ablation protection of our nose cone.

The letter has been consigned to the Smithsonian Institution for as long as they may wish to display it, with the condition that whenever it is removed from display it will be returned to me or my family.

There were some interesting repercussions to the nose cone letter. Much later, on what had by then become a more or less routine test of the full-scale Jupiter nose cone for recovery, some of the people at the Missile Firing Lab at Canaveral put *several* letters aboard for friends or acquaintances who had requested them. Apparently there were some disgruntled folk who had requested the same favor and been denied, for a great flap developed. I had to impound all the letters. Two had been delivered, and I had to send out emissaries to get them back, together with some kind of legal release from the people who had them. The official excuse for the uproar was that "persons unknown had managed to put unauthorized material aboard a test vehicle without permission." This was taken as an indication of insufficient security precautions, although we knew very well that everyone who had access to our missiles would protect them with his life. Such is bureaucracy.

As a result of our success with the small-sized nose cone, Jupiter Missile No. 5 was on time for firing the following May with a full-scale protected nose cone packed with recovery gear. Since we had really learned from our test model all we needed to know, I decided that we could afford to close down the Jupiter C test program with the scale version nose cones. Vanguard was getting deeper and deeper into trouble. We were more and more convinced with every day that passed that we would somehow, some day, get our chance at putting up a satellite. If we had the hardware on hand, we could make a cheap bid; if not, the price would be high and the time scale long.

On August 21, therefore, I issued a directive to stop the Jupiter C test program at once, and to put all Jupiter C hardware into protected storage so that it would suffer no deterioration. The original program had called for twelve shots. We had used three, and had nine precious missiles, in various stages of fabrication, to hold for other and more spectacular purposes. After looking the missiles over carefully, and evaluating the state of readiness of each, I advised General Gavin, Chief of Research and Development of the Army, that we could hold the two most advanced missiles in such condition that one satellite shot could be attempted on four months' notice, and a second one a month later.

We made a whole series of unsuccessful efforts to get some release of information that would let our people take a bow for our success with the nose cone problem, but the Pentagon powers always said no. Finally, it was decided that the President would announce the achievement over TV and show the public the recovered nose cone. We all watched and listened hopefully, but there was no mention of the Army or any of our people.

Meantime, as we drove ahead with Jupiter, the apparently endless struggle with the Air Force continued over whether or not they would give us their requirements for ground support equipment. The Department of Defense still could not choose between Jupiter and Thor, and as long as Jupiter's future was in doubt there was little incentive for the Air Force to furnish ABMA with any information at all.

In the middle of August, the Secretary of Defense finally announced that an Ad Hoc Committee would review all the facts and make the decision. This committee was to be composed of William M. Holaday, Special Assistant for Guided Missiles; Maj. General Bernard Schriever, my opposite number in the Air Force; and myself.

Poor Bill Holaday! I am sure he felt like a large lamb chop suspended between a ravenous lion and an equally hungry tiger. On the one hand, the urgent national need for an IRBM made it impossible for anyone honestly to cancel Jupiter, since our missile had proved itself in terms of actual performance. On the other hand, the combined political weight of Air Force contractors and the pro-Air Force feeling within the Department of Defense overwhelmed any possibility of Thor's cancellation.

The meetings of the Ad Hoc Committee went on for weeks and weeks. General Schriever is an able officer, but temperamentally he and I were completely different. He was a much more detached commander than I was, not so personally or emotionally involved in the activities of his subordinates. As a result, I think it is fair to say that I knew more about the details of Jupiter than he knew about the details of Thor. My people were all at Huntsville, right under my thumb. He had the disadvantage of working through a civilian team of management experts known as Ramo-Wooldridge. This organization, while undoubtedly competent in many ways, was in no hurry to admit its mistakes to General Schriever, or to anyone else in the Air Force. As a result, General Schriever sometimes had a rosier impression of the status of the Thor program than was actually the case.

Three things stand out in my mind when I look back to those

hearings. The first was the efficiency of our Army system of communications, which functioned with superb speed and accuracy. Whenever I wanted a fact, or a set of facts, I could get them in a matter of minutes from Huntsville, or JPL on the West Coast, or anywhere else. The Air Force had no such lightning-fast network, and this gave us a tremendous advantage.

The second thing that made a lasting if somewhat dismal impression on me was the Air Force's system of costs and accounting. This was so snarled up that not even the Defense Comptroller's office could unravel it. Consequently it was very difficult to get an accurate comparison of the costs of the two missile systems.

The third vivid recollection I have concerns the brilliant support of my young assistants, Maj. Don Kohler and Capt. "Hap" Hazard, who were with me constantly. Don knew every inch of the Jupiter program; Hap had been ordered to keep track of Thor. Hap had done his work so well that on one occasion he tangled with a top scientist from Ramo-Wooldridge on some highly technical point, and finally routed him completely, much to my delight.

The decision that came out of these Ad Hoc hearings was really "no decision." In October we were finally told to proceed with the development of the Jupiter missile system, and the Air Force was ordered to co-operate by furnishing us with the necessary Ground Support Equipment data. Given all the pressures involved, I felt lucky that we were able to come out with a draw.

While all this was going on, I kept in touch with the Arsenal by telephone, teletype and courier, and was able to make decisions without hesitancy, just as if I had been in my own office. I was never more conscious of the truth of my own maxim that the power to control is only as good as the power to communicate.

When I look back now, those summer days of 1957 seem almost like a blur. Time spun by so fast that without the aid of a desk calendar on which I crossed off the days, I would have completely lost track of the date and time of the month. Weekends had little or no significance. What had to be done was done when it was needed without regard to days or hours or the time of day or night. The project was the master of us all.

It was ironic that, working as hard as we did, one of our main handicaps was a directive from Washington limiting the money we could spend on overtime at the Arsenal. We were already behind schedule where deployment of Jupiter as a weapon was concerned, mainly because of the delays and difficulties in getting specifications from the Air Force. This was our one area of weakness, and we knew that our competitors would not hesitate to exploit it. The restrictions on overtime just made the problem more acute. We finally got relief on this, but not before a lot of damage was done.

Meantime, we lived with the sword of uncertainty dangling squarely over our heads as to whether the results of all this frantic effort would ever really be used. The days went by, and still no decision was reached as to whether Thor or Jupiter or both would continue into production and deployment.

It was a nerve-wracking situation, but we tried to forget about it and get on with the job. There was nothing else we could do.

CHAPTER XIII

The Beep That Came to Dinner

As the reader will have noted, we had been through a difficult and frustrating year, to say the least. All attempts to do something—anything—to help in getting the U. S. satellite program under way had been blocked. Even an offer to do whatever we could in virtual anonymity—under the banner of the Vanguard program, if necessary—had met with stony silence.

The President had stated publicly long before that the U. S. would definitely launch a scientific satellite during the geophysical year. From where we sat, with intimate knowledge of the Vanguard's efforts and its disasters, we were convinced that the chances of making good on the President's promise, if efforts were confined to the Vanguard, were so small as to constitute a ridiculous gamble.

Meantime, we were haunted by the feeling that time was running out. The components of Missile 29, so carefully put aside against the possibility of launching a satellite, were gathering dust. Without tangible evidence, except a couple of chance re-marks dropped by Russian scientists at an international scientific meeting several months before, we were convinced that the Rus-sians were on the verge of going into space. We were also con-vinced that when they did make the attempt they would succeed on the first, or at worst the second, try.

Our feelings in this connection had been reinforced by the fact that Tass (Russian news agency) had announced on August 26: "A super long-range intercontinental multistage missile was launched a few days ago. The tests of the rocket were successful. They fully confirmed the correctness of the calculations and the selected design." I knew the statement was correct. Their big mis-sile program was ahead of ours, and very obviously they had the power available for a substantial satellite!

It had been announced that Defense Secretary Wilson was to leave soon, and that Mr. Neil McElroy would succeed him. With-out knowing much about McElroy, we still could not shed a single tear over Mr. Wilson's departure. It was our strong feeling that his tenure had been characterized, to put it charitably, by a complete lack of imagination. We felt that we had been some-what less than fairly treated, and that the interests of the country had been prejudiced by a minimum use of our proven capabili-ties. Rightly or wrongly, we were convinced that during Wil-son's regime the Army had consistently been pushed aside in favor of almost unlimited support for the glittering but unsub-stantiated promises widely publicized by the Air Force and its contractors.

This might be as good a place as any to offer a few observa-tions on the role of businessmen in government. It has been my experience, in dealing with civilians in top government positions, that businessmen as a rule are generally less effective than law-yers. In fact, I think one of the mistakes of the last few years has been the policy of appointing businessmen to high defense posts, presumably on the theory that since the Defense Department is about the biggest business in the world, why not call in proven businessmen to run it?

This sounds good on paper, but in practice it doesn't work out so well. And for two reasons. The first is financial. If the appointee is a lawyer, chances are he can take a leave of absence and his law partners go right on working for him. So he doesn't have to worry about money. He can concentrate on his new job.

But the businessman, who is likely to be on a big salary, really gets hurt when he switches over to government pay. What's worse, if he holds stock in a company doing business with the government, he may have to sell it if he's to get Senate confirmation. This is like asking a businessman to cut off his right arm. Besides, the implication is that he can't be trusted not to feather his own nest . . . not a very flattering one.

Finances, though, are only a part of the problem. The real trouble lies in the mental conditioning a big businessman has had before he gets into government work. As a rule, he has risen to the top of his particular field by drive and hard work. But in the process he's become a sort of czar, surrounded by subordinates who carry out his orders and obey his whims without daring to question his judgment. This gives him the illusion that he knows all the answers. He rarely does, outside his own general field.

If you take a man like this and put him into a government job, he's in for a dreadful shock. He'll have a honeymoon period where things seem to go well, and people are patient and kind. But then he begins to find out that there are all sorts of hidden checks and restrictions on him. He isn't a czar any more. He has to fight for appropriations from the Bureau of the Budget. He has to justify his decisions to Congress. Congressional Committees begin to needle him and ask insulting questions. Then what happens? He gets mad. He gets fed up. He wants out.

A lawyer is different. He's trained to evaluate facts in any area, not just one. His outlook is broader than the businessman's because he's conditioned to think horizontally, not just vertically.

He's used to legal battles where his judgments are questioned and fiercely contested. He's not upset by red tape; that's his native habitat. And he knows how bureaucracy works because they taught him something about it in law school.

I think that businessmen are the backbone of the country. But in the Defense Establishment, by and large, they are fish out of water. They might do better to stay home and run their factories and their steel mills and leave government to the lawmakers.

Late in September I received notice that McElroy would visit Redstone on an "orientation" trip before taking office. He was to be with us almost 24 hours! We determined to give him our frank feelings, backed by facts and figures, as to our record for delivering what we promised, when we promised, and for the money originally stated. We now hoped that with a fresh and uncommitted mind the Secretary-elect would grasp the significance of our story.

In the light of later events, I do not honestly feel that the whole story really got across to Mr. McElroy. If it did, it must have been clouded and distorted by the subsequent staff "brainwashing" that seems to be so effectively applied to our appointed civilian chiefs in the Pentagon. In any case, our whole organization was thoroughly fired up with the necessity of giving Mr. McElroy the full and complete story on October 4 and 5, 1957. As it turned out, we were to have powerful and immediate help from an unexpected quarter.

McElroy and his rather sizable party arrived about noon on the fourth. Also on hand were Army Secretary Brucker, General Lyman Lemnitzer, Jim Gavin, and other dignitaries. After an afternoon tour and briefing on the Arsenal we had arranged a cocktail party and dinner to afford an opportunity for the new Secretary-to-be and his party to become personally acquainted with the key members of our outfit. We also wanted him to meet some of the more prominent officials and citizens of Huntsville, upon whose support we depended for a good community background for our efforts.

The cocktail party was under way. After greeting all the guests, McElroy was talking with Wernher and myself in a relaxed and informal atmosphere. Suddenly my Public Relations Officer, Gordon Harris, dashed up and unceremoniously interrupted the conversation. "General," he gasped, "it has just been announced over the radio that the Russians have put up a successful satellite! It's broadcasting signals on a common frequency, and at least one of our local 'hams' has been listening to it."

There was an instant of stunned silence. Then von Braun started to talk as if he had suddenly been vaccinated with a victrola needle. In his driving urgency to unburden his feelings, the words tumbled over one another. "We knew they were going to do it! Vanguard will never make it. We have the hardware on the shelf. For God's sake turn us loose and let us do something. We can put up a satellite in sixty days, Mr. McElroy! Just give us a green light and sixty days!"

While Wernher talked, all the things that had to be done before we could launch were racing through my mind. Hardware to be cleaned and retested. Final assembly to be performed. The crew from the Jet Propulsion Laboratory would have to recheck the small, but effective, payload. Our crews would have to muster strength at Cape Canaveral for final tests and check-out of the solid-propellant upper stages. "Sixty days," Wernher kept saying. "Just sixty days!" Finally I interposed—"No, Wernher, ninety days." It turned out to be a good estimate. Any greater haste would have reduced greatly our chances of success.

By this time everyone was crowding around, exchanging views, protesting that we could have beaten Russia to the punch, literally exploding with pent-up frustration and urgent demands that we be given a chance.

In a far from normal mood, we finally sat down to our dinner. McElroy was strategically placed between von Braun and myself. Other members of the visiting group were spread out among our own people, and I am sure every one of them was subjected to the same drumfire of demanding urgency. The Secretary-designate was in a rough spot. This was a completely new field to him. In our enthusiasm we were all using the familiar technical terms that had grown up inside the business. McElroy must have heard many words, the meaning of which he could only guess. He held his balance very well, but it was obvious that he was caught on the horns of a dilemma. He was certainly concerned about the possible effect of the Russian feat, undoubtedly confused in his own mind as to why we had not been given a chance long ago, and at the same time officially bound to the decisions of Mr. Wilson—at least until he could formally take over the office.

I took great pains to give him positive facts and definite promises. "Missile 27 long ago proved our capability," I told him. "It would have gone into orbit without question if we had used a loaded fourth stage. The hardware is in hand, and so the amount of money needed to make the effort is very small. We must have the chance to make two shots, since there is always the possibility of failure with one. We can have the second missile ready as a back-up to repeat the shot, if necessary, not more than four weeks after the first one. I believe we have a 99 per cent probability of success with at least one of the two shots." I kept hammering away at him, on and on.

I knew that we could hope for no commitment from McElroy on the spot. While we were at dinner, we received a continuous barrage of reports from the local press, TV, and finally a report from our own military radio service of having listened to the *beep-beep* of the Russian satellite. Gordon Harris was bombarded with queries. Some of the calls came from as far away as London.

By the time Mr. McElroy went to bed he had much to think about. Sputnik I was a fact: it was beeping derisively right over our heads. What was still to come was the full story of that achievement in terms of world-wide psychological impact.

Wernher and I stayed behind and talked for a few minutes before heading for home. We agreed that we would reorganize the briefings for McElroy the next morning, and in the more formal atmosphere of the Control Room try to pound home the facts supporting our confidence in being able to put up a satellite on short notice. Our feelings were really very mixed. We were angry and frustrated at having our country so badly outmaneuvered. On the other hand, we were jubilant over the prospect of at last being allowed to get our own satellite off the ground.

The next morning we poured it on. The young officers who were doing most of the briefing emphasized every point of performance and test that would contribute to the certainty of success. We all felt like football players begging to be allowed to get off the bench and go into the game, to restore some measure of the Free World's damaged pride.

The schedule was tight, since McElroy's departure was scheduled for noon. After the briefings, we staged a fast inspection trip through part of the shops to show hardware, and so to the airport. We still had no positive commitment, but by this time we had all managed to convince ourselves that we would get a green light.

After the visiting group had left, I made a few decisions. We had been up to the Pentagon many times with our "6–18" project—six satellite shots for eighteen million dollars. Nevertheless there was no question but that we had to have the best possible information and a firm schedule in Washington bright and early the next week. I had talked briefly with Jim Gavin about our strategy before he left earlier in the morning. I told Colonel Zierdt to get the material together, check it out thoroughly, and send it by officer courier to Washington by Monday afternoon at the latest.

As for Missile 29 itself, I stuck my neck out and directed Wernher to get the stuff out on the floor and go to work on it just as if we had a directive to proceed. I was convinced that we would have final word inside of a week, and that week was too valuable to be lost. If we *still* did not get permission to go, I would have to find some way to bury the relatively small amount of money we would have spent in the meantime.

As matters turned out, I was far too optimistic. Despite the intense world-wide reaction to the Russian success, the United States satellite effort was to remain bogged down in a morass of discussion, argument, delay, and indecision at the Washington level for more than a month. In the meantime the pressures on me became almost intolerable.

Aside from the internal strain and tension, there was continual pressure from all news media—press, radio, TV, and magazines—for statements from von Braun and myself. We decided that nothing would be accomplished by becoming embroiled in the public furor over the beginnings of the space race. In fact, we felt that opening our mouths was probably the least helpful thing we could do. I think the press in general was pretty well aware of the fact that we had a satellite capability, and had been trying to find a market for it. Since the Vanguard program had been unclassified from the beginning, the reporters also knew about the troubles that were haunting that effort. Some newsmen were naturally interested in building up a controversy. We were not. Comparisons, as some wise man said, are odious. All we could possibly accomplish by making statements would be to make one or more important people angry. Such anger almost invariably breeds stubbornness, and even a little stubbornness at that stage could close the door on us for keeps. We therefore agreed to a "no comment" policy, and I so instructed the entire staff and all the technical personnel of ABMA.

As an interesting sidelight, some of our best people were in Spain, attending the annual meeting of the International Astronautics Federation in Barcelona, when the news of Sputnik broke. When the Russian representatives quietly rubbed our people's noses in the sand, General Toftoy, who had gone along as the senior military representative, blew his top. In a press interview that followed, he made some rather incautious remarks about the reasons for our failure to beat the Russians into space. When he got back he had a bit of explaining to do in Washington. Although Toftoy was not under my command, I got caught in some of the backlash. It appeared that Murray Snyder and his press experts in the Department of Defense thought I should be able to control all our representatives by some form of telepathic communication!

By the 9th of October we had work on the satellite missile rolling along pretty well. Meantime, as the final act of his tenure as Secretary of Defense, Mr. Wilson had at last released ABMA from the burdensome restrictions on overtime that had all but put the Jupiter out of business. Final decision had not yet been handed down as a result of the sessions of the Holaday-Schriever-Medaris committee on the Jupiter-Thor controversy, but relief of the overtime restriction was an encouraging sign.

Accepting it as such, we were pressing hard to overcome our disadvantage in the area of the complex ground equipments for the system, and were attempting by every means possible to get some decisions out of the Air Force as to the type of equipment that would be acceptable to them. These were busy days, and the sun set on few of them that had not seen the "panic button" hit at least once.

Dr. Pickering, Director of the Jet Propulsion Laboratory in California, had gotten together with Wernher and myself on an hour-long teleconference to make sure that every action to be taken with regard to the launching had been considered, and every responsibility fully and properly assigned. There were certain areas of disagreement between Pickering and von Braun with respect to some of those responsibilities. I had to sit as arbiter and judge to assure sound and friendly resolution of those differences, and a fair and proper division of the responsibilities. The closest of co-operation was necessary every step of the way, and the willingness of both these distinguished men to accept my rulings and get on with the job had much to do with our ability to maintain our promised schedules.

Meantime, the President had made a public statement to the effect that the United States would definitely launch a small tracking satellite in December, and a scientific payload in March! At Redstone there was a chorus of subdued groans and much private tearing of hair. How far out on a limb could our poor country get? We who could coldly appraise the odds on Vanguard were frankly scared to death. Failure to make good on at least part of that promise would put us in far worse shape before the bar of international opinion than had the appearance of Sputnik I. We at ABMA could do nothing about the first part of the promise—that was Vanguard's responsibility. And since our first effort would have little aboard but tracking equipment, we could do almost nothing about the second part before late March at the earliest.

The confusion in Washington continued. Endless questions were sent down to us. Could we put our missile underneath the top stage of Vanguard so as to boost up the already prepared Vanguard payload without change? (Could Chrysler put a Cadillac engine in a Valiant the day before the public showing of new models?) There seemed to be little or no understanding of the intricacies of matching all elements of a missile or space vehicle into a dependable system. That problem, incidentally, was always with us, and even today there seem to be many who have still not learned how complicated and temperamental these gadgets are. They seem to think that it is very easy to take anybody's booster, bolt on someone else's upper stage, take a guidance system off still another shelf and chuck it inside, hang on any kind of payload that doesn't exceed the weight limitation, and blast off. We could not agree to any such proposal, knowing that the odds against success, particularly under such pressure, were astronomical. We were forced to risk appearing uncooperative, and hold our ground.

Meantime, the Jupiter-Thor problem came to a head. In spite of Secretary Wilson's previous insistence that one was to be canceled, up popped a press release from Washington on October 11 saying that both Jupiter and Thor were to continue until "further testing had been accomplished." But this left us still dangling. We were never to have a pardon, only a reprieve!

Bill Holaday had been given no opportunity to get the word to us officially ahead of the press release. An hour or so later he phoned to confirm the fact that "both are to continue until enough have been fired to assure a successful missile." He and I both knew the real answer. Only Jupiter had so far shown its capability. Thor was far behind on its firing schedule, and beset by troubles known only to the recipients of classified reports.

Thus Jupiter could not by any stretch of conscience be canceled. On the other hand, no one had the nerve to try to cancel Thor in the face of the powerful support of the Air Force, the whole airframe industry, and even Deputy Secretary of Defense Quarles. All of them wanted ABMA to disappear from the missile field. Thor was a major bid by an airframe manufacturer to help capture the missile business for that industry. Our industrial support was confined to our own production contractor, the Chrysler Corporation. So the product of excellence and staying up with or ahead of competition was barely enough to get us a "tie," and keep us precariously in business.

I cannot, in conscience, blame the airframe companies for the pressure they exerted. The signboard was already up, pointing to a steady, but certain, reduction in the requirement for military aircraft. Built up to large proportions when warplanes were in urgent demand, and certain that commercial requirements could not possibly keep a majority of the industry moving at a profitable pace, there was nowhere to turn for possible relief except to the growing field of missiles. We had saddled ourselves with a captive industry, and it could not be waved away or suddenly dissolved without painful results. The ABMA setup was a maverick, there-for a natural enemy in the commercial sense. So I think the stand-off decision was in reality a victory for which we had little logical reason to hope.

The month was spinning by. By now I was far, far out on a limb in connection with our satellite preparations. I had neither money nor authority, yet work was going on. By the end of October I was really sweating, and beginning to wake up in the middle of the night talking to myself. Meantime, a whole new series of flaps developed.

Some of the farsighted people in Washington, notably Jim Gavin, began to worry about satellites as a possible military threat. Very logical. What could we do about a defensive counter-satellite weapon? How soon? For how much? "This could well break extremely fast, as a top priority national requirement," Jim said. "Get us a technical evaluation, engineering outline, time schedule, cost estimate. Day before yesterday will be soon enough."

Fortunately, we *had* been thinking about this problem. Now we threw some of our best people into an around-the-clock exercise to come up with a plan that would be sound and do us credit. We sent a crack briefing team off to Washington with the results, under the impression that everyone was waiting with bated breath to see if we had been able to come up with an answer to this frightening dilemma. By the time they got there, everyone, except General Gavin, was busy with other things. Our people cooled their heels for a couple of days, finally left the material with him and came home. Now, three years later, I can find no indication of any serious effort in that direction, although the problem is a real one, and the threat still highly possible.

With the clock ticking fast and still no actual directive to proceed, we came up at the end of October to the national meeting of the Association of the United States Army. The year before I had had a featured spot on the program, and it was at that time that I first advanced publicly the idea of transporting people and equipment from one point on earth to another by missile transport.

Perhaps it is appropriate here to examine this concept a little, since almost nothing has been done in that direction. I still consider it to be an extremely important approach, and one that should be pushed aggressively. There is no question but that the cost of missile transport for either equipment or men is forbidding at the present time. On the other hand, it has always been hard to justify any new type of transportation when it first appeared to be a possibility, and I strongly believe that the future will make missile transport economically feasible.

A much stronger basis for the requirement at present lies in the military field. If we assume—and we cannot safely assume otherwise—that all types of manned transport will be highly vulnerable to attack, we must recognize that some other means for getting critical supplies or small groups of men to predetermined points is a future essential in military operation. I see nothing on the horizon that can begin to solve this problem except the very high-speed capability of the ballistic missile. We have devoted some exhaustive study to the problem, and there are no insurmountable obstacles from the technical standpoint.

The three-day session in Washington was ended for me in a very unexpected manner by Secretary Brucker. Along with the meeting of the Association, he had called together his Civilian Aides from all parts of the country for special orientation. On the afternoon of October 29th, Secretary Brucker's aide had asked me to join the Secretary and the Aides at a special troop review to be held at Fort McNair. I had no idea that anything personal was involved, but the Secretary had a different notion. Without my knowledge, arrangements had been made to bring Mrs. Medaris and Mrs. von Braun up from Redstone for this ceremony. When I suddenly ran into my wife at Fort McNair, I began to be suspicious. It turned out that the principal object of the exercise was for the Secretary to award me an Oak Leaf Cluster for my

Legion of Merit. The occasion gave him a fine opportunity to pay tribute to the outstanding work of the Army in the missile field. I think this ceremony did much to sustain the morale and confidence of the people at Huntsville. This was most important at the time, because as we moved into the bleak November days we were having great difficulty in getting any solid direction or authorization for our activities.

CHAPTER XIV

Frantic Days Hath November

November found me directing what was in effect a crash effort to launch a satellite without any official sanction for doing so. By the end of the first week in November, I was getting really nervous. I called Jim Gavin in Washington and told him so. I said that I was spending money and man-hours without authority so that we might have a chance of making the March date with a second, scientifically instrumented satellite. His answer: "I'm doing the best I can do to get a decision. Hang on tight and I will support you." Bless his heart! At least I had someone in the high command fighting for me.

On the 7th of November, in a television talk, the President showed our recovered scale-size nose cone to the American people. I am sure that almost every person in ABMA took pains to be watching. We had no real hope that our exploits would be publicly acknowledged, having been through the bitter experience of total anonymity many times before, but there was always a chance. True to form, however, there was not a single mention

165

of the Army, or of ABMA. So far as the public could judge, a faceless and nameless group of unknown characters had come up with the first positive and visible demonstration of man's ability to conquer the so-called "heat barrier" of high-speed re-entry into the earth's atmosphere. We were not too unhappy, however. Whatever was being withheld from the American public, we felt sure that the highest authorities in the nation knew that we had accomplished something of great importance. We hoped they were also aware that we had done it on very little money.

On the 3d of November the Russians put up Sputnik II with a payload of more than 1,100 pounds. This showed us that they were clustering big rockets and were far ahead of us in this critical area. Even Washington was jolted into activity. On the 8th of November, the thirty-fifth day after Sputnik I and five days after Sputnik II, the press wires hummed with the following release from the Department of Defense, which I quote in full only because of the contrast between this public statement and the official directive which we received shortly afterward:

> The Secretary of Defense today directed the Department of the Army to proceed with launching an earth satellite using a modified Jupiter C. This program will supplement the Vanguard project to place an earth satellite into orbit around the earth in connection with IGY. *All test firings of Vanguard have met with success, and there is every reason to believe Vanguard will meet its schedule to launch later this year a fully instrumented scientific satellite.* The decision to proceed with the additional program was made to provide a second means of putting into orbit, as part of the IGY program, a satellite which will carry radio transmitters compatible with Minitrack ground stations and scientific instruments selected by the National Academy of Sciences.
>
> The Assistant to the Secretary of Defense for Guided Missiles, Mr. W. M. Holaday, will be responsible for co-ordinating the Army project as part of the United States satellite program.

That the Vanguard program had *not* met with uniform success in its test program was known to almost everyone. Face had to be saved, even at the expense of veracity. But the worst was yet to come.

Our official directive arrived. It did not say, as had the press release, that the Army would "proceed with launching." Instead, we were told to *prepare* to launch. In effect, there was no clear-cut authority to go ahead and put up a satellite. In the light of previous experience, this was rather easy to interpret. Stripped of official obfuscation, what the directive really said, in very plain English, was about as follows:

"You fellows go ahead and get that hardware ready. You may set provisional firing dates if you want to, but you cannot fire without getting a last-minute release from the Department of Defense. We are going to give Vanguard every possible chance, right up to the last minute, and if by some miracle they do get something up, you can put your toys back on the shelf."

We were sure of the meaning, but just to remove any possible doubt I got Bill Holaday on the phone and asked him point-blank. Reluctantly he agreed that I had the right interpretation. At this point, I blew up. If we were to be called off the sidelines, I certainly felt that we were entitled to at least one shot at the goal whether Vanguard was successful or not. We could not work well without fixed firing dates, against which we constantly measured our progress. We knew we could be ready for the first try before the end of January. Then to have to sit, and slip date after date, waiting for Vanguard to make up its mind, was simply intolerable. If the first shot was slipped too far, the chance to make the second before the end of March began to vanish. We were too old hands at the game not to realize that the chances of success on the first try were not much better than 50-50. Then where would we be with respect to making good on the President's promise to have an instrumented satellite up before the end of March?

I called Wernher in, and before I cooled off, dictated a wire to

General Gavin, with a copy to the Secretary of the Army, to be sent over our confidential lines for their eyes only. In the wire I said flatly that the conditions imposed were unjust and unacceptable, and that if we could not have firm permission to go ahead and fire two attempts, we asked to be relieved of the whole task so we could try to forget about it and get on with our other work. I'm afraid my language was pretty rough. I am thankful that both of the gentlemen to whom the message was directed had the good sense not to show the literal text to anyone in the Defense Department.

Over the phone I told Jim Gavin that if this directive was not altered to give us clear authorization to fire I was ready to quit. I suspect that if Defense had seen my wire I would have been invited to do so at once! I had only one protection. Both Dr. von Braun and Dr. Pickering were with me, and both had insisted that I quote their similar comments in my wire.

The reaction from the Army Staff to my strong message was almost instantaneous. On the 9th of November I had a long telephone call from General Lemnitzer. He began by congratulating me on the assignment to us of the satellite mission. I replied that we were not at all sure that we had an assignment and that when we read the text of the initial directive, we were extremely upset. I am not sure to this day whether General Lemnitzer had read my dispatch, but he took the position on the phone that he had not, without saying so directly.

I repeated to him the circumstances of our protest, and reiterated that if we could not have a solid directive under which to go ahead, we would rather not take the job at all.

It turned out that Lem also had his troubles. He was upset about an interview that von Braun had had with Associated Press representatives on the West Coast during which Wernher had spoken out rather bluntly about the urgent need for getting on with the satellite business. Lem reminded me that the President had taken the attitude publicly that there was no competition with Russia in the space field. He said that Wernher's remarks could be very damaging to what the President was trying to do. He went on to say that they had talked with the head of Associated Press about the text and had persuaded him to take out a few things that were not quite in accordance with good propriety. Lem said that they thought they had weathered this one, although there might still be some flare-back. His purpose in calling was to emphasize that "the time for talking has stopped." He said we should get out of the headlines and that we could do a good deal of damage by talking.

I pointed out to him that this had been our attitude from the time Sputnik I had gone up, but that on the other hand I knew that all of the scientists did not agree with this viewpoint, and that he certainly must recognize that I could not exercise complete censorship over our civilian scientific personnel or their associates at the Jet Propulsion Laboratory.

I pointed out again that the wording of the directive did not give us an unconditional mission and that both von Braun and Pickering were extremely unhappy about the whole situation. I emphasized the fact that the only real control I could exert over nonmilitary people was with relation to information that came under the direct heading of national security. I said that I would try to persuade them to close down, but that the best way to get them under control was to straighten out this directive and get us a real decision with definite firing dates and no conditions imposed as to when and under what circumstances Vanguard was fired. I told him that I had been going ahead this last month with almost no authority and with my head stuck out a mile. I also reminded him that nobody else was being half as reticent as we were, and called his attention to the advertising propaganda flooding out of the aviation industry.

General Lemnitzer said that if there was anything in the wording of the directive that we thought was restrictive, he was sure the Secretary would go to bat to get it removed. He added that he thought any restrictions or hidden meanings in the directive were not intentional, and repeated his strong conviction that we must keep still and go to work.

The conversation was closed with my remark that if he would reconsider the whole background and reread both the press release and the directive, he would find that the restrictions were definitely there and were wholly deliberate.

In the end, we got what we wanted, but it took a long time.

Of the whole of my four years of intimate work with missiles and space, this month of November 1957 was probably the most confused and most exasperating. Behind the scenes we continued to press for firm firing dates for our satellites. Meantime the whole Air Force propaganda machine swung into action to get the aviation industry into the space business. Their propaganda concentrated on military applications in the space field, and the public statement was made that if they could get money and authority they could have an "operational" satellite in 1960. This was certainly contrary to the administration's "peaceful" space policy as expressed to me by General Lemnitzer, but I saw no indication that anybody was trying to close them down and the propaganda continued at a great rate.

During the same period, we went through a great deal of discussion and controversy with regard to security. The Vanguard program had had no military implications and had therefore been open to the press from the beginning. On the other hand, we were going to use much military hardware in our satellite attempts. I took the position that the use of this hardware for an open scientific satellite did not relieve us of the necessity to preserve security as to the nature of the hardware itself. We finally got a check list together to indicate what was classified and what was not, and sent it out to everyone connected with the effort. We left the whole payload uncovered by security restrictions, thus giving Dr. Pickering every opportunity to discuss the whole problem with other scientists and in public statements. Wernher was somewhat unhappy over the fact that this gave JPL an opening for publicity that was not afforded ABMA, but I could find no other solution.

During the same period, we were up to our neck in preparation for HARDTACK, which was the code name for the high-altitude nuclear firings in the Pacific that have since been made public property. To the uninitiated, this particular project may have seemed a very simple one, since our missiles were built to handle nuclear warheads from the beginning. I assure you that it was by no means simple. The co-ordination required to get and prove out the very special instrumentation required by the Atomic Energy experts, and to schedule hundreds of people and hundreds of thousands of pounds of complex equipment into position in the Pacific area on a tight time scale, was tremendous. I had assigned Lt. Col. Glen Elliott to that project and had directed him to pay no attention to our other problems. He did a superb job, as was fully proven by the complete success, on time, of the operations.

During this same period, the matter of whether or not we could keep Professor Oberth in the United States also came to a head. The old man was an extremely valuable consultant, and his years had by no means dimmed his brilliant imagination. To our people, especially the ex-Germans, he was the "elder statesman" and was paying his way many times over. On the other hand, he was on the horns of a real and human dilemma. During his years in Germany before the war, he had fully earned the quite adequate retirement pay of a German professor. He could not, however, take advantage of this retirement income without returning to Germany to live. On the other hand, he was rapidly approaching the age for U. S. Civil Service retirement, and due to his relatively short service with us, had not the slightest possibility of earning a United States retirement income sufficient to keep himself and his wife from starving.

The Oberths wanted to stay in the United States, but economic necessity was dictating otherwise. The Professor had received notice from Germany that if he did not come back by the end of the year, he would forfeit his German retirement.

When this was made public and it was announced that they were returning to Germany, the press struck up a two-day alarm. Many people became concerned over why the United States could not afford to keep such a man in this country. I looked into the situation very thoroughly and came to the conclusion that the only possibility of keeping Professor Oberth here would be to turn up enough money by private subscription to buy an annuity for him and his wife. It turned out that this would cost $75,000. I had telephone inquiries from quite a number of wealthy and important people as to what could be done. I gave them all the same answer and told them I could do nothing officially. The results were interesting. In almost every case, the first reaction was assurance that the money could be easily found, and that they would be in touch with me shortly. This was always followed by a great silence. Finally, when time was running out, I would call them back to see what was being done. Invariably I got the answer that they were very sorry but that it didn't appear possible to do anything. In the end, I had no choice but to tell that grand old man that, much as we would like to have him in the United States, the only way he could protect his own economic future was to go back to Germany. So he went.

About the 19th of November, I picked up the first rumblings of a Defense Department plan to organize a special super-agency to handle space activities and the antimissile missile program. A draft directive was circulating through the Pentagon, but I could not get my hands on it. Finally, there was a press report indicating that such an organization was planned. I was quite concerned over the prospect. Rumor had it that this would be an operating organization, with its own right to make contracts directly with industry or with military organizations, and in general, to operate (rather than direct) these important programs.

I was in Detroit at about that time to talk to the Economic

Club of Detroit, and in a side conversation with Tex Colbert, President of Chrysler, mentioned my concern. It seemed to me that this might easily become another case of duplicating higher headquarters and could well develop into a bureaucratic monster. I had never been in sympathy with this business of meeting every new requirement by creating a new organization. Adequate resources already existed within the structure of the Defense Department. To me it was a simple matter of having someone in the Department with the firm authority to say yes or no to proposals, and the ability to back up his yeses with money. I was all too familiar with the complexities of contracting under existing federal laws and regulations. With all three Services having adequate organizations for the purpose, I could see nothing but confusion arising from the creation of a fourth organization negotiating directly with industry. Even today, I have the very strong impression that most of our difficulties of the post-World War II years could have been handled better by single strong direction within the Defense establishment, rather than by constantly tinkering with the basic organization.

The indirect reaction to my talk with Mr. Colbert was immediate. On the 20th of November I had a call from Brig. General Randall, Military Assistant to the Secretary of Defense, who wanted to know just what was on my mind. I told General Randall the nature of my concern, and tried to make clear to him the distinction between the direction and over-all management of a program, and the actual operation of such a program, which would require a sizable new organization which I was sure would get in everyone's way. Our discussion boiled down to whether contract authority was to be given the new agency and whether we were to have new channels for receiving and reporting on money and progress, or whether it could be intelligently recognized that this was not necessary, and that this new deal could be best set up as a strong individual who would have real, decisive authority.

I asked about the distinction between Bill Holaday's job and the new one, and whether the new man would have greater final authority than had been accorded to Bill. I also questioned whether missile activities as a whole could properly be divided at the level of the Department of Defense from space and antimissile missile work, since it was obvious that in the field the same organizations and industrial units would be doing the work in both areas.

While we had quite a lengthy discussion, there was no particular conclusion. I was given to understand that the new organization would probably have direct contracting authority but "probably won't use it." I let it go with the statement that it looked to me as if I would wind up with one more boss to add to the four or five I already had. It is notable that the subsequent development of the Advanced Research Projects Agency (ARPA) was to stick by and large to the over-all management concept, but only because of the intelligence and forbearance of Mr. Roy Johnson, since they had full authority to become operational if he had so desired.

On about the same day as General Randall's call, we finally got an understanding out of Bill Holaday with respect to our satellite firing schedule. It was some time afterward before we got a directive in writing, but I had enough agreement with Holaday to give me confidence that we would be allowed to go ahead regardless, and I so advised our people. There was a great sigh of relief and a great surge of added enthusiasm. We had already decided on the 29th of January as the earliest practical firing date for our first effort, but we had some long discussions before I finally agreed that the second one would have to be on the 5th of March. I was extremely anxious to get the second effort scheduled as early as possible in case the first one failed, but a combination of conflicting schedules on the range at Cape Canaveral, and the necessity for doing a thorough job on the back-up hardware, prevented an attempt any earlier.

On the 21st of November, at a staff meeting, I spelled out our position on the earth satellite program and set down the following policies:

(1) We are not in competition with anyone in the satellite program. We are engaged in an effort to accomplish everything possible for the benefit of the country by doing the best we can. This viewpoint will be communicated throughout the organization.

(2) In support of IGY, scientific payloads for our satellites will be as co-ordinated with and directed by the earth satellite panel of IGY. Dr. Pickering of JPL has been requested to act as our co-ordinator with the panel and to be responsible for the determination of the payloads as approved by the earth satellite panel. This includes the matter of communications between the satellite vehicle and the ground after launching.

The last sentence of the second policy was very important, since the question of a world-wide tracking net to follow our satellite was a very complex one and required the most careful attention. The JPL approach to tracking our satellites by radio was called "Microlock." On the other hand, the tracking net that had been developed on a more or less world-wide basis to support the Vanguard program used a system known as "Minitrack." The differences are highly technical and I will not attempt to explain them, but I believed then and still believe that the Microlock approach was somewhat the more efficient and accurate.

However, we had only three stations that were strictly engineered to manage the full Microlock capability. One was at Cape Canaveral, one was on one of the islands downrange from Cape Canaveral, and one at JPL on the West Coast. Fortunately, through crash efforts on the part of JPL and with the co-operation of the British, we were able to get two sets of essential equipment into British hands and placed at strategic points on the other side of the world.

Throughout the discussions with respect to our efforts in the satellite field, it became obvious that the whole of the Defense Department was allergic to the term "Microlock." All they could see was the possibility of having to construct an entirely new tracking net duplicating the Minitrack, and this naturally upset them. Fortunately, in building up the Microlock system, JPL had made its frequencies compatible with those that could be received by the Minitrack net and I honestly believe that this is the only thing that saved us. Even as it was, we had to repeat endlessly that the two were compatible and that we were not asking for any more special tracking stations.

In still another way the month of November was critical. We still did not know where we stood in the Jupiter-Thor controversy, and time was fast running out on us. While we were able to take a straightforward position with respect to the development of the Jupiter missile itself, and the preparation for transferring production to Chrysler, we were in no such clean position with respect to ground equipment. In our continued attempts to reach a meeting of minds with the Air Force for the use of the Jupiter, the ground equipment situation had been used continuously as the primary "reason" why Jupiter could not make the deployment dates. It was the contention of the Air Force that our ground equipment was not sufficiently developed, and in any case, would not meet their requirements.

To this day, I am unable to convince myself that this ground equipment squeeze was accidental. Throughout the months since the issuance of Secretary Wilson's directive assigning operational responsibility to the Air Force, we had made repeated efforts to get specific directives from the Air Force as to the qualifications that had to be met by the ground equipment. In this we had been uniformly unsuccessful. In the meetings of the Ad Hoc Committee, this point had been turned around to try to show that while we had a successful missile we could not possibly have the system as a whole ready to meet Air Force requirements by the required time of deployment.

We had used every known method we could possibly find to

determine the specifications of their requirements. Lt. Col. Glenn Crane, in his office at the Air Force Ballistic Missile Division in Santa Monica, had done an outstanding job of ferreting out every piece of paper that he could get hold of, legally or illegally, that might shed some light on the subject. We believed we had a fair idea of the specific requirements in terms of stand-by capability and reaction time, but we were not so naïve as to believe that we could not be thrown a curve by a minor but all-important change in any one small specification.

We had been unable to get a directive from topside to B.M.D. to insist that they give us the details required, probably because no official decision had yet been made as to whether the Jupiter was to continue on to production and deployment. Meantime, if we were to have any chance to make the time schedule, we had to be prepared with some kind of hardware to show. The fact that in November and December 1957 my organization produced hard mockups of the complete and complex ground equipment required to support the fixed base concept of the Air Force, while still preserving the possibility of mobility in case of need, was to my mind one of the real technical miracles of the entire period. Yet, because it was less spectacular than the firing of missiles, it received little attention. That achievement was such, however, as to make it impossible in the end for the Air Force to insist that we could not meet the deployment schedule.

Finally, a committee of Congress indirectly brought the situation to a head. The new Secretary of Defense was to appear before the Lyndon Johnson subcommittee of the Senate on the 27th of November. He knew that one of the critical questions to be asked by the committee would be with respect to the Jupiter or Thor deployment. He was, therefore, more or less forced to make a decision, and did so by including the following in his opening statement.

"Gentlemen—Mr. Quarles, Mr. Holaday, and I are glad to be with you and to make ourselves available to you for any questions you may want to ask us. However, before you begin your questioning, I have a brief statement to make which will, I believe, represent an action which we are taking today which will be of considerable interest to this committee.

"We have been undertaking during the past few days an intensive reassessment of our position with respect to the testing and development program of our IRBM missiles, the Thor and the Jupiter. We have been greatly encouraged by the success that has been achieved in the recent tests of both of these missiles. It is now clear that, while neither of the missiles can be regarded as having completed its development phase, they both are at a point at which we believe we can, on the basis of judgment, make a sound decision to program additional production for operational purposes.

"Accordingly, we are today authorizing the placing into production of both the Jupiter and the Thor missiles.

"By making use of the production capacity now available for both the Jupiter and the Thor, an operational capability can be achieved by the end of 1958 in the United Kingdom, and as soon as necessary arrangements can be effected in other appropriate locations.

"The Department of the Army has assured the Air Force, which has the operational responsibility for the deployment of the land-based IRBM, of its full support in training of personnel and other ways in which it might assist in making these weapons operational at the earliest practicable date.

"In reaching these conclusions we have been benefited by the advice of Dr. J. R. Killian, recently appointed special assistant to the President for science and technology.

"While we cannot at this time define just what new appropriation and other authorization by the Congress will be required, we expect to submit any needed proposal to this end soon after Congress meets in January. We believe, however, that we will not have expended our commitments beyond a manageable point before Congress may have had an opportunity to indicate its decision in these matters."

This statement was flashed to us immediately, and you can be sure that we were greatly relieved. On the other hand, this particular statement set in motion a train of events that included the worst single example of indecision and vacillation in the complex structure of the Department of Defense that I ever encountered. Which is saying a good deal. From that standpoint alone, the month of December 1957 deserves full and complete treatment.

CHAPTER XV

The Valley of Indecision

Secretary McElroy's announcement that both Jupiter and Thor would be carried into production and would be deployed opened a veritable Pandora's box of maneuver and countermaneuver.

Immediately following the Secretary's announcement, it developed that the deployment date of Jupiter was to be advanced to a point nine months earlier than anything previously discussed between ourselves and the Air Force. No training had started, and the matter of the exact make-up of the ground equipment was still undetermined, yet we were committed to deploy in little over a year.

Although the Army had been banished from long-range missile operations by Secretary Wilson's directive a year before, the Army Staff now got back into the act on the basis that in order to make the deployment schedule it might be better to retrain an existing Redstone group rather than start from scratch with new Air Force personnel for the first Jupiter squadron. Training was, of course, a key element in our ability to make the schedule. When question arose as to where and how training could be conducted, I recommended what to me was the only logical solution —that we do the training at Redstone Arsenal, beginning with Redstone equipment as a point of introduction to large ballistic missiles, and moving on to Jupiter equipment as soon as we had one complete prototype available. By doing this, we could also make use of the skilled instructors of the Ordnance Guided Missiles School.

The operational side of the Army Staff was always allergic to the idea of having tactical training on a technical installation. We were immediately embroiled in an internal dispute over whether ABMA was to hold the responsibility or whether this was to be taken over by the Artillery.

I needed, and got, the vigorous support of Jim Gavin. It was my contention that any attempt by the Army to inject Army tactical control into the Jupiter picture would meet with immediate and justified resistance from the Air Force, who would see the maneuver as an attempt to get the Army's foot back in the door with a view to employing Jupiter eventually as an Army weapon.

We had planned the Jupiter as a mobile system from the beginning. The missile was no larger over-all and no more difficult to handle than Redstone. The same techniques, with the addition of refinements and improvements that we had developed in the meantime, would have made it possible to use Jupiter anywhere in the world where a spot of hard ground could be found. This was, of course, incompatible with the basic Air Force idea of handling their strategic weapons from fixed bases, with the troops permanently housed and the weapons supported by permanent buildings. Since it was planned as a mobile weapon, many of us felt that there was great logic in having Jupiter manned by Army troops particularly trained to operate while on the move. In this way, the entire Army support system, including communications and the survey capability of engineers, could be used to support the weapon.

However, the battle for operational control had been lost on the 26th of November, 1957, and it seemed to me that it would be very foolish to let it appear that we were challenging that decision or to give the Air Force any cause to doubt our willingness to co-operate. I therefore recommended strongly that the Army tactical staff stay out of the Jupiter picture. I asked that arrangements be made with the Air Force so that I could deal directly with the Strategic Air Command, the ultimate user of the weapon, in all matters pertaining to the characteristics of the final prototype.

I had a reason for this. Since the Air Force Ballistic Missile Division of the Air Research and Development Command was in direct competition with us through their sponsorship of Thor, I knew I could not expect any sympathetic treatment from them. On the other hand, SAC was in no such position. They were to be the users for both missiles. I felt that if we could deal directly with SAC, we could establish a friendly and co-operative interchange which would help us meet the commitment for deployment and keep us out of the area of bitter rivalry. Later events were to prove that I was right.

The Air Force themselves had some difficulty in figuring out how they could manage to train people to man the first squadron. In the end, they decided to select some of their very finest personnel for the first squadron, in order that their training could be condensed into a minimum of time. They did an outstanding job of picking the people, and it worked out very well.

These problems were minor compared to the indecision that we continued to encounter at the top of the Defense structure. It was true that we now had a directive which said that both Thor and Jupiter would continue to deployment. Such a directive sounds good, but to the operators responsible for the production and preparation of the hardware it means nothing until numbers of missiles, quantities of ground equipment, a time schedule for production, and the money to support these things are decided and made definite. This was where the real problem lay, and where we were to encounter endless frustration in our attempts to get firm guidance.

The first roadblock was an indication from the Department of Defense that they did not want us to continue with our plan to transfer Jupiter production as quickly as possible to the Chrysler plant at Warren, Michigan. Our whole plan from the beginning had been based on that concept. We did not consider it appropriate for a government-operated research and development organization to get itself tied up with long-term production. If we had been compelled to accept full responsibility at ABMA for production of the squadron equipment to be deployed, we would have tied up our capability for several years and put ourselves out of the research and development business. Our production and assembly areas were not adequate to support both research and development, and at the same time carry a production line on missiles.

By this time, the pressure and the tension were so great that we were seeing hobgoblins under every bed. Some of our people even suspected that this pressure to carry out production at ABMA constituted a deliberate attempt to saturate our capabilities and keep us out of advanced research and space work.

The accelerated time schedule made it impossible to get the first missiles for deployment out of the Chrysler plant. We were therefore compelled to do *some* production at ABMA, but I considered it vital that we get out of that business and get all production into Detroit at the earliest possible moment. Throughout December of 1957 and January of 1958, we went around and around on this subject. We had already committed the money necessary to provide tooling for the Detroit plant, and this was not recoverable. That fact was of critical importance, because the whole effort to keep production at ABMA was at least outwardly based on cost. We were infested with visitors from the Department of Defense Comptroller and the Bureau of the Budget, all apparently trying to establish the fact that it would cost more to have production moved to Chrysler. While there was no question that there were costs involved, my contention was that these costs had already been paid through our investment in plant and facilities at Detroit, and through our having many Chrysler people in our own shop for training throughout the period from early 1956 on.

We could not really come to grips with the problem of production at Chrysler, however, until we got a firm decision as to how many missiles and how many ground equipments were to be produced and how fast. This question alone occupied more than six weeks, and it was late in January before we got real numbers that we felt would hold up.

Even then, we did not have money support for those numbers. The Department of Defense had decided that production and deployment costs were to be borne by the Air Force. The Air Force contended that they did not have enough money in their budget to meet our estimated costs. This hassle was so protracted that the Army finally had to advance the funds to support the production of Jupiter for many months before reimbursement from the Air Force was forthcoming. Money was to be a bone of contention between the Air Force and ourselves throughout the whole period of our getting Jupiter produced and out to the NATO countries, and many times I was able to continue only because the Army advanced me money while they battled the situation out with the Air Force.

Were I to add up the thousands of man-hours that were unproductively devoted to this apparently simple question of getting a decision as to quantity, time, and money, the figure would be hard to believe. In order to protect the capabilities of our technical personnel, we kept them out of these battles, and when they required immediate decisions, I made those decisions on my own responsibility. Meanwhile, however, a large proportion of the time of the military and civilian supporting staff was consumed in the endless exercise of estimate, re-estimate, statement and restatement. Whatever we did or in whatever form our figures on money or schedules were submitted, someone could think of another way or another form. I cannot honestly say that there was ever a complete resolution of the problem, but each element was finally resolved by being overtaken by time, leaving no alternative but to confirm that which had already been done.

It is impossible to assign the responsibility for this kind of appalling delay and waste of manpower to any one individual. The system we have created to operate our defense establishment is so complex that hundreds of people are necessarily involved. It is apparent that no one individual, short of the President himself, can take the final responsibility.

Even if it were possible in such complex cases to lay all the facts directly before the Secretary of Defense, without the intermediate evaluation and interpretations of his voluminous staff, and even if he were to make a complete and whole decision as to what should be done, that decision still could not be accepted as certain until the Bureau of the Budget had satisfied itself through its auditors and accountants that the money was required, and what is much more to the point, had decided that it approved the action and was willing to apportion the money!

It is precisely here that the apportionment process operates to deny the directive power short of the President, since he is the only common boss of the Defense Department and the Bureau of Budget.

As the date for our first space shot approached, excitement grew steadily more intense. At the same time, we were deeply involved in critical activities connected with both our major weapons systems, and could not allow ourselves to forget that these were after all our primary missions and the real reason for our existence. Thus, I had to husband resources very carefully to see that everything was covered.

Our feeling of urgency in the field of space exploration had, of course, been intensified by the fact that Russia had successfully fired Sputnik II. When on top of that the Vanguard blew up on the pad on the 6th of December, we were more convinced than ever that any chance to make good on the President's promises was going to devolve on us. We reminded ourselves that this meant that we had to be doubly careful in checking out everything connected with our first flight, since its chance of success had to be increased to a maximum. This was particularly true since we could not make a second attempt before early in March, and the psychological impact of Russia's successes on the rest of the world was daily showing itself to be more serious than anyone had anticipated.

The final testing of Redstone tactical prototypes was continuing with uniform success. We fired a complete missile on the 10th of December, and for an extra dividend put some of the special instrumentation required for the Hardtack exercise on board. Another fully successful missile carrying all of the Hardtack instrumentation was fired on the 14th of January.

In the midst of all this activity, we ran into difficulties with the engine of the Jupiter. The firing of Missile No. 4 on the 18th of December confirmed our suspicions that we had definite problems with the high-speed turbine pump. We set about most urgently to run a very special set of tests, and for the purpose created almost overnight a test rig that would enable us to run the Jupiter turbine at the Arsenal under vacuum conditions closely resembling those that existed in flight.

Now that the space door was opened, we felt it to be extremely important that there be a continuing follow-on program to carry the United States deeply into the exploration of this new environment. We knew that no one had been thinking about these problems as long or as thoroughly as Wernher von Braun and some of his people, so we put a few of the best of them off in a closed room to come up with a 12- or 15-year national space program.

This group was told that they must not try to build a program that would use only Army equipment, but must consider all existing hardware and boosters under development, including the

ICBM, since it was the considered conclusion of both von Braun and myself that if the space program was organized properly there was more than enough work for all the qualified groups of technical people and all the existing resources. By mid-December we had completed the job, but we didn't know what to do with the document. We had no space mission as such. Finally, we discreetly distributed a limited number to the Army Staff, to our friends at JPL, and to the Chief of Ordnance, General Cummings.

The essential elements of the von Braun program, as I remember them, were as follows:

Spring of 1960—2,000 pounds in orbit.
Fall of 1960—soft lunar landing.
Spring of 1961—5,000-pound satellite.
Spring of 1962—circumnavigation of the moon with *adequate* photographic coverage.
Fall of 1962—two-man satellite.
Spring of 1963—20,000 pounds in orbit.
Fall of 1963—manned expedition to circumnavigate the moon and return to earth.
Fall of 1965—20-man permanent space station.
Spring of 1967—3-man lunar expedition.
Spring of 1971 (13½ years)—50-man lunar expedition and permanent outpost.

These goals were to be achieved by what might be called a leapfrog technique. While one group of capable people moved forward to capitalize on capabilities with existing vehicles, another group moved on to develop the next generation. As soon as that generation was available for use, the first group would quit using obsolescent vehicles and start into developments for the next jump forward.

As I remember it, the program placed us in the position by spring of 1968 to handle enough weight and size to do almost anything we decided to do.

The total cost for a 14-year program was estimated at approximately 21 billion dollars, or an average of 1.5 billion per year. This average, however, allowed for about 400 million a year to be expended in supporting research and development of components to handle future activities, with approximately 1.1 billion devoted to the production and use of current vehicles.

As I write these words, it looks to me as if we are spending pretty close to that amount now, but because of duplication and lack of a long-range coherent program, we are not getting anything like the intended results except in a few isolated areas.

Meantime, the Air Force, through BMD, was busily extending and increasing their plans. They took the position that previous approval of what was known as the 117L Program gave them the right to go ahead on a satellite project with any money they could find. Colonel Crane made inquiries as to their plans and found the door was shut completely, and that there was an internal directive that no information on satellites would be released to ABMA. The only thing I could do defensively at the moment was to retaliate in kind, so I also closed the door and told our people to give the Air Force no information on our satellite plans or activities. This was preposterous, but it was the only lever I had. I had Colonel Crane inform BMD that this position would be reversed at any time that they were willing to reciprocate.

The whole business of the public release of information was also in a big flap. The press was actively pursuing every lead, and I had no time to operate with the Army Staff on a case-by-case basis. I insisted on getting some definite written guidance and finally succeeded about the 8th of December. The guidance required that all releases of public information be submitted to the Department of the Army for approval unless it was a matter of purely local nature having no national significance. It also prohibited anyone from appearing on live, unrehearsed radio or television, except myself. The statement was made that since I had good and current knowledge of the situation at the seat of

Government, I could so appear when I believed it to be advisable. This, of course, put the responsibility to keep out of trouble squarely on my own head.

The first indications that there might be more satellites in the offing came with a request to send representatives to talk with Dr. Killian, who had been made the President's scientific advisor, and Doctors York, Kistiakowski, and Piore with respect to our capabilities for follow-on work in the satellite area. In the meantime, the space committee of the Rocket and Satellite Panel of the National Academy of Sciences had been formed, and Dr. von Braun had been made a member.

Wernher and I talked long and earnestly about the approach to be taken, and finally agreed that the best thing to do was to use our previously prepared national space program as a basis for his recommendations to that committee. Not knowing what tactics the Army Staff had planned, I consulted with Jim Gavin and he agreed that it was all right to use that as a basis. While there were many variations in detail, the final outline program still very closely resembled our initial approach.

The same thing occurred later on when Dr. von Braun was asked to participate with the National Advisory Committee on Aeronautics in developing an outline space program, after it became apparent in the spring that a new civilian space agency would probably be built around NACA. It is interesting to compare our original document with the final recommendations of the NACA committee. They are almost identical. It is also interesting to note that the space program as it has developed bears little resemblance to the coherence and steady progress laid out in that document.

At the end of 1957, as I reviewed our general situation, it did not seem too bad. I knew that we knew our business, and I was naïve enough to believe that if we produced the goods, we would get a chance to do more. I could not then foresee that our successes would bring us more and more difficulty.

Just before New Year's, I took a summary reading of the whole situation and it looked about like this:

In the space business we had a definite commission to fire two satellite attempts. We had more hardware of the same kind on the shelf, and were busily engaged in negotiating for payloads and additional money and authority for a follow-on program. We were well along in the engineering of a second-generation space vehicle, to use the Jupiter booster and to increase the power of the solid-propellant upper stages so that we could get significant scientific payloads into orbit. This later became the Juno II.

In our original mission to weaponize and deploy the Redstone, we were on schedule. One group was well trained and on their time schedule for actually firing a practice missile in the spring of 1958.

Where Jupiter was concerned, we still had no really firm basis for production, but we had established very friendly working relationships with the Strategic Air Command which would be responsible for the readiness of deployment of the missile. We had managed under great pressure to put together an array of real hardware representing our idea of the ground equipment for Jupiter, and in a big review conducted by the Air Force had succeeded in convincing most of their people of both our capability and our willingness to co-operate. A Jupiter office was being set up by the Air Force at ABMA, and we felt that in spite of all the difficulties at the Department of Defense and Department of the Air Force levels, our working relationships with the people who would actually use the weapons were good.

Plans were under way for celebration of the second birthday of ABMA on February 1. We were determined to make this a real event, and since the first satellite firing was scheduled for the 29th of January, we had every confidence that we would have a real achievement to brag about.

On New Year's Eve, I looked forward to the customary official military reception the next day with feelings much different from those that had had my head bowed and my spirit beaten a year before, when I had known that the Inspector General was on his way and that we were in deep trouble, but had not known what kind or how seriously. This year I knew that there were many problems and difficulties ahead, but the morale of the organization was very high. With their spirit and confidence I felt that they could achieve anything, short of the impossible. I knew they would even have a swing at *that*, if I asked them to!

CHAPTER XVI

On the Threshold of Space

January was filled with furious activity, and the demands on my time got worse as the month went on. I had hoped to take a week's leave toward the middle of the month, but this plan was steadily eroded until in the end I had only two days.

I also felt the urgent necessity for visiting the West Coast, to be sure that all the loose ends were tied together with JPL and that we had no differences of opinion or neglected areas of responsibility. I scheduled myself to go on the 6th of January, which was Sunday, but as it turned out I had to put the visit off for another week and then make it a real flying trip, straight out and back.

On the 2nd of January, I was advised that I had been selected as one of the participants in the special midyear program of Rollins College at Winter Park, Florida, which is called the "Animated Magazine," and was asked to be in Orlando on the 22d, 23d, and 24th of February to participate as a speaker and to receive an honorary degree from Rollins. My schedule was already very crowded, but after looking over the quality of previous participants and the background of this affair, I felt that I should not neglect it. So, in the midst of other matters, I had to give careful attention to the preparation of my speech for this occasion. Later on, in the fall of 1958, that talk was recommended to the Freedoms Foundation, and I received an award for it the following February.

This month of January 1958 saw the beginning of a long struggle over the question of publicity connected with our firing. It was my very strong belief that there should be no information about any of our projects in advance of the firing, and that the build-up of advance publicity was unwise from several points of view.

First of all, it focused the attention of the press and public on the Cape at the time of our scheduled effort. It meant a substantially increased number of official visitors actually at the Cape to witness the effort, and this seemed to increase the pressure on the firing crew. Two years of close personal observation had convinced me that the chances of success on any important firing effort were in inverse proportion to the number of VIPs present. Where there was no particular attention focused on the effort, the firing crew, under Kurt Debus, worked in a relaxed atmosphere and did not hesitate to hold a missile to the extent necessary to assure that everything was in proper working order before firing command. There was no hesitancy about postponing a shot at the last minute for one or two days, if it appeared advisable to make a major correction. But with a considerable number of important people standing around waiting for a shoot, there was a very human tendency to decide in marginal cases to go ahead and accept the risk rather than disappoint the visitors.

Throughout the year I had made it a point to be present at most important firings, and to take upon myself the responsibility for delaying or scrubbing a shoot in order to fight this tendency. More than once, I had asked Kurt Debus to call a "hold" just because I could hear the rising tension of voices on the intercom net that indicated the crew was under too much pressure. The uncertainty involved in a highly instrumented research and development firing is very great and does not remotely resemble the conditions under which a tactical missile would be fired in combat.

I knew, however, that since Cape Canaveral was perfectly flat and there were no restrictions with respect to people on the beaches for miles in either direction, observers with field glasses could always note the presence of a missile on the pad and the increased activity that went with preparations for a firing. In fact, the news agencies had regular watches established to alert them whenever there was the probability of an effort to fire a major missile. Thus a policy of complete secrecy was impossible to maintain.

Maj. Gen. Don Yates of the Air Force, who commanded the Missile Test Center at Cape Canaveral, is one of the most reasonable, co-operative, and objective officers I have ever met, and I have nothing but praise for his handling of our problems at the Cape throughout these difficult periods. The primary burden of handling the press at the Cape naturally fell on his shoulders. Over the years there have been many debates over his activities and policies, but I for one am convinced that he did the best that anybody could do under almost impossible circumstances.

General Yates finally reached a gentlemen's agreement with the press that divided Cape efforts as between regular tactical missile firings and special efforts in the space and recovery areas. On the tactical missile shots, he would give them nothing in advance, and only brief announcements after the missile had been fired. In connection with the special missions, he agreed to have the press in ahead of time and give them an off-the-record briefing with the understanding that they would release nothing until the missile had actually been fired. With few exceptions the press respected the agreement and the resulting co-operation was excellent. The arrangement was in jeopardy several times when some irresponsible member of the press could not stand the pressure and would break an exclusive ahead of time. Don's only weapon in these cases was to bar the offending agency, and this, of course, created a great furor each time it happened.

One of the major problems was concerned with the text of the releases after any firing. I had made the point most vigorously to both Assistant Secretary of Defense Murray Snyder, the Defense public relations chief, and to Don Yates that great damage was done every time greater success was claimed for a mission than was in fact achieved. The people intimately connected with the missile programs always received classified, complete, and factual reports of the results. To have a release made which claimed that "the test of X missile was fully successful and the missile impacted in the predetermined area," when those on the inside technically knew that the guidance system had gone haywire and the missile was 50 miles off course, invariably created jealousy and very human pressures on rival missile personnel to leak the real results to the press.

I insisted, therefore, that great care be taken to claim complete success only when the missile did do *everything* that it was supposed to do. I also insisted that those responsible for approving the releases get information in advance of the event as to what the particular test was expected to achieve, so that there could be a predetermined objective against which results might be fully measured.

Over the entire period of 1958 and much of 1959, the text of these releases was a point of major dispute. Those in charge of some projects at the Cape seemed to have developed a very fine technique for making the headlines by announcing the objectives of a special mission as "apparently having been fully accomplished," and then the next day a very small inside paragraph of the newspapers would say that "after full analysis of test results it appeared that all missions were *not* fully accomplished." These and similar techniques of inter*project* rivalry were the source of much bitterness that was often wrongly attributed to "inter-*Service* rivalry."

The arguments over the kind of publicity that was to be released on our first satellite attempt, and over how, when, and by whom it was to be released, were really in the frantic category. My very able PIO, Gordon Harris, was up to his neck in this controversy throughout the month of January, and it is a wonder to me that he didn't wind up with a colossal case of ulcers.

Early in the flap, it became quite obvious that every effort would be made at the national level to suppress the Army's participation in this enterprise, and to credit the whole business to the scientific personnel controlling the IGY effort. From a practical standpoint the idea was rather ridiculous, since the most inexperienced reporter was fully familiar with the circumstances, and with who was doing what. I might say, in passing, that the most bitter disappointment of my entire life occurred when the President congratulated Dr. Allan Watterman, the head of the National Academy of Sciences, on the successful achievement of orbit by Explorer I, and neither directly nor indirectly sent any such message to either Dr. von Braun or myself. If there was a man in the United States who had little to do with Explorer I, it was Dr. Allan Watterman, and this is said with no intent to disparage that very fine scientist.

The final public relations plan was a document complex enough to have rivaled the final and complete war plan for the invasion of the European continent in 1944. It stipulated the kinds of camera coverage, how picture and movie film would be transported and to whom, where secrecy screening would take place, and who would finally authorize release of this material. The package of factual information, including payload data and the nature of the intended orbit, was screened so many times that it was dog-eared. Again, almost every reference to Army-developed hardware was stricken from these documents and they became pure recitals of scientific and technical data. Since JPL was an independent organization operated by the California Institute of Technology, much greater latitude was allowed in releasing information on the payload, tracking, and upper stages, and Dr. Pickering and his fine people received much more credit than was given to our group of dedicated civil service employees. It seemed that the military was to be suppressed as completely as possible, in a rather dishonest attempt to make our first space triumph look like a civilian effort.

We were told that the people at the Cape in charge of the firing would appear before the press immediately after the event. We were positively directed, however, to discuss nothing in such an interview except the propulsion vehicle itself. Since much of that was classified military hardware, our area of discussion was greatly restricted. All information with respect to orbit and information derived from the payload was to be released by the scientific IGY group in Washington, and only by them.

In the hope that some credit would fall where it was due, we divided our forces and—much to Wernher's disgust—decided that he and Dr. Pickering should be at the Washington end, prepared to participate in the IGY press conference if and when orbit was achieved. I would be at the Cape, with Kurt Debus in charge of the firing operation, and Jack Froehlich, JPL's project engineer in charge of the upper stage and payload checkout, and co-ordination of initial data on the orbit. We would also be the ones subjected to the press conference at the Cape.

Against this developing background of debate I was scheduled to appear before the Lyndon Johnson subcommittee in Washington on the 7th of January. I was making every possible effort to keep the intended firing date concealed, but leaks were appearing from all sorts of places. Necessarily, many people in Washington were informed that we intended to fire on the 29th. Nonetheless, every time there was evidence of a leak I was asked to see if our people had been talking. The truth was, our people were just as interested as I in keeping the date covered until the last minute, and these leaks certainly did not come from them.

The Johnson committee hearings exploded a whole new series

of activities into our lap. In the middle of the hearings, public announcement was made that the Joint Chiefs of Staff and the Secretary of Defense had just approved for the Army a project to build a medium-range ballistic missile to be smaller than Jupiter, highly mobile, and to have a greatly reduced reaction time through the use of solid propellants. This was to be the Pershing. In view of the fact that the announcement stated no range limitation, there was an immediate storm from the press as to whether this constituted a complete setting aside of the Wilson directive which had limited the Army to a 200-mile range.

The fact was that it did represent such a break. No range limitation was specified, and the very cute approach was taken of laying down a maximum gross weight for the missile instead of saying anything about the range capability. To anyone familiar with the business, the gross weight specified was ample to permit exceeding the 200-mile range by a substantial amount. It presented us with a very challenging situation, since we now had to attempt to get every mile of range we could out of a given total weight of missile. This was an entirely new approach to missile design and put a great premium on technical efficiency.

Right after the Johnson hearings, I was subjected to an immediate interview by the press and TV, and had to resort to some fancy footwork to cover the situation, both with respect to the intended firing date of our satellite effort and what we were going to do about the new missile. I flew back to ABMA on Tuesday, the 7th of January, carrying a hatful of new problems. How fast could we react to the challenge of the new project? What could we achieve within the limitations imposed without stretching the state of the art to a point where success would not be fully assured? Just how would we plan all this within the manpower limitations of the gross total of 5,000 people that had been imposed on ABMA, and still leave ourselves with resources and people to do what we believed to be invaluable follow-on work in the space area, while at the same time crashing the Jupiter into production and carrying the initial burden of that production right in our own shops? I knew that if I underestimated the future in the space area and kept too much of this production burden in the house, we would either break down under the load or find that we had to turn down challenging future work. On the other hand, if I overestimated the future space work and got rid of in-house projects, our people might not have enough work to keep them busy.

All these things were going around in my head as I flew my plane the three hours required to get back to home plate. I could only decide that the Lord would have to guide me, since there was no measure of the future except intuition and a combination of experience and judgment. I knew without being told that it would be impossible to get any sound direction from the Department of Defense with any planning figures on which we could rely with certainty.

By the time I got back to Redstone, I had more or less made up my mind as to how we would approach the problem. Calling a conference of our top technical people the next day, I laid down the guide lines for a vigorous attack on the technical and engineering factors involved in meeting this challenge. One thing was obvious—we had to get maximum co-operation from Chrysler in getting Jupiter out of the house as fast as possible.

A considerable amount of my time during the balance of January was occupied in laying out preliminary plans for the assault on the Pershing Project. Meantime, the auditors were still in my hair in connection with the costs of the transfer of the Jupiter to Detroit. The Air Force Operational Planning Conference on Jupiter the 9th and 10th of January went off very well. The basis of co-operation with SAC that we laid down at that time made it possible for our people and the Air Force to live together in peace and harmony throughout the rest of the Jupiter operation.

As the days flew by, I attempted to keep the main line of my thinking and attention clear, and focused on our upcoming satellite shot.

Vanguard was scheduled for a full-scale attempt 11 days ahead of our proposed firing date on the 29th. I was worried about this situation because, based on the record of the Vanguard program, the odds were very great that they would not get off on time. If their schedule slipped back too far, our firing date would be in peril.

Even if they were successful, the tracking net, and particularly the computation center of the Smithsonian Institution in Washington, would require several days to track the Vanguard carefully and pin down its orbit. During that time it would be unreasonable, if not impossible, to ask them to take on the heavy chore of following the initial flight of our satellite. Confusion could result which would be disastrous to both programs.

It became a question of arriving at some agreement as to how far back Vanguard could slip their date before they would have to scrub altogether and give way to our firing. Our record for promptness in maintaining our schedules had been outstanding, and as a result we felt that we should have a right to maintain our established date of the 29th, with at least three days' latitude behind it for postponement if this became necessary.

The first approach from the IGY committee was to the effect that we would have to allow five days from a Vanguard firing before we could go. This meant that if complete priority was given to Vanguard, and they postponed beyond the 24th, we were in trouble. I felt that the morale and confidence of my organization were so tied to the whole idea of having a definite schedule and maintaining it that we should be allowed to keep our date. Our people did not take kindly to the idea that they might have to sit around and twiddle their thumbs until Vanguard got off.

I finally got Don Yates' support to the idea that our date should be protected by requiring that Vanguard scrub until after our firing if they did not get off by the 24th. Armed with that support, I argued the question through the Pentagon and finally got the firm decision that I wanted. Our range time was now protected and we were safe.

As it turned out, Vanguard had lots of trouble and did not come down to a firing until the 5th of February. If we had been in the position of having to take second priority and wait for Vanguard, our whole plan would have been upset.

In the midst of all this, I spent what seemed to be most of January going to Washington at the behest of Congressional Committees. I stood by on the 5th, 6th, and 7th of January, waiting to be called by the Senate Preparedness Committee, only to go back to headquarters and take care of a little urgent business and be called again to Washington to testify on the 10th.

One of the problems of a commander in the field who has to testify before Congress is the fact that there seems to be no way of pinning down the schedules of these committees ahead of time. They start out with a general plan, but the committee extends the time with any one witness as much as any of the Congressmen feel is necessary, and the schedule for the rest continues to slip. These committees are also affected by what is happening on the floor of Congress, and frequently hearings are recessed in order to permit the individual Congressman to answer quorum calls on the floor. As a result, I have cooled my heels in committee anterooms many, many hours and even days throughout the last seven years. Most top officers of the Armed Services, and even the Secretaries, have done likewise. I do not know the answer, but it certainly does cause a great waste of the time of our senior commanders and their civilian chiefs.

After testifying before the Senate Committee on the 10th, I was put on stand-by for the House Armed Services Committee on the 24th and 25th of January, only to have that committee recess without my appearing at all. Finally, I put everything else out of my head and took off for Patrick Air Base on the 27th.

The elongated Redstone that was to launch Explorer I had been on the pad for some time. Since the upper stages were solid propellant, and therefore more hazardous to handle, they had been separately checked out and the balance corrected. We had to be absolutely sure that when the tub with all these rockets inside started to spin on top of the missile, it would do so smoothly and without destructive vibration.

The problem was much like the balancing of a tire on an automobile. In normal manufacture, it is almost impossible to get the weight distributed on an exactly uniform basis all the way around the tire, and if there is any spot heavier than the corresponding point on the other side, vibration and possibly "shimmy" result when the tire spins on the road at high speed. So we have to have our tires "balanced," with little bits of metal attached where necessary to make the wheel and tire spin evenly.

We had to do just about the same thing with the upper stages of these early space vehicles.

We could not spare the weight that would be required if we put extra mechanism in the upper stages to keep those stages perfectly aligned with the proper path as they were being fired and brought up to tremendous velocity. This was one of the penalties we were paying for not having a big enough booster. To have anything at all for payload, we could not put any guidance above the Redstone's first stage. Our upper stages were two rings of rockets, with seven in the outer ring, three in the next ring inside, and finally, a single rocket as the last stage attached to the payload. No matter how precise and careful the preparation and loading of these rockets, they would not all turn out exactly the same amount of push at exactly the same instant. If the whole assembly was not spinning, any little irregularity of that kind would push it off course, and just a couple of degrees of change in the direction of thrust would be more than enough to wreck the possibility of getting into orbit. So we had to make this whole tub containing these rockets spin. By having it spinning in flight, the irregularities would be canceled out, and even fairly large differences in the thrust of the individual rockets would not have any substantial effect on the course of the whole assembly.

Balancing a tire, however, is vastly different from balancing a spinning tub full of eleven rockets, all of which are hazardous, and all of which must be tied together with wiring connecting the ignition devices with the timing mechanism that would fire them at the right moment. We had hastily put together, in an isolated spot on Cape Canaveral, a device to permit spinning this assembly and balancing it correctly without exposing the people to the danger of an explosion. It was a difficult problem, requiring ways of watching the spinning tub from a distance, measuring its vibration and unevenness, and then applying the necessary weight correction.

The problem was even more complex than that. From our early experiences with the nose cone re-entry test program, we had learned that the speed of the spin had to be varied with the speed of the vehicle and the consequent pressure. We could not simply decide at what speed to rotate the assembly in flight. It had to be turned faster at take-off than it would be later. We found that if this speed program was not perfectly worked out, there would be a dangerous vibration that could tear the whole vehicle apart.

Before my arrival at Patrick, the preliminary checkout of the upper stages had been completed and they were now assembled on top of the long Redstone. To assure the safety of the people working around the missile, the ignition devices had not yet been installed. This would be done at the last minute by one lone man, just before everyone left the pad.

The whole towering and complex vehicle was lovingly enfolded in the arms of our gantry tower. At the last minute those arms would be opened, and the enclosing structure would be moved back several hundred feet to leave the missile standing alone.

Arriving at Patrick on the afternoon of the 27th, I had a talk with Don Yates about plans for handling the press. I fully agreed with his intention of notifying them a day in advance and giving them a full off-the-record briefing as to the time of the firing and our intentions. They, in turn, had agreed to release no information on the date or time until the missile actually took off.

On the 28th, I made the first advance check on probable weather conditions, and ran into very disquieting information. The jet stream, the very high-velocity river of air that is always over some parts of the United States at altitudes varying from 25,000 to 45,000 feet, had unexpectedly moved southward, and the southern edge was over Patrick. The stream was moving at an extraordinarily high velocity, in the neighborhood of 165 to 175 knots.

The speed of the jet stream as such did not bother us, since any missile moving in a solid stream of air is not upset by how fast that whole stream is flowing. What did bother us were the sharp lower and upper edges of this stream. Penetrating it suddenly with a relatively fragile missile would be like putting a long slender pole in the quiet waters on the edge of a river and then thrusting the end of the pole abruptly out into fast-moving and turbulent rapids. The difference in pressures could well break the pole.

This particular vehicle was longer and more slender than any tactical missile. We had lengthened the Redstone itself as much as possible to get more fuel aboard, and then on top of that were these spinning rockets and the slender payload. As a result, the whole vehicle did not have the strength to withstand the shearing forces that it would encounter in suddenly moving from the fairly slow air streams of the lower air into the sharp edge of this specially high-speed jet current.

The weather experts at Patrick had sent up instrumented balloons to measure the velocity of the air stream at all altitudes to 50,000 feet. We took their results and drew a diagram showing how the edges of these fast winds would look to the missile, and what the differences in forces would be. By teletype we sent this plot up to our computing laboratory at ABMA, and asked our structural analysis engineers to calculate the maximum shear forces they thought the missile could safely accept. The first results on the 28th showed conclusively that unless the speed of the jet stream dropped down or it moved off from overhead, we were facing a great probability of losing our missile when it hit those high velocity winds. What to do?

Predictions of even the best weathermen with respect to the behavior of the jet stream are at best only educated guesses. Until a good weather satellite can measure great areas of weather conditions from above, they will be no better than that. And yet, that jet stream has a very potent effect on all weather on the earth's surface.

Don Yates himself is a pretty fancy weatherman. In fact, he was the weather specialist who predicted the conditions for General Eisenhower at the time of the invasion of the European continent. In the present case, he was so interested in our problem that he gladly joined with us and with his own weather experts in trying to interpret the situation and make a reasonable forecast of what might happen.

We could find little encouragement in the results. The jet stream would only have to move 40 to 50 miles further north to let us be free. The velocity, if it stayed overhead, would probably have to go down to 125 knots or less if we were to be safe, unless the blanket of air from 5,000 to 30,000 feet speeded up so that there would be less difference. The latter was not likely.

It came down to a question of what that confounded jet stream was going to do. Kurt Debus and I lived with that problem day and night for three days.

Our decisions had to be made early, for if the missile was fueled with the very special fuel we were using, and with its liquid oxygen, and then left standing on the pad for several days, it was very likely that leaks would develop in the system through the effect of the fuel on the seals and valves and washers, or even that the protracted cooling effect of the liquid oxygen could upset our delicate instrumentation.

The checkout schedule for this complex missile had been carefully worked out. We knew it was good because we had used it on Missile No. 27 and on the two previous nose cone re-entry experiments. Because of the time required in checking out all of the complex instrumentation, it was necessary to fuel the missile at least seven hours before firing time. This meant that each day we had to make a decision by 10 or 11 o'clock in the morning as to whether we were going to try to fire that evening.

On the morning of the 29th, our scheduled firing date, the weather people sent up another series of balloons. They had to use two. One balloon rose slowly and the wind took it out of accurate measurement range before it reached the altitude of the jet stream. So another fast-rising balloon had to be sent up to measure the higher altitudes. The measurements would not be as accurate as those from the slow one, but would give a sufficiently good picture of the velocities on the edges of and inside the jet stream.

When the results were on hand and plotted, we huddled over that picture of the wind profile and sadly shook our heads. Just to be sure, we sent the figures up to ABMA for a quick trial on the computer, but even without that, it was obvious to us that any attempt to launch would be extremely hazardous.

I am sure that a lot of people, particularly the press, were extremely puzzled when we said we would have to postpone on account of weather. The weather on the ground was beautiful, with a soft breeze blowing and hardly a cloud in the sky. We tried to explain the situation to them, but I had the feeling that it didn't quite get across and that some of them thought we had a problem that we didn't want to admit.

We queried the weather people almost to death. All day long we were asking for new forecasts of changes or any indication that things would get better. There was none. They told us we would have to wait patiently and hope, and take another reading the next morning. We spent our time nervously going back over every step of preparation, reviewing our tests, and checking and rechecking to assure ourselves that nothing had been overlooked. The mental strain was terrific, but at the time it was not apparent to us because we were so absorbed in what we were doing.

The morning of the 30th was a repetition of the 29th. There

had been a little reduction in the speed of the jet stream, but the edges were, if anything, sharper than ever. Now time was running out. The weekend was approaching, and it would be both difficult and expensive to maintain the entire range crew and downrange instrumentation people on stand-by over that period. The ABMA birthday party was scheduled for Saturday, and I had a whole host of VIPs coming to Huntsville for the celebration—if any. This was Thursday!

To make matters worse, Vanguard was now on top of us, and had tentatively scheduled firing on the 3rd. This meant that our positions were reversed, and if we did not get out of the way in a reasonable time from our original planned firing hour, we would be pushing them back. In the meantime, we had gotten word from the IGY people that they could not handle two satellites unless they were launched at least three days apart. This, plus the fact that the 31st was a Friday, meant that we had an absolute deadline of the evening of January 31st.

Meantime, the strain in Washington was as great if not greater. Arrangements had been made for open teletype circuits between our station at the Cape, ABMA, the Jet Propulsion Laboratory on the West Coast, and from ABMA to the big conference room in the Pentagon where the teletype messages would come up on a big illuminated screen. Von Braun and Pickering were standing by in Washington, helpless to do anything and in worse shape than we were, because not being on the ground, they couldn't even be sure we were doing all we possibly could. The Secretary and key members of the Army Staff were on stand-by to go to the Pentagon and be in the conference room whenever we decided to fire. Kurt Debus, Jack Froehlich and myself were being constantly asked over the wires, "What's happened? What are you going to do?" Obviously, we didn't know ourselves. We could do nothing but wait.

I checked and rechecked the communications that had been set up, and our detailed plan of action. In a quonset hut behind the big assembly building of ABMA at Cape Canaveral, JPL had established a communications center, with teletype connections to ABMA's computation lab, the comp lab at JPL, and to the tracking station at Antigua in the West Indies. There were also telephone connections to the conference room in Washington and to JPL and ABMA, and those lines would all be standing open during the firing. A crew was standing by for fast computation of initial data and to feed the results from the local tracking station and the one at Antigua to the computation center. There was one office at the end of the quonset hut reserved for a few of us to use during the critical period after launch and until we had at least initial results. This could not be less than 45 minutes and might well run to an hour or more. I knew it was going to be the longest hour of my life!

A late weather reading on the 30th began to give us some hope. The jet stream had begun to shift perceptibly to the north and the velocity was dropping a little. After lengthy consultation with the weather people, we reached the conclusion that there was some possibility that we might be able to get off Thursday evening. We decided to start the clock, and at noon on the 30th work began, heading for a scheduled firing time of 10:30 that night.

The critical point in the countdown would come when it was time to put liquid oxygen aboard. If we scrubbed after that, we would have to defuel and dry out the missile. For this shot, we were using a special fuel which gives a higher thrust, but it is not a very practical fuel to handle and for that reason has never been accepted for field use. If that particular fuel was kept in contact with the various seals and washers in the fuel system for a long period of time, those seals would go bad, and this would mean a major job of disassembly and replacement.

Kurt Debus and I decided that we would fuel and carry the countdown to the time of putting in liquid oxygen and then make a final decision. At the same time we decided that if we could not go by the next night at the latest, we would have to defuel the missile and replace seals.

Early in the evening the weather people flew some more balloons for us, and we waited impatiently for the results. About 7:30 we had them in our hands and had plotted the wind. It looked better than it had in the morning, but it was too close for us to make the decision ourselves. We had to wait while the Computation Laboratory at ABMA ran the final analysis. At 8:20 we put the missile on "hold." We were all ready to put in the liquid oxygen, but did not want to start without being sure we could go on and shoot.

At 9:20 the word came back from ABMA: *Highly marginal— we do not recommend that you try it.* We looked at one another wearily. Then we canceled the firing. This left us one more chance to meet our promise to put up a satellite in January. If we could fire the next evening, all our tightly knit plans would still fit together. If not, we were in a mess.

A number of us got together that evening for the mutual support that comes from a few friendly drinks in a group where everyone is being gnawed by the same worries. Sleep came hard, but knowing that if we did fire there would be little the next night, sleep we did.

CHAPTER XVII

"Goldstone Has the Bird!"

Next morning, right after the 7 o'clock weather run, word was flashed to us: *Things look good. The jet stream has moved off to the north and by evening should be down to not more than 100 knots.* That still sounded like a lot of wind, but it meant the difference between a strain that we knew the missile could stand and one that was dangerous.

The men were tired. They had been working long and irregular hours, snatching sleep when they could. Everyone was going on sheer nerve. The day before we had taken the countdown to minus 125 minutes, but now we had to go back and run the checks over again. We were aiming once more for a 10:30 firing time. It was essential to make these shots at night, because we had some special pyrotechnic flares in the satellite itself that would help us tremendously in tracking the early stages of the flight before the path could be pinned down by radio signals alone.

At 1:30 in the afternoon we picked up the count at X minus 480 minutes (8 hours) on the chart. This would still leave us with an hour's margin for unexpected delays. I kept in touch with the blockhouse by phone until late in the afternoon. The early work would be routine, and the critical point would not come until 6:30 or after. I made final arrangements for our schedule after the shoot, and arranged for a last weather check about 5 o'clock in the afternoon. In between I got a few catnaps, because I knew that if the shot went as expected I would be up most of the night and would still have to fly to Huntsville early the next morning.

The late afternoon balloon flights confirmed the earlier forecast. The wind was down to tolerable limits, and the weather looked good. Only some unexpected problem with the missile or the payload would stop us now.

By the time I got to the pad at about 6:30, we had lost some time and then gained it back. We had had to hold for half an hour because the work had not gone as fast as we calculated, probably because the men were tired, and under no circumstances did we want to rush them. Just before I got there, however, we had picked up 30 minutes and were now almost on time at X minus 190 minutes at 7:25. This meant that if we could not pick up any more, we would be just 5 minutes late.

At 7:30 we checked all of our communications circuits. By 8:00 we had our phone lines open and operators on all the teletypes. We alerted Washington that we were approximately on time, and got back word that the people were on their way to the conference room.

Our blockhouse at the Cape is different from most in that the people inside can look out through heavy safety glass and actually see the launch pad and what is going on. Most missile blockhouses are built so that they are completely closed up on the side facing the missile, and the only view that the operators inside have is by television. Having watched many firings, I am convinced that better work is done and there is a much greater sense of teamwork when the crew boss can actually see the missile and what is happening around it.

All the key people on our firing crew were linked together on a single intercommunication net. All wore head phones and had microphones around their necks so that, while using their hands freely for their work, they could still talk to one another. I had my own station inside the blockhouse and was able to listen to all of the conversation and reporting going back and forth. The whole communications system is broken up into segments, and while the key people in each area can talk together, each one is also on a separate net with his own working crew.

Every single move in the final countdown of a big vehicle is important. Much of the uniform success of the ABMA firing crew can be attributed to the stability of the people involved. Since there was very little turnover, they became so accustomed to working with one another and so conscious of the importance of each little task, that carelessness just did not happen.

Even for the firing of the ordinary big long-range missiles, tension in the blockhouse is very high. There is nothing that I have ever encountered to equal the feeling of suspended animation that comes during those last minutes. One's mental processes are so speeded up by the adrenalin being pumped into the bloodstream that the clock seems almost to stand still. There is no sense of haste because of this peculiar phenomenon. In fact, one almost feels that every move is made in slow motion.

On this critical night, the feeling was far more intense than for any of our previous shots. Every man on the crew was conscious that the hopes of a Nation were riding with us. Our satellite was small, but it was efficient. Its success would prove that the United States did have the capability to go into space, even though we were lacking the brute force necessary to match the Russian achievements.

We even felt that Vanguard would have a better chance if we were successful, because the pressure of having to get something up to make good on the President's promises would not be on their backs, and they would be thus less apt to make mistakes.

Coffee was consumed by the bucket. As long as men were

working on the pad, we could circulate freely in and out of the blockhouse. I made repeated trips out to the firing platform and twice took the work elevators and visited each level where men were working.

We had a snack bar on a truck outside the blockhouse. I don't know why it is that tension makes me hungry, but it does, and when I checked the time and realized the truck would have to pull out very soon, I dashed out and got under the wire for a final ham-and-egg sandwich.

All responsible supervisory personnel were like restless ghosts. None of us could be still. We would go from station to station inside the blockhouse and then out to the firing pad and then back in to listen on the intercom for a little while.

Dr. Jack Froehlich of JPL was in charge of the crew that had full responsibility for the payload and tracking. We got a brief scare when for a short period the broadcast from the payload, which had been turned on and was running steadily, could not be picked up at our primary station. Jack asked one of the other stations on the Cape, and they said it was coming in loud and clear, so we relaxed, knowing that the problem was with the receiving set. If the payload itself had gone off the air, we would have had to go back into the missile—with the probability of another postponement.

When checks were made with the range control, where the safety officer for General Yates had his station, we found that one of the radars was not operating. Capt. Ray Clark, who had the hot line between the blockhouse and range safety, was arguing with the range as to whether we could go ahead with only one radar. He finally won the argument. It later became academic, because the other radar came back in.

Between 8:45 and 9:30 the destruct package was armed, and the upper platforms of the tower were opened up away from the missile. This destruct package is the device by which the range safety officer can destroy the missile in flight if it wanders off course in a direction that might be hazardous to people or property. Actually it can be operated from either the blockhouse or the range safety officer's station. A coded radio signal does the job.

We have often been asked whether these missiles could be blown up by deliberate sabotage, broadcasting a signal on the right frequency, or by a stray radio signal coming in from elsewhere. The latter, incidentally, is a frequent problem, and more than once we have had to stop sensitive work on the Cape to locate a stray signal. Based on freak atmospheric conditions, we have even had interference from taxicabs in Rio de Janeiro. The fact is, however, that none of these could possibly trigger the destruct package, because it responds only to a carefully devised combination of signals of specific pattern, and this pattern is frequently changed. No ordinary radio signal on any frequency, no matter how strong, could thus blow up the missile.

Now the pad was cleared, and the whole great structure that had had its arms around the Jupiter C was moved back on its tracks out of harm's way. Floodlights were turned on and the missile stood like a great finger pointing to Heaven—stark, white, and alone on its launching pad. The crew that had been working outside came into the back of the blockhouse. All the vehicles, including the chuck wagon, were sent beyond a roadblock about three quarters of a mile away. Everything from here on would be handled by remote control.

Bob Mosher has been ABMA's Chief of the blockhouse crew since my first connection with the organization. He is the only person who cannot move around, but must keep his station in the middle of the blockhouse, with the countdown check sheet in his hand, the clock right in front of his eyes, and final responsibility for being sure that each piece of required work has been accomplished and its accomplishment reported.

Bob is a tall, self-possessed young man who came into the business by way of a two-year induction in the Army. He is an engineering graduate and was screened out for participation in the Army's special program for scientific and professional soldiers. These specially selected individuals are given 8 weeks of basic military training and are then sent to some station where they can actually use their professional education while fulfilling their obligation to the country for military service. At various times we have had as many as 400 of them at Redstone Arsenal. These youngsters have been a very fine source of recruitment for our engineering staffs, and over a period of years about 20 per cent of them have taken Civil Service posts with us when they completed their military service. Bob was one of these, and when he took off his uniform, he kept right on as a civilian engineer with Dr. Debus' Firing Laboratory. He is a tower of strength at shoot time and has the ideal temperament for the job. His calm and unhurried attitude and tone of voice, even during the final hectic minutes, gives assurance that nothing will be overlooked.

At 9:45, with the count exactly on time, we got another scare. Hydrogen peroxide was apparently leaking out of the tail. A "hold" was called and men went out to check it. This could mean anything from a very small problem to one that would cause us great trouble and require bringing the structure back and going into the missile. Kurt and I stood and smoked furiously until the word finally came in that there had been peroxide in the flexible fuel line that had not all drained out. When the line was drained there was no further leak, and the count was picked up at 10 o'clock, now running 15 minutes late.

At X minus 12, the motors were started to spin the top stages. Slowly they picked up speed, and the automatic counter gradually moved toward the red mark that indicated the required speed for lift-off. As that speed was reached, the power sources on the missile were all checked and found to be in good shape, and power was transferred from the ground power supplies to onboard sources. The missile was now ready to operate on its own, independent of any connection with the ground. As it lifted off the pad, it would separate the last cable connections that permitted the crew to stop the whole process, or check the operation of any component.

By now the build-up of tension was terrific. There is no actual time kept during this last interval, but instead each of the many final steps is accomplished and the responsible individual reports to Mosher, who checks it off on his sheet. Only when these tasks are accomplished can the firing command be given. This method is responsible for small variations in actual firing time, even though the countdown clock may be beyond zero-time. In order to be able to count time after lift-off, the clock is held momentarily so that it will register zero on firing command. Another clock over the board in the back room, where the missile's path can be followed by the signals it sends back, is started automatically when the missile lifts, and counts the exact seconds of flight.

Over in the ABMA hangar, Dr. Stuhlinger, top research scientist, with Mr. Mrazek, Chief of the Structures Laboratory, and a couple of others, were charged with calculating the exact time to fire the second stage. In later operations we were to go over to an automatic system, but for this one the time had been too short to turn up any method that could be considered dependable, so this crew of fine scientists and engineers had developed a high-speed method for figuring against the velocity reported by the Doppler track exactly when the missile would have reached its absolute apex.

The so-called "Doppler effect" that permits keeping exact track of the velocity of a missile is the same that makes the tone of a train whistle seem to rise as it approaches, and fall again as it goes away. The proper type of radio signal will behave the same way, and by reading the apparent frequency of the received signal, the change in velocity can be determined. When the velocity jumps, as when another stage is fired, there is a corresponding "Doppler shift" that tells the story.

The Redstone booster was to push the missile as high as possible. The booster would drop off as soon as its energy was expended, and the upper stages attached to the conical compartment containing the guidance and control equipment would coast on upward. During that time, special jets in the sides of the guidance compartment would gradually turn the missile into a horizontal position.

This turning of the missile would not slow it down, since it would not begin to turn until it was well up above the atmosphere, where the near-vacuum of outer space presents no resistance. If the missile could get high enough to give us a little margin for error in the direction in which the thrust of the upper stages would be applied, so that it would neither go so far out and away from the earth that it would fall back into the atmosphere when it returned, nor be pointed down so much that the missile would be caught by the atmosphere before it cleared the other side of the earth, then the full power of the upper stages could be applied to give it the velocity that would put it solidly into orbit.

I had watched Stuhlinger and his people go through the drill required to figure the apex many times during the past few days, until the calculations had become almost automatic. Stuhlinger had developed a special slide rule which could be used for the final computation. It was his job to decide when to push the button that would fire the second stage.

The following ignition of the 3rd and 4th stages was controlled by a simple timer, which would allow the full thrust of each to be applied before the next stage fired.

In those last few seconds of countdown, it seemed to me that even the stars in the black Florida sky were waiting and listening. The last "Rogers," acknowledging the responsibility for work done, snapped over the intercom. A breathless half-second of silence. Then, from Bob Mosher, "Firing Command!"

From that point on, all anyone on the ground could do was to cut the missile down or shut it off immediately if it did not appear to be behaving properly. There are two possible firing methods: you can hold the missile down, or let it stand free. At ABMA, we favored the latter method, letting our missiles stand free on the launch pad so that when the necessary power builds up they can rise without interference. Which system is better can hardly be proven technically. Holding the missile down adds some assurance, in a way, since it is possible to measure the thrust and be sure that full power has been built up before the missile is released. On the other hand, this adds considerable complication to the firing platform. A device must be built which will let go quickly, smoothly, and evenly all around, because the slightest unevenness in release can throw the missile off balance. Any device that is added to a missile firing can be a source of failure, so it is a question whether the added assurance is worth the price that is paid in terms of complexity.

In any case, other factors dictated our choice with respect to both Redstone and Jupiter. Both missiles were developed for use in the field, with the capability of being moved from one place to another. The firing platform, therefore, had to be as light and as simple as possible. It would be highly impractical to provide a means of holding the missile down unless the platform itself were thoroughly anchored, and for a mobile missile this would not be feasible. Since we did all our static testing, which of course requires holding the missile down, back at ABMA, we had no reason for creating an especially big and anchored platform at the Cape. Thus in all our programs we used the same type of launch platform that would be used in the field by troops firing the missile in anger.

"Firing Command" does not actually fire the engine on the missile. Turning the key in response to firing command merely sets in motion an automatically controlled sequence of events that will result, some 20 seconds later, in lift-off. Pressure on the fuel and oxygen is controlled by the overflow valves, and vents will automatically close. The igniter that is inside the chamber of the motor is fired, and the bootstrap operation that will bring the turbine up to speed and inject the fuel at full rate is initiated. Each condition required for proper performance is automatically checked, and if within the allowed fractions of a second the proper condition is not met, the whole process automatically shuts itself off.

Finally, if the igniter generates enough heat fast enough to burn through a very carefully calculated fusing wire within a specific fraction of time, the great valves controlling the main flow of fuel and oxygen are opened, and with a tremendous roar the main stage of the motor comes to life. As these automatic events are happening, they put their signature on the control board inside the blockhouse, and these few seconds are filled with voices as each event is loudly reported by the responsible individual. The final thrilling sound is "Main Stage!"

Kurt Debus, myself, and several others spend these last seconds at the safety windows watching the missile. Dozens of high-speed cameras are recording every action, and a big master tape is making a record of every voice. Each instrument makes a permanent record of its own readings so that if something goes wrong, the records can be checked back and carefully matched to find the cause. Although an instrument also records "main stage," it is never needed, for every man watching the missile will shout in unison as the great engine bursts in full flame and the missile starts almost immediately to move majestically upward.

In the very last seconds before ignition, some instrument (and neither Kurt Debus' memory nor my own can recall which one) suddenly dropped off to zero and was reported by its watcher. It was a heart-stopping moment. Was it serious enough to hit the cutoff button, knowing that if we did so we would have to recycle back to at least X minus 60 and begin over again? Was it merely a malfunction of the instrument itself with no effect on the performance of the missile? All I can remember now is that a lightning sequence of thought flashed through my head—and I know Kurt Debus had the same reaction. For an instant we looked at each other with raised eyebrows. Then both our thumbs went up, and almost in a single voice we said, "Forget it! Go ahead!"

The air in the blockhouse seemed literally charged with electricity. As the missile started its slow, majestic rise you could hear almost every voice in a chorus that sounded like a prayer, saying, "Go, baby, go!" It did! Up and up. Faster and faster.

As the missile reached the point where the top of the windows kept us from following it farther, we rushed to the panel in the back room where we could pick up the signals already coming in. Until the missile was well clear, the blockhouse would be kept locked, and we could not go outside to watch it. Those who were out at the roadblock, and the press and visitors on top of a radar platform a mile away, got a much better view than did we. They were able to follow the flame track as the missile gained speed and started to tilt in the proper direction out over the Atlantic. We had to follow the same drama through the medium of impersonal and unexcitable instruments.

The group of instruments that records the early path of a missile means little or nothing in terms of the actual success of the mission. I believe it does, however, prevent some heart attacks, because if that firing crew had to sit blindly and wait until they could get out, or have someone telephone them as to whether the missile was behaving properly, I don't think they could stand it. The firing itself is the climax of thousands of hours of dedicated work, and when the missile starts to rise every member of the team literally has his heart on board.

Special instruments have been set up in advance to show what the normal performance is expected to be. There is a curve on one chart that reports the proper build-up of velocity, and a needle follows that curve if velocity is being acquired at the rate it should be. Another inked curve shows the horizontal path of the missile as it should develop, and again a needle indicates whether or not it is following that path.

Three small needles are set to show the attitude of the missile as it pitches over on the proper program, and continuing proper performance from the reference platform on board. So long as those needles stay on the zero mark, everything is going as it should. Down in the right-hand corner is a high-speed printer, tapping out in figures the velocity being reported by the Doppler system, but we are much more concerned with the velocity curve, since those figures cannot be immediately translated as good or bad.

In some of our earlier work we had gotten some nasty shocks when halfway up the curve the needle would suddenly start to shake and drop off towards zero. When this happens it is supposed to indicate that the engine has shut down, or for some reason thrust is no longer being applied. We learned, however, that as the missile tilted over there was a particular point where the ballooning flame from the engine set up interference with the transmission of the Doppler signals to our particular receiver. They would still be coming in loud and clear at stations that were set to one side or the other of the path. The blockhouse receiver, however, was right in line with the flame, and for a few seconds we would get no response. The first time that happened, we thought we had lost a missile. Now we had learned to wait until the transmission would pick up again. But even knowing this to be the case, there still was and always would be a shock, a deadening of the nerves, and the question in one's mind when that needle knocked off.

A few feet to one side Gordon Harris, on the telephone to the teletype room, was saying over and over, "It looks good. It looks good. Still looks good. Still going good!" As far as I was concerned, he could keep on saying just that.

The 400-odd seconds that were to pass before Dr. Stuhlinger would press the button for the upper stages seemed like forever. The velocity curve stayed up where it belonged, and the missile was right on track. The engine cut off when it had been expected to, and the instrument indicated that separation had occurred and the guidance system was beginning to tilt the upper stages over to the horizontal position. Every new indication on the instruments was announced by everyone who could see them. We were really talking out loud as we waited for the flashing light that would indicate that Stuhlinger had hit the button.

Finally the clock showed that apex should have been reached. Still no signal. We learned later that the velocity was just a fraction low, and so it took a little bit longer for the missile to get to the top of its arc. As we were about to question Stuhlinger frantically on the phone, suddenly the red light flashed SECOND STAGE IGNITION!

From there on we were wholly dependent on careful analysis of reports and graphs of reported velocities to determine whether all four stages had fired. In accordance with previous plan, the minute the blockhouse door was opened, the roadblock was released and priority was given to two cars to take a few of us over to the Communications Center at JPL's quonset hut.

I admit that we could gain nothing by being in a hurry. The missile was out of our control, and we would not have final results for some time. Nonetheless, the tension of the moment was such that we could not be satisfied with anything less than high speed. The cars had right-of-way, and we covered the several miles in nothing flat!

By the time we arrived, there were enough indications from the Doppler results to give us fair confidence that all upper stages had ignited on time. But we still could not know whether they had performed in full, and whether the velocity was what it needed to be. It takes very little difference in performance to represent the margin between successful orbit or a missile falling back to earth. We could only wait. We did tell Washington that, so far as we could possibly tell, everything had performed as it should. Antigua had picked up the signal exactly when it should have, and both the Cape Station and Antigua were solidly locked onto the signals coming from the satellite.

Meantime the press had flashed the news of the launching of the satellite vehicle. We were specifically forbidden to make any statement or give any indication to the press as to success or failure, since that announcement was being reserved for the President. To avoid any possibility of mistake, the satellite would not be accepted as successful until it came around on the other side and was picked up by the western tracking stations. We would be permitted to give out the information that all four stages had been fired, provided analysis of our figures assured us this was true.

The waiting seemed interminable. Signals from Antigua were passed to ABMA and JPL, and the computers went to work. Meantime, we settled down with big cups of coffee to sweat it out. Jack Froehlich had gotten someone to make up some big china mugs with an outline of the Jupiter missile on the side, and there was one for each of us. I kept mine at the Cape until the middle of 1959, and finally took it home to be sure nothing would happen to it. I still have that mug—one of my most prized trophies.

We had indicated to Washington that we hoped to have some answer in about half an hour or a little more. The half hour passed, and we went after the group in the computing room to see if they would give us any information. They, too, were playing it very cagey, and refused to be committed. We could only go back and wait. Meantime, we did find that every tracking station in reach had been solidly on the bird.

After about 40 minutes I got a plaintive message over the teletype from Washington. Secretary Brucker wired down: I'M OUT OF COFFEE AND WE ARE RUNNING OUT OF CIGARETTES. WHAT DO I DO NOW? The only answer I could send back was SEND OUT FOR MORE AND SWEAT IT OUT WITH THE REST OF US. I have never seen the clock move so slowly.

Finally, information trickled out of the communications room that the firing of all four stages had been verified by careful matching of Doppler velocity figures, and that the final velocity was adequate. With this, the only remaining question was whether or not the missile had been at the correct horizontal attitude when it was finally injected into orbit. There were no instruments aboard which could have told us the answer. We were so hard up for weight that there was nothing in the last two stages or on the satellite itself that didn't absolutely have to be there. As a result, after the second stage fired, and the upper stages and satellite swooshed out of the tub leaving the guidance compartment behind, we could get no information except velocity.

Since we knew that we had enough velocity, and had fired all the stages, there was nothing more we could wait for there. The next announcement would have to come when the satellite was picked up on the West Coast, if it came around successfully. That was figured at a little over 90 minutes.

We all took off for the Post Theater at Patrick, where we were to confront the press. The actual launching had been at 10:48, and it was now midnight.

As Debus, Froehlich, young Dr. Lundquist, and several of the others walked into the Post Theater with me, we were the immediate target of the usual battery of flashbulbs. We leaned up against the front of the stage and told the press we were ready to answer questions. I started the proceeding off by telling them as much as we were permitted to, but I am sure from my general attitude they all got the impression we were quite confident of the result. I told them all stages had fired, that we had gotten the required velocity, and that we should know before long whether we were in the right orbit.

Questions came thick and fast. We were bone-weary, but the letdown had not come yet and we really did not know it. We tried to answer all the reasonable—and unreasonable—questions that were fired at us. Most of the press at Canaveral was pretty well informed on the missile business, and asked questions that could be answered intelligently. There were always a few, however, who felt they had to ask a question and really didn't know what to ask.

A connection had been established to Washington so that we could hear the official announcement whenever it was made. Suddenly in the background I heard a voice on that loudspeaker, but not loud enough for me to hear what was said. At the same instant, someone came up and shoved a piece of paper in my hands, on which were these magic words: *Goldstone has the bird!* This meant that the big radio tracking station in Earthquake Valley, that had been put into position in record time, had picked up the satellite on its first trip back around over the United States. The orbit was wider than we had thought and the bird was a few minutes late, so we had been sweating and wondering why no word had come.

I have a full-sized copy, sent to me by *Life* Magazine, of a picture taken by a *Life* photographer just as I read the words on that slip of paper. It is the most highly prized photograph I own. Whenever I am inclined to be depressed, I go and take a look at it, because it is the picture of one extremely happy man. I doubt if I shall ever feel quite that way again.

I repeated the words on the paper out loud. A cheer went up from the newspaper people. Then someone turned up the loud-speaker, and we heard the President announcing that the United States had successfully launched an earth satellite. Neither then —nor later—was there any reference to the Army, to ABMA, or to any of us as individuals.

Finally—and now it was about 2 o'clock in the morning—we escaped from the press and headed back to the Trade Winds Club in Indialantic, 18 miles south. As it turned out later, I was pursued by a bevy of newspapermen and photographers trying to get special pictures or special interviews. By this time the letdown had hit. Every bit of energy seemed drained out of my body, and I was overwhelmed with just plain exhaustion.

When I arrived at my cottage, good old Tom Doherty, who owned the Trade Winds, was up and on hand. In fact, he had some of his people out to help in keeping intruders away so that I could get a little rest. He had a drink made before I got in the door, and few things have tasted so good.

Reluctantly I agreed to give a couple of news hounds about five minutes. They were nice enough to stick to their promise and left promptly. In the meantime, Tom had been having his troubles with one slightly inebriated citizen who insisted that he had to see me. Tom had chased him off about three times, but he kept coming back.

Finally I asked Tom what the fuss was all about and he told me about this character. "He says that all he wants to do is shake your hand, but I think he might be hard to handle."

I walked to the door and opened it. Our more-than-slightly squiffed citizen was standing right there. I stuck my hand out and said, "I'm General Medaris." He grabbed hold, pumped enthusiastically, mumbled something incoherent and wavered away.

So ended the longest and happiest day. I finally tumbled into bed for about three hours' sleep before I had to get in my plane and return to Huntsville for the Birthday Party. One thing was sure—we now had plenty to celebrate, and the success of our birthday party was guaranteed.

The town of Hunstville, where most of our people lived and worked, had already started celebrating before I got to bed back in Indialantic. The news that the satellite was up hit Huntsville about midnight. The local paper put out the biggest extra edition since the Civil War. They didn't wait for the President's official announcement. Bells and whistles set up a clamor, and the local radio stations began asking everyone to come down to the town square and help celebrate.

From what I hear, almost everyone did, and I was not the only one who was short of sleep the next day. If I remember correctly, it took Huntsville about 48 hours to change the signs on the outskirts of town from HUNTSVILLE, ALABAMA—THE MISSILE CENTER OF THE USA to HUNTSVILLE, ALABAMA—SPACE CAPITAL OF THE UNIVERSE! ! !

CHAPTER XVIII

The Road Starts Downhill

Early in 1958, Secretary McElroy set up a new agency in the Defense Department. The Advanced Research Projects Agency, generally known as ARPA, was in a sense a stopgap solution to the widely felt need for some instrument to promote the national space effort, pending a decision as to a permanent organization. It was to be a small task force or management team for advanced research in weaponry and space projects that might have military significance. Above the level of the three military Services, having its own budget, it would be able to concentrate on the new and the unknown without involvement in immediate requirements or inter-Service rivalries. Such was the theory, at least.

Mr. Roy W. Johnson, a former vice-president of General Electric, was put in charge of ARPA. He turned out to be, in my opinion, one of the most intelligent, objective, and really able people to have any influence on the space and missile programs.

Politically speaking, his back was finally broken by the layers of bureaucratic superstructure that were piled on top of him, and by the endless confusion of missions and authorities. To me this was one of the real tragedies of those hectic years.

At ABMA there was no letdown after the successful firing of Explorer I. Explorer II, with a more sophisticated payload, was scheduled for early March as the second of the two attempts we had been authorized to make. By this time the space race that had started with Sputnik I had generated all sorts of interest, conflicts, and competition. People to whom "space" had been a dirty word only a few months before were now clamoring to get into the act.

We had been given authority to go ahead with Pershing. At the same time we felt most strongly that momentum must be retained in the space program, and that there must be immediate agreement on a follow-up program. We had nothing to contribute on a short time scale except our Jupiter C hardware with its maximum 25-pound payload capacity. In order to use it with any promptness, decisions had to be made right away. The process of readying a really productive scientific payload and testing it to be sure it will perform properly in outer space is a long and difficult one. We could control the preparation of the vehicle, but for the payload there had to be agreement among the scientists of the National Science Foundation as to the most important experiments to be carried out, then long and careful work with the responsible scientist or scientific group to develop the means for the test.

We had been fortunate in having as our first assignment an experiment proposed and developed by Dr. James van Allen of the University of Iowa. The purpose was to measure radiation in space. Our association with Dr. van Allen was to be long and fruitful, and the results of the experiments were to be of enormous significance.

Our second attempt to launch a satellite was a failure. Roy

Johnson went with me to Canaveral to watch. Take-off was perfect, but within an hour we knew that the fourth stage had failed to ignite, and the payload had fallen back into the ocean. We didn't know why, because our very small weight capability did not permit putting enough instruments aboard to keep track of every function—one of the worst penalties of not having big enough boosters to work with.

We had brought along a duplicate missile and payload as back-up, so that we could make a substitution in case something went wrong before firing. That same evening I received authority from Mr. Johnson to fire the back-up missile as soon as possible. Allowing time for thorough check-out and preparation, it was scheduled for three weeks later.

Explorer III was fired on time, and sent back solid data that clearly established the existence of the "van Allen belt" of radiation around the earth. This excited the entire scientific community and emphasized the need for further experiment as soon as possible. Explorers IV and V were approved for this purpose, to be fired in July and August. Their firing was co-ordinated with high altitude nuclear experiments, so that we might not only define and measure the normal pattern of radiation around the earth, but might also measure the effect on that pattern of nuclear blasts in outer space.

Explorer IV did its job well. Orbiting on an elliptical path, first close and then farther from the earth, it was able to "paint a picture" of the radiation pattern, and its varying strength. Explorer V failed on 24 August 1958 when separation occurred a bit too early and the residual thrust operating on the booster caused it to overtake and bump the upper stages, knocking them off course. So our score was three out of five—not a bad batting average for a first series of attempts, each of which was stretching the capabilities of available power plants to their absolute limit.

In the meantime the February Vanguard effort had failed, and finally in March that program achieved its first success by putting a 3¼ pound "grapefruit" into orbit. It's still there. April and May attempts to put up a full 21½ -pound satellite also failed. Finally using up its hardware, Vanguard would close out in September of 1959 with nine failures and three successes, having finally put 21½ pounds into orbit in February of 1959, and a heroic 50 pounds up on its final try in September of that year.

Meantime, the competition for any kind of space project was becoming intense. Our old friends in the Air Force, whose space interests had previously been confined to a long-range approach to a possible reconnaissance satellite, were now bidding for every type of project. The Thor program, having been started on the "lots of hardware" concept, had produced a large number of missiles that were not needed for the IRBM. These became our competitors for the next generation of space boosters. The hardware was offered virtually free.

The limitations that had been imposed on us, on the other hand, left us with almost no Jupiter boosters that could be spared from that program, now on a crash basis for deployment by the end of 1958. Our only chance was to bid in the few missiles we had, using the already developed upper stages of our Jupiter C on top of the bigger booster, which would let us get close to 100 pounds in orbit, or send about 15 pounds to or beyond the moon. These were puny loads. Since no upper stages were immediately available for Thor, the Air Force was in a position to take advantage of all that had been learned, and come up with a combination (later the Thor-Able) that would be considerably more efficient from the load-carrying standpoint. They could "calculate" 200 pounds in orbit, and about 45 pounds on a lunar probe. The only thing we had on our side in this competition was speed, and a reputation based on proven on-time accomplishment. It was enough to keep us in the picture for the time being, but not enough to carry us on to bigger and better things.

By April I was facing a real dilemma in planning intelligently for the future. We had approval to develop the Pershing, but we could only see over the next hill insofar as space missions were concerned. We had authorization for a maximum of five missions with the Juno II (the Jupiter booster with virtually the same upper stages as we had used for Explorer I). These were spread out over more than a year, and the total work involved did not represent a significant load on ABMA. The Jupiter IRBM was being moved out to Chrysler as fast as possible, since we felt it would be disastrous to tie up expensive research and development facilities with a continuing production job. While we had to exert every effort of which we were capable to get the first Jupiter squadron out by the end of 1958, it was clear that our work at ABMA would slack off fast after March of 1959.

Here I had to make a choice that could have a far-reaching effect on the future of von Braun's superb organization, and very possibly on the ultimate success of the nation's bid for position in the space race. If we decided to develop Pershing entirely in-house, with our own resources and our own people, the task would follow the end of the work on Jupiter and keep our people fully occupied. But this would also mean that we would be unable to accept any significant role in future space developments without very considerable expansion of both our resources and our personnel. Bitter experience had taught me that there wasn't a chance of getting approval for such expansion. It was clear to me that if we started on Pershing, we would be out of space by the middle of 1959 at the latest. Yet our people had demonstrated the highest capability for the successful penetration of this new frontier.

Still another consideration had to do with the application of solid propellants to tactical missiles. With respect to Pershing there was no question but that solid propellant should be used. On the other hand the disadvantages of solids in the space field were considerable. It was a virtual certainty that liquid propellant engines would dominate that field until nuclear propulsion could become a reality at some point in the distant future. We had developed an expensive and efficient installation devoted to the testing and integration of liquid engines into big missiles. Both the talent and this multimillion-dollar test facility would be idle if we committed ourselves to Pershing. This certainly would not be in the best interest of the nation either from the efficiency or the economy standpoint. The same kind of resource would have to be built and developed elsewhere to do the same work, and the poor taxpayer would take another beating.

The missing element of information was whether or not ABMA could count on a significant amount of follow-on work toward future projects in the space field. I went to Washington to get the answer.

I talked the problem over with Secretary Brucker, and he took me with him to see Neil McElroy. After reviewing the situation briefly, I put the question straight to him. "Mr. Secretary," I said, "recognizing that the Army has been assigned no basic mission in space, and that work in that area will have to come from the Defense Department (ARPA), will ABMA be given significant future work in the field of space vehicle development and operations?"

Mr. McElroy gave us definite and straightforward assurance that we had a secure future in space work, and I *thought* I had my answer. I decided to put the major share of the work on Pershing out on contract to industry, retaining for ourselves systems engineering, technical supervision, and the development of the guidance system. The latter would be a miniaturized outgrowth of the system that had proved so reliable and accurate for the Jupiter, and gave much greater assurance of success than any other.

With the approval of Secretary Brucker, therefore, we buttoned up the plan for Pershing and got it under way. The ink was hardly dry on the contract before I was to question the wisdom of my decision, and wonder why I hadn't learned that no one man's assurance can be taken at face value in the government. We found that we had to fight for every dollar and every job we were to get in the space field, and that even after they were assigned, tasks could be canceled on the flip of a coin. Not until our authorization to proceed with the super-booster came around in the spring of 1959 were we to see any daylight, and even then Saturn—as this giant rocket was to be called—was to become the vehicle for kicking the Army out of space.

Roy Johnson was sympathetic and did his best for us. But he had to get money to support our projects. In June, just a few short months after McElroy's assurance to me, we were almost down and out again. We had been told that out of the fiscal-year budget, we would get a space program of 48 to 58 million dollars. Suddenly the figure changed to 18 million.

I went to see Roy Johnson and spoke rather bitterly on the subject of good faith. I also asked him where the money had gone. It seemed that several of the projects that had been given to the Air Force, such as the reconnaissance satellite, were now going to cost a great deal more than the original estimates. Having approved the projects earlier, Johnson was on the hook. If he satisfied the increased needs for money to keep them going, there was nothing left. If he did not, money already committed might be wasted.

I reported to Secretary Brucker, and as usual he gave us his most vigorous support. I don't know where the money came from, but we finally got back up to around 40 million, which was about the minimum on which we could maintain any reasonable momentum.

Meantime, we had finally come to grips with the problem of a more efficient organization to manage the Army's technical resources in the whole field of missiles, together with such tasks as were assigned in space. It had become increasingly clear that the splintered organization that resulted from the original decision on ABMA was not the right answer, and that consolidation would improve efficiency, give greater flexibility, and assure maximum use of all the skills and physical resources available.

The Army finally agreed that the "timing" was all right, and that it was "politically" feasible to approach the Department of Defense for approval to create the U. S. Army Ordnance Missile Command, and bring at least the major elements of the resources of the Ordnance Corps devoted to missile work under its wing. These were to include ABMA, the Redstone Arsenal with its combined technical and housekeeping mission, the White Sands Missile Range where all overland testing of shorter-range and air-defense missiles was performed, and the Jet Propulsion Laboratory. JPL was not a true military establishment, but was operated by contract with the Army as a nonprofit enterprise under the California Institute of Technology. All the facilities, buildings, and equipment were furnished by the Army, so that it was, in fact, an Army-owned, Contractor-operated establishment. However, the fact that it was a nonprofit institute, and that all work was paid for strictly at cost, made it possible to consider JPL as an integral part of the Army resources.

Why that reorganization and the constitution of the new command had to be taken to the Defense Department for approval in the first place I could never understand. Additional funds were not required, neither were more people. Nonetheless the Army, in its all-too-usual timid way, would not move until it had been "blessed." I am quite sure that neither of the other two Services would have delayed any such move for the same reason. Perhaps it is this sort of unneeded "consultation" that has served more and more to invite the interference of the Department of Defense staff in the internal affairs of the Military Departments.

In any case the Command was approved. The target date for setting it up was March 31. In January and February, I tried unsuccessfully to get the news released, so that all of our people might know of it, and plans could move forward on a broad front to prepare for the new situation. Until the information was released, I had to do all my planning with a very small group, under tight secrecy. The operation was called "Green Door" from the song title of some years ago. Everyone knew there was a "green door," but could only speculate as to what was going on behind it! The announcement was finally released on the 20th of March, and I had only ten short days in which to bring everyone aboard, allay the fears that always accompany a reorganization, and bring some semblance of control to the whole far-flung enterprise.

I entrusted the day-to-day management of ABMA to the capable hands of Jack Barclay, who had been my Deputy from the very earliest days, and turned a great deal of my attention to the numerous other missile projects of the Army, the control methods to be used, the degree of central control to be exercised, the reorganization required to get the housekeeping job for the Arsenal out of the hair of the technical people, and the business of bringing the White Sands activities into closer and more productive relationship with the rest of the operation.

I could not disengage myself from the job of "front man" for the organization, however, and my visits to Washington, entanglements with the Army, the Defense staff, ARPA, the Congress, and later with NASA became, if anything, more intense and more frequent. The special delegated authorities remained in my hands, and I could not delegate them to any of my subordinates. These special authorities were limited to the high-priority programs— Jupiter, Pershing, space work, and eventually to Nike-Zeus. Handling part of my programs with those authorities and part without (through so-called "normal" channels), I was in a unique position to observe the difference. I found, not to my surprise, that it took from a minimum of 30 days to a maximum of six months longer to accomplish a given action through the "normal" channels than was required for the others. In such cases, papers went back and forth to Washington in a steady stream, and not until every one-feather Indian in the Pentagon was satisfied, or had gotten interested in something else, could final authority to act be expected.

It is surely an expensive way to do business, but since no one in authority can be expected to trust a major general unless he is stationed in Washington, and only staff officers can be expected to have brains, I am afraid the nation will continue to suffer from this plague of overcentralization.

CHAPTER XIX

Wanted: One Million Pounds of Thrust

As the weeks and months of 1958 flashed by, everyone was becoming increasingly concerned over the fact that there was nothing on our immediate horizon that looked like a space vehicle big enough to challenge the Russian lead or carry really significant loads. In January, in my first appearance before Congress in connection with U. S. space activities, I had made the flat statement that the U. S. must command at least one million pounds of take-off thrust by 1961, or by 1962 at the latest, if we were to have any chance of overtaking the Russians. My judgment was underlined when, in May, Sputnik III put almost 3,000 pounds into orbit. Events since have only served to add further confirmation, and so I am still of the same opinion. There were signs of the first faint genesis of such a capability in the project for the Nova engine. However, this plan for a single huge motor was barely on the drawing board, and very modestly financed. Any realistic appraisal of the problem led to the conclusion that

Nova could not possibly meet such a time schedule, within several years. How to do it faster?

When you have to do something faster, you look around to see what facilities are already in existence, and then try to build on that. As a result, when ARPA made known its need for a super-booster, our technicians went to work on plans for a giant rocket that became known as Saturn. In an effort to get the extra margin of reliability that heretofore had been so sadly lacking, they were shooting for not just a million, but a million and a half pounds of thrust. To achieve this, they planned to cluster eight Jupiter-type engines. All these engines, firing simultaneously, would enable us to put a busload of astronauts in orbit, achieve a soft landing on the moon, and accomplish many other desirable objectives, both peaceful and military.

Although there are many complicating factors, there are also a host of good reasons for clustering several smaller motors to get a lot of power.

First of all, clustering engines makes it possible to take advantage of the considerations of safety and reliability that have led to the universal adoption of the multi-engine airplane as the safest mode of air transport. Thus, if the capabilities of the vehicle are not stretched to the limit, and something less than the last pound of possible weight is carried, a space mission can be completed with one or more engines out of action or functioning at less than full power.

Next, there is the question of control. Driving a missile up through the atmosphere is like balancing a billiard cue on the end of your finger. If it starts to tip (and because the weight is up near the top it is essentially unstable and *will* start to tip) the force applied by your finger must immediately change direction to push the base to one side and bring it back into line. This is done by having the gyros of the guidance system immediately sense the change of attitude, and through the control system swivel the motor so that the thrust of the jet will point a little to one side and force the base in the required direction. In some of our missiles, the larger engine stays still, and small extra motors on the sides of the tail change direction to control the attitude. Since the thrust of these motors is much less than that of the main one, control is less positive, and the demand on the guidance system is correspondingly greater.

Now it takes considerable leverage to move a big rocket motor at full power, and if the motor is big enough and heavy enough the movement of the motor itself may tend to tip the missile still more and make the job still harder. Also, the bigger and heavier the motor to be moved, the harder it is to move it quickly and sensitively, and with every fraction of a second of delay in correction there is more risk that the missile will tilt over too far to be straightened out, or will turn so fast that the structure cannot stand the strain and will break up in flight.

If a cluster of motors is used, not all of them will have to be designed for swiveling. The center ring of engines can be fixed in position. At the same time, each of the outer motors can do more than just control the vertical attitude of the vehicle. By moving them all in the same radial direction, the vehicle can be caused to "roll" around its own long axis. Thus the same guidance system, applied through the same controls, can keep the vehicle on a steady path, correcting for error in all three axes—roll, pitch, and yaw. Being smaller, each motor requires less force to move, and can move more quickly and delicately to do its job.

Finally, clustering motors permits the use of engines that have already had considerable flight testing in smaller missiles. A really new motor designed from scratch, such as the Nova, is bound to have quite a few "bugs" in it. An exhaustive pre-flight test program on the ground can catch many of them, but not all. Inevitably there are a few defects that will not show up until the engine is sent out into space. This process is expensive and time consuming, and usually involves the loss of at least a few test vehicles before the engine can be considered operationally reliable. On the other hand, the relatively minor changes that are required to adapt a proven motor to a new type of vehicle can be accomplished faster, and with substantially less risk. Thus, the clustering of existing motors shortens the time scale and increases reliability.

Tooling is also a factor in the time required to bring a new vehicle to the flight test phase. Using the single million-pound engine would mean the design of a whole new set of tanks and missile structure. We had tooling on hand for tanks of the Redstone diameter, and of the Jupiter size. Why not cluster tanks also? If we could do that, two ghosts could be laid. We would waste neither the time nor the money for new tank tooling, and we would not have to tackle again the problem of sloshing in a tank many times bigger than the Jupiter.

Satisfied that they were on the right track, our engineers went to work with vigor and enthusiasm to outline, analyze, and come up with the preliminary designs for a booster that would deliver not just one million, but one and one-half million pounds of thrust.

In terms of both peaceful space exploration and military space requirements, the Saturn—as this huge booster was called—would fulfill a host of requirements. The Air Force, for example, was working on a manned space-bomber project known as Dynasoar. In this concept (outlined long before World War II by a brilliant German scientist named Sanger) a bomber hurled into space by a giant booster would descend into the atmosphere and "skip" for hundreds of miles, like a flat stone skimmed along the surface of a pond. Such a space bomber might easily circumnavigate the globe without refueling. But it would require a booster with enormous thrust to put it up in the first place.

Little did we know, as we began work on the Saturn, that already in Washington events were under way that would first threaten to split the von Braun team in two, and ultimately would succeed in divorcing it from the Army altogether.

By the fall of 1958, we had hammered out a follow-on space program of sorts. In October, we used up the last of the Jupiter C's in a premature attempt to launch a 12-foot-high visibility sphere with a carrier much too small to handle the job properly. Meantime the Hardtack high-altitude nuclear shots had come off in good style, and were finally officially acknowledged as having been carried by the Redstone. We were busy cleaning up on the Jupiter program, and scheduling test shots in sufficient quantity to satisfy the atomic energy people as to the reliability and safety of the fuzing and arming system.

We also got from ARPA general authority for about six probe and satellite attempts with the Juno II. This used the Jupiter booster, but the upper stages were somewhat the same as with the Jupiter C. The energy in the solid propellant had been upgraded a bit, and covering shrouds were designed to protect the whole spinning tub and payload during the brief exposure to fairly high heat that would be encountered on the way up through the atmosphere as a result of the increased velocity.

There was much discussion and delay in deciding upon missions for these vehicles. It was finally agreed that the first two would be used for probes to the vicinity of the moon and beyond. As we discussed dates, we suddenly found ourselves back in much the same situation as we had encountered with Vanguard and our first satellite. Thor-Able was to make its debut in the space business, and for its first effort was to tackle the moon probe. To complete the comparison, they were to make three efforts, and we were to wait until they had had their three times at bat before making our first try in December. Our second moon try with Juno II was scheduled for March of 1959, and other satellite shots were set up for July, August, and October. Except for the two moon-shots, all dates were very indefinite. The scientists were debating as to what payloads should be assigned, and decision in that area would finally control the schedule.

Meantime, in July, the National Space Act had been passed, and the National Aeronautics and Space Administration (NASA) began to move into the picture under the direction of Dr. T. Keith Glennan. This civilian agency, which was designed to emphasize the nation's desire for a peaceful role in the exploration of space, was built upon the existing structure of the National Advisory Committee for Aeronautics, an organization of some 8,000 people and three laboratories that had been in existence since 1915 and was usually referred to as NACA.

NACA's research had always been confined to manned aircraft. They had done fine work, and as an organization could take much credit for many of the most advanced scientific and engineering concepts in the business of airplanes, both military and civilian. They had *not* however had a mission in space, or work directed to that end. There were few people in the organization who could honestly claim to have devoted much effort in that direction. Now, however, great activity arose, all intended to prove what was later said publicly, that "NACA has for some time been devoting a considerable proportion of its most advanced work toward space research, and can, therefore, be expected to contribute materially to this effort."

The most ironic example of this came after Dr. Glennan's appointment to head NASA, when Dr. Abe Silverstein, who had been Deputy Director of the NACA laboratory in Cleveland, was appointed to head "Space Operations" for NASA. Few people knew, as we did, that only a few months before Sputnik, Dr. Silverstein had been the chairman of a committee appointed by the Secretary of Defense to determine future requirements for large rocket engines. After considerable deliberation the committee came out, over Dr. Silverstein's signature, with the pontifical declaration that "there appears to be no foreseeable need for any rocket engines of thrust greater than that now being developed for the ICBM"!

During the Congressional hearings that led to the passage of the Space Act, I had found myself in a very difficult position. I was in favor of anything that would get us some positive action toward a really progressive space program, but I was completely opposed to the fanciful idea that space as a scientific arena could be divorced from space as a future military environment, and I saw here workings of the pernicious tendency toward the creation of wholly new organizations just because there is a new problem. I could see no reason why ARPA should not be capable of directing as much space program as the nation was willing to finance, and do so with just a small headquarters. It was obvious that NASA, if created, would promptly become fully operational rather than a directing agency. To me this looked like wholly unnecessary expense and the creation of another large government bureau to no good purpose.

Very shortly after the creation of NASA, Dr. Glennan moved to take over direct control and funding of all projects that could be properly classified as "civilian scientific."

As Commander of AOMC, my first requirement was to determine what NASA's policies and attitudes might be expected to be, and to assess the effect upon our own future course of action. Through direct discussions with Glennan, examination of his statements to the Congress, and some exchange of ideas at the technical level, it became crystal clear that NASA intended to be fully operational and build whatever resources were necessary.

It was also clear that NASA was having no part of us. Offers to make our top people available for any consultation, advice, or planning assistance that might be required got a pretty cold shoulder. I was told, in effect, that due to jealousies between the Services and pressures arising from commercial elements of the missile industry, Dr. Glennan felt that as long as ABMA belonged to the Army he would be unable to face up to the storm of criticism that would arise if major responsibility for any element of NASA work were assigned to our group.

Not even Dr. Glennan, however, could deny that the von Braun team had the only clear record of straightforward space accomplishment. Consequently, in October, he moved decisively to take it under his wing.

What Glennan wanted, actually, was the whole top structure of scientific and engineering talent and about half of the rest of Dr. von Braun's division, plus all of the Jet Propulsion Laboratory. He made a great case for the capabilities and special talents of both groups, with which I could easily agree. He pointed out that each had special talents which were not duplicating, but complementary. Since their development had been planned that way, I was pleased that he had reached that conclusion. However, my contention was that what he was requesting was not within the intent of the law, and that the results from any point of view would be disastrous.

By this time the Development Operations Division of ABMA (the von Braun team) consisted of a little over 4,000 people, all tightly integrated. The loss of even 100 of the top scientists and engineers, plus half of the best technicians, would have made the remainder useless for anything. A highly successful organization would be hopelessly ruined. Over 90 per cent of their work was on weapons systems and some space work from ARPA on the military side, for which Dr. Glennan had no responsibility. Even JPL, almost entirely a scientific and engineering organization, was more than 50 per cent engaged on Army weapons systems.

In addition, the NASA budget showed no signs of being able to accept the responsibility for the operation of the two groups. However, Dr. Glennan seemed to be proceeding on the assumption that if he could get the people and the resources, someone would have to provide the funds and projects to keep them busy. I must say, I rose up in wrath, and Wernher, eager as he was for space work, was equally perturbed at the prospect of breaking up a winning team.

The whole matter could easily have been resolved if the Army had received any shadow of reason or support from the Department of Defense. Deputy Secretary of Defense Quarles, who was handling the entire matter, apparently took the attitude that the Army had no business in space, or in large missiles, and that therefore the von Braun team had no business in the Army. As official representative of the Department of Defense, Dr. Quarles would accompany Dr. Glennan to the White House and state to the President that Defense had no objection to the proposed transfer.

By the terms of the law no presentation to the Congress was required if the transfer was effected before January 1, so the Executive Order could be issued immediately. Secretary Brucker's strong protests were brushed aside, and as a sub-Cabinet officer he had no direct access to the President to make his views known. Not knowing that there was any disagreement over the matter, the President had no reason to delay a favorable decision. It began to look very much as if the Congress, the press, the Army and the public would be presented with a neat *fait accompli*.

I had been in Washington discussing the whole matter with the Army Staff and with Secretary Brucker. I had reported on the attitude of von Braun and his people, and my fear that such a division of the organization would mean that some, at least, of the top scientists would accept readily available and much more profitable jobs with industry. I had also provided facts and figures as to the distribution of our work, and had analyzed the impact of such a raid on our important weapon responsibilities, which after all constituted our first priority mission. All of us were equally indignant, but after the Secretary's personal efforts were brushed aside, there was nothing left in the way of official recourse. I consulted my conscience, reappraised the situation as objectively as possible, and decided the next move was strictly up to me.

It was late in the afternoon. The President had an appointment with Glennan and Quarles the next morning. Time was very short. There was nothing in the whole situation that could be construed as a matter of security or classified information. If the same move were made sixty days later, the whole matter would *have* to go before the Congress, and be subjected to public scrutiny.

It seemed to me that thus to convert the whole business to a star chamber proceeding simply on the basis of the legal right to do so at that particular moment was fundamentally wrong. I felt that, at the very least, the President was entitled to know that there *was* strong opposition to the move. If, with full knowledge of that fact, he still signed the order, he had the perfect right to do so, and his decision would have to be supported. But, isolated as he was at the apex of the pyramid, it was entirely possible that he did not know.

For obvious reasons, neither Secretary Brucker nor I could go over the heads of our superiors to appeal to the President. If we had done so, discipline would have demanded that the offender be sacrificed, regardless of the justice of his cause. It didn't matter so much where I was concerned, although I certainly had no appetite for being shoved into retirement under a cloud. But in Secretary Brucker we had one of the best, if not the best, Secretaries of the Army ever, and only the Army would suffer if his neck went on the chopping block.

I had one particular friend in the press, whom I had found over the years to be honest, reliable, objective, patriotic, and thoroughly dependable. He was Mark Watson of the Baltimore *Sun*. I telephoned Mark and asked if he could meet me as soon as possible to discuss a matter of great urgency. He responded, as I knew he would, and within about an hour we were together in Washington.

I laid the whole situation before Mark and asked his opinion. If he had told me it should be let alone, I would have heeded his advice. However, he too recognized the gravity and essential unfairness of the situation, and agreed that the only proper thing to do was to make sure that the President knew that this was a highly controversial matter. We felt that if the President knew that much, there would be sufficient delay to assure adequate and reasonably objective evaluation of the situation.

Mark left, and almost within minutes his dispatch hit the press wires outlining the plan, stating the situation as he saw it, setting forth the attitude of von Braun and of the Army, and expressing concern over the outcome. He followed with what I thought was a brilliantly written analysis in the morning edition of the *Sun*.

Almost immediately press representatives began to call the White House for comment. In other places, the press sought out important members of Congress and asked their views. Some of these Congressmen sent messages to the White House, and at least one prominent Senator dispatched a telegram. Our point was made. The President knew the problem. As a result, the morning meeting was called off, and serious discussions between Glennan and representatives of the Army took the place of a directed verdict.

I really believe we would have won our whole case had not some of the Caltech people thrown their weight in the direction of transferring the Jet Propulsion Laboratory to NASA. Long before, the sentiments of JPL and the Caltech administration had been partially alienated from the military by inept handling of some of their problems by people in military control of JPL operations. I knew all this, and had done what I could to rectify it. Now, however, the appeal of space, plus the remnants of this old hostility, had their way, and Caltech plumped for NASA.

The resulting agreement transferred JPL to NASA, but left the von Braun group intact. This, too, was to go a year later, but with a major program in hand (Saturn) to assure its future, and with the whole organization rather than just half of it. The intervening time has given me no cause to question my conviction that acceding to the original request would have resulted in substantial damage to important Army missile programs, and the reduction to impotence of the nation's best space team.

CHAPTER XX

The Last Mile

A whole book could be written on the accomplishments and the defeats of 1959, but there is space for only a few. Earliest came the moon-shots.

As decreed, Thor-Able had its chance. The first effort exploded in the air 77 seconds after launch, but they got the second out to 71,300 miles before it fell back to earth. Much could have been learned from that second shot, but unfortunately something went wrong with the instrumentation on board and little if any intelligible data was received. The third effort in November was unsuccessful when the upper stages failed to ignite.

Our first try in December suffered almost the same fate as the second Thor-Able, and after climbing to 63,500 miles also fell back and was burned up. However, as a scientific experiment it was an outstanding success. Instrumentation on board was designed to measure again, and much more completely, the quantity and pattern of radiation in space. The result was the discovery that there are in fact two different and distinct belts of fairly heavy to heavy radiation, one the inner Van Allen belt discovered by our earlier satellites, and the other much further out but just as clearly defined. Out through both and back through both our little messenger painted a portrait of the whole area of radiation affected by the earth's magnetic field.

Our second try was in March, and this time everything worked perfectly. JPL, in addition to being responsible for the upper solid propellant stages, was also the designer and monitor of the small, but highly efficient, payload. When Pioneer IV passed the moon on its way to permanent orbit around the sun, JPL was jubilant. Of course they were now part of NASA, and so had much more opportunity to claim credit for their accomplishment.

By this time, NASA had settled on a program to put a man in space. This program, involving the now-famous astronauts, is designed to send a man into orbit around the earth in a capsule with the Atlas ICBM as the booster. We managed to persuade NASA that the initial trials and essential experiments should be done with Redstone and Jupiter, without orbit. Redstone especially has the demonstrated reliability to justify giving the astronaut his first "check ride" out and back on the nose of that booster. Of course, all the astronauts were chosen either from the Air Force or the Navy, another indication of the official policy that the Army must be kept out of space.

My major efforts in the first half of 1959 were directed toward getting firm control of the Army's other missile projects, and disciplining their management through the Rocket & Guided Missile Agency of the Command to the point where contractors and project officers could really be held responsible for performing on time and within planned money limitations. One by one I went through a careful evaluation of each program. I recommended that the Dart antitank missile be canceled, since it was not showing progress consistent with cost and its defects could not be cured within a reasonable time or with a reasonable amount of money. Other weapons could do the job better before Dart could be made ready.

By direction, I stayed out of the Hercules-Bomarc battle. Nike-Hercules is a fine weapon, and capable of dealing with *any* air-supported weapon, manned or unmanned, that may be brought against us in the foreseeable future, with the single exception of a very low-altitude attack. The U-2, for example, would be highly vulnerable to Nike-Hercules. (This year, 1960, Hercules capability was underlined when it accomplished the successful interception of a Corporal ballistic missile. A bullet *can* kill a bullet!) By mid-1959, Hercules was battle-ready and being deployed to sites in the United States.

The Air Force Bomarc is essentially a pilotless aircraft. If successful, it was supposed to provide a more distant intercept of incoming aircraft. Of course, if Hercules were sited farther forward on our northern defense perimeter it could do the same. In any case, Bomarc had rung up a spectacular series of failures in test. *If* its problems could be overcome and *if* it finally turned out as forecast by its hopeful admirers, it might still be ready for use just about the time that there is little or no probability of any attack on us by airborne weapons. By that time the missile threat will have taken over completely, if it has not already done so. There was, then, no real excuse for not canceling Bomarc. A year and a new budget later, and with the economic pressure somewhat relieved by the assignment of the Dynasoar (space bomber) program to Boeing, Bomarc is not only not dead, but showing increasing ability to survive and absorb defense funds.

Hawk was designed by the Army to meet the threat of low-altitude attack. It had performed extremely well in test, but required some changes and considerable push to convert it to a producible and dependable weapon. The necessary spotlights were turned on, and the contractor went after the job with renewed vigor. That one was in hand.

So we went through the whole list. Most of what we did must remain under security cover. I can only say that no Army missile program, present or proposed, escaped searching evaluation. Some of my recommendations had only mediocre success. The Army makes mistakes too, and like all other elements of government hates terribly to admit them.

In my opinion, however, a man or an organization should be judged on its batting average, rather than on any requirement that each and every action be perfect. This viewpoint is not accepted by any of the investigative elements of the government. The General Accounting Office, Bureau of the Budget, Audit Agencies, and even the Congress take the position that there must be a hue and cry over every error, no matter on what good faith or logical reasoning it was based.

The results are highly unfortunate for the progress of our country and the efficiency of our government. In an effort to avoid even the smallest of mistakes, no action is taken without over-lengthy and detailed examination, delay, and buck-passing designed to keep responsibility from ever being fixed on an individual. Another equally bad result is to cause almost everyone to go to any lengths to avoid having to disclose an error, or change a decision. In the technical field especially, it seems much easier to hide a mistake than to correct it. The result is more delay, less effective weapons, and wasted money.

None of this can be changed unless public opinion can be directed to the support of government officials who do a good job over-all, and the press persuaded not to make a field day out of an honest error. The alternative is a faster slide down the hill of governmental inefficiency, since the best men will not accept assignment to a position that will inevitably expose them to the constant harassment and personal criticism that follow the naïve attitude that an individual in government must be perfect.

One small illustration will do. After the law was passed that reorganized (again) the top structure of the Defense Department, and in particular provided for the now extremely powerful post of Deputy Secretary of Defense for Research and Engineering, quite a few months passed without any sign of an appointment to that post. In a casual conversation with Bill Holaday one day I asked him why the post had not been filled, since it was obviously considered a very urgent matter. His answer was a classic. "That's easy," he said. "Every man who is smart enough to do that job well is much too smart to accept it." A few weeks later Dr. Herbert F. York was appointed.

By midsummer I was literally exhausted. I don't know how to coast on a job, and so it is all or nothing. A summer vacation in the mountains didn't help much, and in August I faced the problems of a new fiscal year with the feeling that I was nearing the end of the line. Mental exhaustion breeds mistakes, and mistakes are not allowed. Maybe, I told myself, I'd better quit while I was ahead.

In thinking of retirement, what I wanted to avoid above all else was any inference that I was quitting either in a personal or an official huff. At the moment things were quiet, but I knew that if a battle should develop later in the fall, and it should appear that the Army, ABMA, or that I personally were on the losing end, then any announcement of retirement was bound to be interpreted as a protest.

I had realized long before that there was no other post in the Service that demanded my particular capabilities, and so my own future was completely tied to the Missile Command. On the morning of August 25, therefore, I made up my mind. I would give immediate official notice of my intention to retire shortly after the first of the year. This would allow sufficient time for selecting my successor, and would give me a chance to make some plans of my own for the future.

Retirement from the professional military service, and particularly from an important command assignment, is a wrenching dislocation. Having previously spent some time in civilian life, I knew it would be a little easier for me. But nothing can relieve the heartache that comes with laying aside the cherished uniforms worn so long with so much pride. Retirement from a position of responsibility in a civilian corporation must be difficult also, but it does not carry with it the complete severance of ties and associations, the instant departure from familiar scenes and trusted comrades, and the total change of one's way of life that follows so immediately on receiving the last commander's parade, the last thrill to the lift and dip of the passing colors, and the final handshake with still-active friends and associates in the military.

The prospect was saddening, but it had to be faced. Without plans for the future, but with a conviction in my heart that I had no other real choice, I told the Chief of Ordnance, Lt. General Jack Hinrichs, that I would exercise my right to retire shortly after the first of the year.

As it turned out, my timing was good. Within a very few days it became apparent that ABMA was in the fight of its life, with little chance to win, and that if I had not made and announced my decision just when I did, I might have been compelled to stay and preside over at least a partial dismemberment of the magnificent organization that was as close to my heart as my own family.

Behind the scenes, and beyond my ken, a deep-rooted fight had been going on over the future organization of the Defense Department for activities in space. It had been precipitated by the need for careful organization of recovery operations related to the Mercury program, where for the first time not just hardware or monkeys, but man himself, would have to be brought back safely from a trip into the outer void.

NASA had very properly requested the Defense Department to provide the resources and handle the recovery end of the job. All three Services would be involved. Early trials with Redstone and Jupiter were to be launched by ABMA. Launchings would be from Air Force operated ranges, primarily Canaveral. Army, Navy and Air Force communications were all involved in the initial tracking, the world-wide tracking net, and communications to operational elements needed to find and recover the capsule and the astronaut. Air Force planes and Navy vessels would have the final job, with the Navy holding the paramount requirement for snatching the precious cargo from the sea.

The Joint Chiefs considered the problem, and finally came out with a "split" paper, the Army and Navy recommending a Joint Command with all three Services participating, and the Air Force holding out for the entire responsibility for command and control.

The fate of that paper, and the final results, represent as clear an example of the evils inherent in the present Joint Chiefs system as one could possibly ask for. Once again the fact that the Chiefs disagreed invited the civilian staff of the Department of Defense to enter the field and make final decisions.

The Secretary of Defense, already expecting to bow out of office before too long, referred the matter to Dr. York, a civilian scientist whose job as Deputy Secretary for Research and Engineering actually carries no authority over military operational resources.

After much delay, and "staffing" by the professional civil service staff, a really weird paper was issued and referred to the Joint Chiefs for "comment." The paper stated that there was no prospect of sufficient space operations in the near future to justify the formation of a Joint Command, and went on to assign all development, production, launching, and related operational activities connected with space vehicles to the Air Force. A bone was thrown to the other Services by the assignment to each of one satellite mission, with the accompanying statement that the Army and Navy would have to purchase the vehicles and all related services from the Air Force in order to get their satellite into orbit.

Actually, the reference of the paper to the Joint Chiefs was pure formality. Objections by the Army and Navy were summarily brushed aside. The Secretary of Defense summoned the Joint Chiefs before him, and in essence said he was acting on Dr. York's recommendation, and that the directive would be issued. I'm sure Gen. Thomas White of the Air Force must have had a very satisfied smile on his face, although I have a feeling that the action was beyond what even he had considered as a reasonable possibility at the time.

This was a classic example of how the inability of the Joint Chiefs to agree removes the professional military experts from any effective role in the decision process. The end result of this situation is the transfer of *operational management* of the Armed Services from the hands of the top-ranking military commanders of the Services to a combination of short-tenure appointed civilian secretaries supported by permanent, professionally unprepared, civil service civilians.

In this case, Secretary Brucker made one last desperate attempt to stop the steam roller and bring some reason to the situation. He called on the Secretary of Defense and recommended urgently the creation of a Joint Military Command, with the participation of all Services, to have full responsibility for the development and production of missiles *and* space vehicles, and all operations in space. He offered on behalf of the Army to contribute to such a command any Army resources and personnel that could be of assistance. His offer apparently received no serious consideration. The directive was issued the next day, and the Army was out of the field in which it had been the Nation's pioneer.

While all this was going on, the Secretary had very kindly taken time to try to talk me out of my plan for retirement, but I was more convinced than ever that my time was up. Secretary Brucker understood my feelings as few could, and agreed that I had fully earned the right to withdraw.

Through the whole last part of the year we were fighting a succession of rear guard actions, trying desperately to preserve some semblance of order in the face of attack after attack. In spite of Russian progress with their ICBM, and in spite of the challenging demonstrations of space capability represented by the January, September, and October Russian space probe and moonshots, Dr. York, obviously with plenty of support, was determined to cancel or transfer the Saturn—cancel the Nike-Zeus—get rid of ABMA—get the Army out of space. We all felt strongly that the Nation had an urgent need for both Saturn and Nike-Zeus, and were determined that regardless of how it all came out, the outstanding organization of scientists and engineers headed by Wernher von Braun must be preserved as a national asset.

By mid-October the scoreboard was marked up. Saturn was reaffirmed as a national requirement, but transferred from the Department of Defense to NASA. Nike-Zeus was preserved—barely—but with the development budget trimmed tight, and no apparent possibility of getting any approval at all for the essential actions that would start it on the road to production and deployment. The Development Operations Division of ABMA—the group headed by von Braun—was to be transferred to NASA as soon as the necessary formality of submitting the transfer to the Congress could be fulfilled, and the Army was faced with the serious problem of reconstituting the capabilities of ABMA with respect to the important Army missile programs for which they were responsible.

The constant and nagging question of the last four years—"What are you going to do with ABMA?"—was finally answered. The splendid capability so lovingly developed and nurtured by the Army since 1945, in which the Army had invested many dollars and uncounted quantities of sweat and tears, and which had managed to carry the United States flag out into space in the face of tremendous opposition, was to be handed over, for good or ill, to NASA. And there was to be no compensation of any kind to the Army for its investment—no extra resources provided to help recover from the blow.

Those last months of struggle showed a peculiar, and at times almost incredible, pattern. Enough so that they deserve a special chapter.

CHAPTER XXI

The Project Snatchers

It has been an interesting study in human nature to watch the various phases of Dr. von Braun's reaction to the transfer of his team to NASA.

In the fall of 1958, when NASA first requested that *part* of von Braun's group be transferred to them, Wernher and his whole crew were bitterly opposed, because they knew that this would mean a division of their team and its associated resources right down the middle. We weathered that storm with the aid of the press and the Congress.

Beginning in the middle of 1959, we were subjected to a series of threats to our existence and to the continuance of the Saturn program. By this time, the whole von Braun group was deeply immersed in Saturn work and we were all convinced that this was the most important project in the country so far as United States achievements in space were concerned. At first we could not take Dr. York's threat to cancel Saturn seriously, but finally, after a big conference where Dr. York was face to face with Secretary Brucker, General Lemnitzer, Wernher, myself, and others, it became obvious from his attitude that he had every intention of canceling that project.

I think the whole campaign, that began with a hold-up of our work on the upper stages of Saturn, was one of the most carefully planned and executed maneuvers I have ever seen.

We had gone through the whole process of selecting upper stages and had made our recommendations to ARPA. We had indicated very clearly that we were willing to accept either the Atlas or Titan as the basis for building the second stage. The real difference was that in one case we would be using the Atlas engines and associated equipment, built by North American, while in the other case, we would be using the Titan power plant built by Aerojet. Largely because of the multitude of different projects that had been saddled on the Atlas, we favored the Titan. Convair builds the Atlas, and we had great confidence in Convair's engineering, but this was overshadowed in our mind by the practical difficulties of getting enough Atlas hardware. However, we assured ARPA that we would take either one.

The time scale was important. In order to get an operational vehicle in the air as soon as possible, and be able to match and possibly exceed Russia's capabilities, we recommended the first flying vehicle to be made up of Saturn as the first stage and a second stage built with the Titan power plant. We also recommended using the tooling available at Martin for the airframe. We felt that by the time we got through the second-stage tests, the powerful new Centaur oxygen-hydrogen engine would be in good enough shape to become the third stage. We then calculated that a year afterwards, or perhaps a little later, we could begin to come up with a second-generation satellite vehicle that would cluster the Centaur engine for the second stage.

Our people made extensive presentations to both ARPA and NASA during the late spring of 1959, always taking the position that we could work with either combination that was agreed to by both. We were anxious to have them agree, because it seemed obvious to us that the nation could not afford more than one very large booster project. We believed that the resulting vehicle would be enormously useful both to the Defense Department for advanced defense requirements, and to NASA for its scientific and civilian exploration of space.

We finally got a decision. We were told that we could begin designing the complete vehicle along the lines that we had recommended, namely, with the Titan as the basis for the second stage. So far there was no sign of trouble.

Remembering the difficulties that we had had in connection with our requirements for North American engines for Jupiter, with the North American people largely under control of the Air Force, we knew that if we were to get on with the job properly we had to make our contract direct with Martin for the second stage work, and with the Convair/Pratt & Whitney group for the adaptation of Centaur to the third stage. We asked the Air Force for clearance to negotiate these matters with the companies concerned. The Air Force (BMD) refused, and insisted that we let them handle all areas with the contractor. They used the old argument that they as a group could handle the responsibility much better, and that if they didn't handle it, there were bound to be priority problems connected with the military programs for Titan and others.

We knew that the Air Force had no technical capability of their own to put into this project, and that if we gave them the whole job, they would be forced to use the old Ramo-Wooldridge organization, now known as the Space Technology Laboratories, as their contract agent to exercise technical supervision and coordination. While we knew and respected a few good men in STL, we felt that we had ample cause to lack confidence in the organization as such. As a matter of fact, when the House Committee on Government Operations looked askance at STL with respect to their position as a profit-making organization, some of the best men had left the organization. We threw this one out on the table and said that we would not, under any circumstances, tolerate the interference of STL in this project. We knew that we had all the technical capability that was needed to supervise the over-all system, and could not stand the delays and arguments that would most assuredly result were that organization to be thrown in also.

Both sides presented their arguments to ARPA, and finally, after letting both General Ritland and myself appear personally and state our positions, Mr. Roy Johnson ruled that we could go ahead and contract directly with Martin and others as required.

It is understandable that the Air Force took this decision with poor grace. It represented a major setback to their system of absolute control over their own contractors, no matter for whom those contractors happened to be doing work. It also left them pretty much on the sidelines with respect to major participation in or control over any portion of the Saturn as a space vehicle.

With the amount of money still available to us from fiscal year 1960 and with our authorization from ARPA, we proceeded immediately to negotiate engineering contracts with Martin. We thought that since Mr. Johnson had complete control over this program, we had gotten over the last important hurdle and could get on about our business. Little did we realize the hornet's nest that had been stirred up, and less did we realize that winning that battle was finally to mean that we would lose the war, and would lose von Braun's entire organization.

We had only a few weeks of peace and quiet. From events that occurred later, I think I can make a fair estimate of what happened during this short period. Having been overruled by Johnson, the Air Force took a new approach. They decided that in view of the importance and power that was given the Deputy Secretary of Defense for Research and Engineering by the 1958 changes in the defense organization, Dr. York represented their best avenue of approach through which to get back in the war.

For reasons of economy we had recommended, and it had been approved, that in building the second stage, we would use the same diameter as the Titan first stage—120 inches. The major costs of tooling for the fabrication of missile tanks and main structure is related to the diameter. Changes in length cost little or nothing in tooling. How the tanks are divided internally, or the structure reinforced inside, or the kind of structural detail that is used at the end in order to attach the structure to a big booster below, or to a different size stage above, have very little effect on tooling problems. However, a change in diameter sets up a major question of tools, costs, and time.

Suddenly, out of the blue came a directive to suspend work on the second stage, and a request for a whole new series of cost and time estimates, including consideration of increasing the second stage diameter to 160 inches. It appeared that Dr. York had entered the scene, and had pointed up the future requirements of Dynasoar as being incompatible with the 120-inch diameter. He had posed the question of whether it was possible for the Saturn to be so designed as to permit it to be the booster for that Air Force project.

We were shocked and stunned. This was no new problem, and we could find no reason why it should not have been considered, if necessary, during the time that the Department of Defense and NASA were debating the whole question of what kind of upper stages we should use. Nevertheless, we very speedily went about the job of estimating the project on the basis of accepting the 160-inch diameter. At the same time it was requested that we submit quotations for a complete operational program to boost the Dynasoar for a given number of flights. As usual, we were given two or three numbers, rather than one fixed quantity, and asked to estimate on each of them.

By this time, my nose was beginning to sniff a strange odor of "fish." I put my bird dogs to work to try to find out what was going on and with whom we had to compete. We discovered that the Air Force had proposed a wholly different and entirely new vehicle as the booster for Dynasoar, using a cluster of Titan engines and upgrading their performance to get the necessary first-stage thrust for take-off. This creature was variously christened the Super Titan, or the Titan C. No work had been done on this vehicle other than a hasty engineering outline. Yet the claim was made that the vehicle in a two-stage or three-stage configuration could be flown more quickly than the Saturn, on which we had already been working hard for many months. Dates and estimates were attached to that proposal which at best ignored many factors of costs, and at worst were strictly propaganda.

During this same period, the total defense budget was in difficulty. As had happened so many times before, the real needs of the Services had been virtually ignored in the submission of the fiscal year '60 budget. The total figure had been established on a basis virtually identical to the year before. As it came time to consider releasing 1960 money, which meant approving specific projects for specific amounts of money, it became obvious that the budget would not cover the needs.

The picture looked even blacker for 1961. Major weapons systems of any kind increase steadily in annual costs as they go from initial development into final development and then into production. Projects approved and begun over the last two to five years were now getting to the big expenditure stage.

Within my own command, I had been fighting this problem in a very serious way, and had found that just to stick with my previously stated requirements meant that every program for which I was responsible had to be pared to the bone. For example, we had to accept almost the limit of calculated risk in Pershing, and reduce the number of projected test firings to an irreducible minimum. From the maneuvering going on in the Pentagon, it was obvious that all Services were having the same trouble, and the demands for more money for the B-70, Bomarc, Atlas, Titan, Polaris, Dynasoar, and a host of others, to say nothing of the need for production of Zeus, brought the total to a figure impossible to meet within the budget.

Dr. York was faced with the monumental problem of handling this situation, and it became obvious that he was ready to snap at anything that promised the possibility of spending less money. In fact, from the challenges posed and discussions held, it appeared that he was determined to cancel one or more of the most expensive programs in an effort to balance the situation. He took the position that by junking Saturn and taking the Super Titan, he could get "everything we need at two-thirds the cost." So now we not only had to change the Saturn in such a way as would increase the costs, but compete for its very life against a true "paper tiger."

In the meantime, rumblings began to reach my ears of other coincidental assaults upon the position of the Army in space work, and the existence of ABMA specifically.

By this time, von Braun and I knew we were in the fight of our lives. We mustered every bit of knowledge and ability and information that we had in an attempt to prove conclusively, to a man who did not want to listen, that Saturn was absolutely essential to the country's future efforts in space and that there was no possible substitute. In one conference this brought a rather incredible retort from Dr. York to the effect that even if Saturn was essential to the future of the United States in space, the Defense Department didn't have to have it militarily, and therefore he had no intention of supporting it. I say this was incredible because the discussion indicated very clearly that Dr. York had no intention of looking beyond his own money problem, and cared little what happened if he could find a way to get the project out of the Defense budget.

Dr. York set up a committee, including himself, to have a showdown over whether there was or was not an absolute requirement for Saturn. In telling us of this, he took the position that there was no doubt in his mind but that the decision would be to cancel. I asked him specifically who was presenting to that committee the military requirements for payloads. I knew that there *were* military requirements which, if they were to be adequately satisfied in the next few years, demanded the size and total thrust of the Saturn. If those projects had to settle for the Titan C, we would have the whole heartbreaking situation again of having to peel everything out of the payload at the expense of reliability to get within the weight limitations as to the total poundage that could be put into proper orbit.

Dr. York's answer was that the top people on the committee knew about the payload needs, and some of the scientists from ARPA could tell them more. General Lemnitzer asked why it was that the military were not being called upon officially to state the *military* requirements in space, but Dr. York merely brushed the question aside.

Finally in frustration, and I must admit some anger, I said, "Dr. York, it seems to me that we are being asked to present a case to a stacked jury that is expected to give a directed verdict in accordance with the way you have made up your own mind!" Although Dr. York disclaimed this, it was certainly reflected in his attitude that day.

In the midst of these frustrating and fruitless discussions, I began to pick up rumors to the effect that Dr. York had initiated conversations with Dr. Glennan about the possibility of handing ABMA to NASA. After the abortive attempt of the year before, Dr. Glennan had made the statement that he would not again request the transfer of ABMA. He was holding to his word, but this time the discussions were being initiated from the Defense Department at a higher level, and he was virtually being offered the von Braun team on a platter. The whole diagram began to fit together and to indicate that each move was a related part of a definite campaign to get the Army out of the space business.

The reasoning went something like this: if the Army could be forced to give up ABMA to NASA, either the Saturn would be canceled or the responsibility for the project transferred. In either case, there was a sizable chunk of money to be saved in the Defense budget. If this did not work by itself, we were to be starved by holding Saturn at an extremely low level of money, thus making it very difficult to put enough work into Dr. von Braun's group to keep them fully occupied.

In defending Saturn against Dr. York's attack, we suddenly received important assistance from a source that could not be ignored. Dr. George Sutton was a respected member of the scientific staff in ARPA, and a recognized authority in the rocket and space field. He made a thorough analysis of future payload requirements based on recognized defense needs. He knew, as did we, that the success of our space efforts was being imperiled continuously by our inability to allow enough weight to assure the dependability of the satellite or space probe itself. He knew that the proposed military operational projects, such as the communications, navigation, and reconnaissance satellites, if they were to be effective and dependable in proportion to their cost, would demand the capability of putting up plenty of weight.

I have tried to emphasize many times in this book how stupid and highly wasteful it is to spend several millions of dollars to get up a satellite to do a specific job, and then find that because of the failure of one element aboard the satellite the mission cannot be accomplished. Many such failures can, in my opinion, be charged directly to the fact that vital equipment aboard cannot be made sufficiently dependable, or duplicated as it should be to provide dependability, because the project is constantly fighting weight. In a communications satellite, it is entirely possible to have two or three transmitters, power supplies, communication relays, and other vital elements of the mechanism. If this duplication can be on board, then it is relatively easy to arrange it so that if one fails, a switchover to a reserve unit can be accomplished immediately. This so-called "redundancy" is almost the only way to assure with relative certainty that the millions of dollars involved in getting the satellite into position will result in a useful instrument for a sufficient time to warrant the cost.

George Sutton wrote a brilliant paper, and demonstrated beyond a shadow of a doubt that no vehicle of less take-off power than the Saturn could possibly meet the future requirements with any degree of assurance and reliability, and that some well-fore-seen defense needs could not be satisfied at all with a less power-ful vehicle.

Roy Johnson, who by this time was thoroughly disgusted with the whole business and had made up his mind to quit, sent George Sutton's paper to the Secretary of Defense and to Dr. York with a strong letter insisting that Saturn was a vital requirement.

In spite of Dr. York's determination to get his committee to agree to the cancellation of Saturn, it would seem that Dr. Sut-ton's paper and Mr. Johnson's letter, now on the official record, made it impossible to cancel Saturn without being assured of either present or future indictment before the bar of public opin-ion. As a result, Dr. York's committee was forced to reaffirm the requirement for Saturn.

This action, however, settled only one of the numerous attacks. In spite of George Sutton's paper, Dr. York did not then admit nor has he or any top administration official, up through March of 1960, admitted that there was a solid defense requirement for the Saturn booster. In fact, the President's message to the Con-gress requesting approval of the transfer of Dr. von Braun's or-ganization to NASA contained a specific denial of such a re-quirement.

By sticking with the twin conclusions that Saturn was an im-portant requirement for United States activities in space, and that at the same time there was no immediate foreseeable and definite defense requirement for the services of this big booster, the ground work for transferring Saturn responsibility out of the Defense Department and onto the NASA budget had been laid very effectively.

By this time it was crystal clear to both von Braun and myself that we were faced with a Solomon's choice—either we could hold firm in an attempt to keep the von Braun group in the Army, being sure that in doing so we were guaranteeing that their space capabilities would die on the vine, or we could support the effort to take the von Braun organization out of the Army and hope that a fond and wealthy foster parent could be found.

Only two such possible parents were available—the Air Force, which now had the entire defense mission in large space vehicles and seemed to be able to find money for whatever it really wanted to do, and the National Aeronautics and Space Administration. We had all taken the position, repeatedly, that the really essential point was that the organization as a whole should be preserved as an indispensable national asset—in the Army if possible, but if that was not possible, then wherever it could be assured of having the opportunity to serve the nation. We were convinced of the fact that there were important defense requirements for a high-performance space vehicle, and we felt that it might be best to plump for transfer to the Air Force.

However, there were some very dangerous possibilities in that course of action. First of all, we recognized the dependence of the Air Force on the aircraft industry, and we had seen those interests continuously attack the concept of government-operated in-house major activities in the missile and space field. With, I believe, some justice, we were afraid that if the Air Force did take the von Braun organization, it would be under continual pressure to get it out of the hardware business and restrict it to engineering. Since we believed that engineering cannot remain effective unless there is actual productive work done, we felt that if this were to happen the organization would decay, and many of its people who liked to see the tangible results of their own efforts would leave for more profitable jobs in industry.

Wernher and I finally reached the conclusion that the least bad alternative was to throw what influence we might have in the direction of NASA.

I sent Secretary Brucker a long personal telegram in which I recited my conclusions and recommended that the Army support the transfer to NASA. We had discussed the possibility of a joint command, and Secretary Brucker had recommended to Secretary McElroy that consideration be given to the formation of such a joint military organization to take over the major missile projects and all space activities of the Department of Defense. The answer was that such a plan would take much too long to accomplish and the money problem was immediate. The Army's offer to provide to the joint command any needed facilities and resources belonging to the Army was thus spurned.

Dr. Glennan was still adhering to his position that he would not again ask for any part of ABMA, but now this was not necessary. The child was being put up for adoption, the sole condition being that NASA also take over the responsibilities for and funding of Saturn. Naturally, Dr. Glennan cheerfully accepted the offer.

At this point, there was still a question-mark in Wernher's mind. Saturn was operating on insufficient funds, the transfer would take his people out of the military missile business quite rapidly, and the real question of their future depended on the extent to which the organization could be supported financially. It was obvious to us that within the current NASA budget there was not going to be too much money available for Wernher. For this reason, anyone who reviews his statements at that time will find repeated references to the fact that he thought the move was probably a good one provided that sufficient resources were available to do a job.

It was interesting to watch what happened immediately after the transfer plan was accepted, the action approved by the President to include the transfer of Saturn, and the whole submitted to the Congress. That which had been previously impossible now became completely possible. Having been told repeatedly that we could not conceivably expect a supplementary appropriation in 1960 to relieve the financial shortage in the Saturn program, a supplement for NASA to increase the rate of effort on Saturn was promptly made available. The Saturn budget for 1961, which under Defense was set at an absolute maximum of 125 million dollars, was immediately raised to the highest total that could be effectively used considering that time had already been lost.

All this was presented to the Congress with enthusiastic administration support. Where nickels had been hard to get, dollars began to appear. VEGA, which had been a pet project of NASA for the interim period, was promptly canceled. It appeared that some of the money saved was to reinforce Saturn. The morale of the von Braun group went to an all-time high, and their enthusiasm for the transfer was naturally complete. Any worry they may have felt over being deprived of the kind of support that only the Army could give disappeared under the glittering prospect of at last having sufficient money to do the job.

I give great credit to those who engineered this whole project. I do not believe these highly synchronized actions could all have come about by pure accident. The child was first starved, criticized, and deprived of a sense of purpose in life. Then, when the natural parent turned it over for adoption by others, the foster parents promptly forgot all their antagonism and proceeded to satisfy all of the child's wants and desires.

I am glad to see the Saturn project being justified by any means whatever. But I do not see that the series of actions has in any way helped the American taxpayer, since the dollar bill spent by NASA still comes out of the same American pockets as the dollar bill spent by the Defense Department. I hope that the taxpayer will not be further wounded by having the Defense Department, through the Air Force and its official mission, develop another expensive space vehicle which is totally unneeded.

On the latter score, I can only say, "I hope."

CHAPTER XXII

A Long Look at the State of the Nation

During my last days in uniform, reviewing what had been done, what had not been done, and what might still be accomplished, I found it difficult to avoid pessimism and discouragement. I felt—as I feel today—that this country has only a lease on freedom. If we stop paying the price—which is discipline and self-denial and sacrifice—we may very well lose the lease.

In these troubled times, with summit conferences collapsing and the threats of our enemies growing ever stronger, we cannot settle for anything less than the most efficient military establishment in the world. Yet I cannot honestly feel that we have it.

The root of the evil is this. More and more the balance shifts from civilian policy control of the military to bureaucratic dominance and day-to-day operation of the Armed Forces by professional civil servants whose main objective in life is the protection of their own position and the perpetuation and growth of their personal empires. The appointed and Senate-confirmed representatives of the administration are insulated, isolated, and brain-

washed by this immense Department of Defense staff to prevent
the possible penetration of their screen by the professional military. Under the guise of enforcing civilian control, a principle
which has never been challenged by the military, layer upon layer
of authority without responsibility is erected.

Finally, civilian authority reaches down and assumes political
control of promotions *within* the Armed Forces. The price of
ascent to high military position becomes conformity. The voice
of dissent and disagreement is stilled under the blanket of "review
to assure conformance with policy," and the detached objectivity
that for so long characterized the dedicated uniformed officer
corps is on the way to oblivion.

In addition, under the guise of so-called "business methods"
of operation, totally unrealistic systems of control and of evaluation of results are foisted upon the Services, crippling the capacity
of the Armed Forces to fight and win any kind of armed conflict
that might threaten us. Corporation accounting methods are
forced into a system that cannot cast up a profit-and-loss statement or price its product, except when the chips are down and
all must go to the profit side if we can win, or all becomes a
loss if we lose. Accountants and bookkeepers have been multi-
plied fourfold, replacing leaders, strategists, and tacticians, and
not one dime of the taxpayers' money has been saved in the process. For every dollar of mistake identified, always too late to
correct, ten dollars have been spent in the finding.

An almost rigidly fixed distribution of the defense budget between the three Services takes no account of changing requirements, creates plenty where there is no real need, and poverty
where needs are urgent. From the management side of this rigid
distribution there arises a form of fiscal immorality that would
not be tolerated elsewhere in our society. When tasks are taken
away, projects transferred, or whole plants and installations
moved from one Service to another or to some other government
agency, there is no compensation for past investment, and no ad-
justment of future budgets to balance this robbery. Thus the

responsible heads of the Services must carefully avoid spending money for anything that conceivably might later be transferred to someone else. Imagination is stifled, courage is killed, and self-preservation demands the injection into decisions of artificial considerations that hamper the defense of our country.

Meantime, in Washington, empire is piled upon empire. The number of Assistant Secretaries has been increased to provide one as a direct supervisor for every responsible military staff chief. If the military organization does not submit to straight control and direction by one of these people, the organization is changed until it does conform. In this fashion, one after another, the missions of the Armed Forces have been brought directly under a civilian element of the Department of Defense, operating from the Pentagon.

It would be a disservice for me to hold forth at such length on the mistakes and organizational errors inherent in our present system if I were totally unable to suggest constructive action. I do feel strongly that a cure is possible, but the cure will require surgery—radical surgery of a sort that has never before been successfully accomplished. History says, and Parkinson's law supports the statement, that a government bureaucracy continues to grow in size and number regardless of need, and never diminishes. Yet to cure our present problems there must be a clear recognition of the fact that one person can truly do more work than seven, and do it better, if the one has both authority and responsibility, and the seven have only permanent tenure on the public payroll.

Correction must start at the top of both the civilian and military systems of the Department of Defense. Let us first consider the military.

As an absolute minimum, the Army and the Air Force must be recombined into a single service. This has been recommended and documented by the House Sub-Committee of the Committee on Government Operations, under the able Chairmanship of Congressman Chet Hollifield. I entirely agree with the committee.

I might add that the Association of the United States Army disagrees forcefully.

Careful attention to justice and equity would be essential in any such merger so that the earlier promotion and thus greater seniority (time in grade) of many Air Force General Officers would not completely submerge the top talent of the Army. There should also be an enforced end to the class consciousness of the flight-rated officer, and thus recognition that a pair of wings is not essential to the exercise of command. It would be best if flight pay could be discontinued, substituting greater government-paid insurance benefits, so that the basic rule of equal pay for equal rank and responsibility could be restored. This re-unification is the only way I can see to end the rivalries and quarrels that stem from the assignment of missions based on tools or weapons, rather than on tasks to be performed.

The crying need for a single Chief of Staff of the Armed Services, with the heads of the services as advisors only to him, must be accepted and the post created. The ancient ghost of "militarism" that has so far prevented this vital step must be laid to rest. A Chief of Staff, as the military head and direct commander of all Joint Commands and Theatres, and as the direct military advisor to the Secretary of Defense, is the only means by which we can eliminate the present nightmarish situation in which the command of military forces is exercised by a quarrelsome committee. It is also the only means of restoring a sense of responsibility to the professional officer corps of our country.

A system of selection for such a Chief of Staff should be devised, and established by law, which would guarantee that the choice of the most able officer for that high post would be completely free of political bias or a requirement for "conformity" as a prerequisite. Thus only can the Congress, the Executive, and the people be assured of the best available military advice. In my opinion, this action—the creation of a single Chief of Staff—is essential whether a way is found to recombine the Army and the Air Force or not.

Of almost equal importance—and probably most difficult to achieve—is the reduction of the civil service staff of the Department of Defense, above the Armed Forces, to about one tenth of the present number. I am personally satisfied that if this were brought about overnight, more would truly be accomplished the next day than had been done the day before. Combined with the next step, the result would be closer and much more effective contact between the appointed representatives of the Executive and the senior responsible military officers, with consequent improvement of communication, much greater understanding, and a very great speed-up in the decision process.

Next, I would reduce at least by half the number of Assistant and Deputy Assistant Secretaries of the Department of Defense and of the several Services. I would also like to see the law specify the responsibility of each, to assure that none would become merely the single civilian boss of one military staff officer, but instead would exercise policy supervision over broad areas.

Finally, it seems essential that the budgetary process be revised if any possibility of prompt and decisive action is to be achieved. Let the Bureau of the Budget exercise its influence and advise the President with respect to the preparation of the budget *before it is presented to the Congress*. After that, funds voted by the Congress should be directly available to the Secretary of Defense and the Secretaries of the Services in accordance with the budget. If changing conditions should require that money approved by the Congress not be used for the intended purpose, the administration should be required to come back to Congress for approval of this decision. Only thus can delay be taken out of the decision process, and any *affirmative* power restored to the Congress.

I know these remedies may seem drastic, but the disease seems to require drastic treatment. There may be other ways to restore sanity to our defense establishment, but I have not been able to find them. Every attempt to date has resulted in more people, more complication, more money, and less decisive results.

So much for the main organizational deficiencies and remedies. Now let us take a look at the state of our national defenses themselves. Here we must define our objectives. This is essential if we are to have something against which to measure our position.

As a first measurement of the state of these defenses, we must identify the types of threats that are known to exist, and also those that we may anticipate. Not all the dangers threatening us are based on military force. Some of the most perilous are internal in their origin and, therefore, difficult to recognize. The Communist threat within our own society seems to have diminished in recent years, but it most certainly is still there, and should never be ignored or forgotten.

Other threats, still short of armed attack, may be raised against us by the attitudes and international operations of other powers. Provocation and assaults upon our sovereignty have become almost daily occurrences in this period of burgeoning nationalism. Sometimes, in our desire to make common cause with those who seek independence, we seem blithely to have tossed aside what should be our proper concern with the preservation of our dignity as a sovereign power. It is hard to know, sometimes, where patience ends and spinelessness begins.

Identification and evaluation of all these threats is our first problem. The second is to make sure that our military power is capable of meeting all such threats and yet will not be applied in such a way as to create more havoc than we can possibly cure afterward.

In measuring the position of our defense against this yardstick, I am led inevitably to the conclusion that something is sadly lacking. For example, funds have been liberally provided to design, develop, and launch earth satellites equipped with advanced electronic systems for the purpose of detecting hostile action on the part of our enemies. Even more funds have been provided to develop ground-based early warning systems to extend far out the radar picket fence guarding our perimeter.

The missions of both the earthbound and the space systems

are to detect and identify ballistic missiles as soon as possible *after* they are launched from pads thousands of miles away. Now, no one can quarrel with the principle involved—to obtain vital information about any possible nuclear weapon that can traverse continents and oceans in a matter of minutes. But the record fails to indicate what, other than immediate resort to the whole course of retaliatory nuclear annihilation, we propose to do if we detect any such missile presumably fired against this continent.

Can we take time to make certain that this missile rushing upon us has not been fired by mistake? Can we stave off the requirement for such a flash-decision by attempting to meet and shoot down such an apparent threat? Such an approach would seem to be the one dictated by reasonable prudence. Yet funds are still being denied for the production and deployment of the only presently visible potential means by which we might gain time to think—an antimissile missile. At the moment, we must simply accept the incoming destruction as inevitable, and resort to the flaming sword of retaliation, thereby admitting that all is lost and condemning mankind to Armageddon.

Surely certain retaliatory capability is the most effective *deterrent* against the possibility of an all-out, massive enemy attack. But if that power of destruction is ever used it has failed in its purpose. At the moment, there is no hesitancy to appropriate all the money required to develop and maintain a retaliatory power on a scale sufficient to destroy the world and all its people. But this would be sheer, negative, destructive revenge. Unless we are willing to see civilization destroyed, we must devote our energies and resources to finding a suitable alternative.

As a third approach to measuring the state of our national defense as related to the threats against us, I feel strongly that we must develop and maintain the capability to move selectively as the exact circumstances demand to counter any threat to our freedom and safety, or our position as a sovereign nation. Such a capability for lightning intervention must exist, it must be known to exist, and it must be sufficient to meet and cope with any threat anywhere.

At the moment, I am convinced that it does not exist. Whatever effective and selective military power we have developed in our Army, the capability of moving the necessary force to the required point is far from sufficient. Furthermore, the force responsible for meeting limited threats anywhere in the world does not have direct access to the means of transport, but must beg from those who have what airlift is available the means essential to carrying out the basic mission of the Army. This is one more reason why Army and Air Force should be re-united.

Fourthly, if we are to measure correctly the state of our defenses, we must recognize that our way of life is embroiled in a struggle to the finish against a resourceful and ruthless opponent. Basic to our total defense capability is the unquestioned public will to use our national power if necessary, and without delay. Our present stature in the world is the result of a continuing national determination—reflected in firm decisions—to resist aggression whenever it has been raised against us. If we ever lose this determination, we are finished.

This consideration leads directly to my fifth and final yardstick for the measurement of our defense situation. Whatever may be our determination, or however carefully tailored our defense resources, unless these strengths are supported by a process of national decision that will permit the rapid and decisive use (or restraint) of military power, the resources themselves are of no value. This fifth yardstick, therefore, is concerned with the efficiency of the decision-making process.

Once more the fact is not consistent with the need. Our national process of arriving at decision has become so confused, weakened, delayed and compromised by the multiplicity of forces acting upon it as to be a real hazard when it comes to national defense. We have worked out a countdown for firing rockets, but we have no countdown for decision.

It seems to me, after watching this area carefully for eight long years, that a great part of the delay in our process of arriving at vital decisions is traceable to the intrusions on a day to day basis of innumerable pressure groups into the executive processes of government. By their very nature, all pressure groups are divisive, since each supports one set of desires at the expense of other objectives. When these varied pressures act continually upon the executive process, the result is the achievement of a balance of compromise dictated by expediency. The end product is relative inaction. We seem to have forgotten that indecision is of itself a decision, and that in the light of history a vigorous mistake is often more effective than no action at all.

If we, as a people, continue to exert such daily pressures as to vitiate the capabilities of those we have elected to make our decisions, there is little possibility that our defense structure can be precisely tailored to our requirements, or that our national power can be promptly used as needed.

Varying and opposing pressures stemming from such considerations as the desire to receive the benefits of government spending, to preserve the *status-quo,* to support current employment levels in specific areas—such elements seem to me to do more to distort and upset proper decisions where national defense is concerned than any other group of factors. The most glaring example, of course, is the pressure from the aircraft industry which was called into being during World War II to meet an urgent need, but which has been fighting desperately against technological displacement ever since. It would be an expensive solution, but I truly believe that in the long run money would be saved if the government were to buy up surplus airplane plants and put some in mothballs and simply close others down.

In the meantime, delays in decision pyramid the cost of new weapons. Literally, we buy obsolescence and pay a staggering price for it. Our programs seem often to be shaped to suit the needs of specific industries rather than being tailored to the dictates of weapons requirements. We seem to be determined to use existing skills without regard to the basic question of whether those skills are advancing our technology and our production capability or holding us back. In this fashion we often achieve political and economic peace, but we do so at the risk of international impotence and finally of military defeat.

As I turn now for a moment to an evaluation of what we have achieved by way of major weapons systems, I would remind the reader that there is no quick or easy solution to the problems I am discussing. By the nature of the critical lead time involved in any change of direction in the development and production of modern weapons systems, there is little we can do which would substantially change our military posture during the next four or five years. My concern, therefore, relates to the military situation as it will exist in 1964 or 1965, rather than in 1960 or 1961. We must make the decisions today that will provide the capabilities we may need most urgently five years from now.

The nation's defense today appears to be dedicated to the philosophy of over-kill, of wholly unnecessary redundancy and of costly duplication in the provision of means to execute massive destruction. Almost without regard to anything a potential enemy might do, I wish we could come to an understanding of two basic facts:

First, any weapon is useful so long as it is capable of doing the job for which it was designed, and

Second, our weapons of retaliation are quite sufficient so long as they are capable of inflicting unacceptable damage upon any aggressor. Anything beyond that quantity or quality is unnecessary and should not be provided at the expense of more important objectives.

In my considered opinion, the combination of atomic striking power represented by the Strategic Air Command and our other retaliatory forces more than satisfies a reasonable counterstrike requirement. Given any means by which 50 to 100 megatons of atomic destruction can be placed on the territory of an enemy, the potential damage becomes more than he can afford. Beyond that reasonable amount of assurance, there is no further justification for continuing to pile up relatively useless destructive force.

Consequently, I am forced to conclude that the approved programs for the development, production and deployment of intercontinental ballistic missiles involving many billions of dollars will go far beyond the basic need. If those programs are carried out to the last rocket, we will have many times more than enough to guarantee unacceptable damage upon any enemy.

Three separate ICBM systems—Atlas, Titan, and Minuteman (and now Titan II)—are simply too many. By what logic we continue to pursue so many ways to provide the same deterrent, I do not understand. It appears that the fear engendered by Soviet rockets has destroyed prudent judgment, for it is exclusively in this area of massive retaliation that such expensive duplication is permitted to exist. A prominent Senator estimated last spring that our present stockpile of atomic weapons represented the equivalent of 10 tons of TNT for every man, woman and child on earth. We seem to be preparing not for retaliation but for obliteration.

A single land-based ICBM system (Atlas) will, in the next fiscal year, require the further expenditure of approximately one and a half billion dollars. A like amount will be required to support another system (Titan) which has yet to be deployed. Half a billion more will be spent in the next year for a brand-new ICBM system (Minuteman) that is supposed to render obsolete its costly predecessors in a few years. The figures assume almost astronomical proportions. Since 1950, approximately 25 billion dollars has been spent for all our missile programs. The over-all investment in two liquid-propellant ICBM systems is estimated to be nearly 10 billion dollars, and this will buy more than twice the amount of nuclear destruction that I mentioned as being required.

The Polaris submarine-transported system will cost approximately 9.9 billion dollars, to provide 45 submarines costing about

$100,000,000 each with the required complement of missiles at a million dollars apiece.

I think one is forced to ponder the over-all impact of these programs upon the national economy and to recognize the not-too-remote possibility that some day we may find ourselves fully equipped with the tools for total human destruction, and with little else.

Personally, I consider the Polaris system the best bet for the retaliatory striking power for the near future. It offers the advantage of concealment to a much more realistic degree than the entombment of concrete-protected, land-based missiles. Its mobility is far superior to any land-based system, if ever such a system is made mobile. Its range, coupled with its underwater capability, provides a flexibility that will meet most requirements.

If there is a question as to the vulnerability of fixed-base ICBM's, I believe the next best alternative to be the Air-Launched Ballistic Missile (ALBM), now under development by the Air Force. Carried by a large, high-performance bomber such as the B-52 or the B-70, the ALBM, along with Polaris, possesses what is to me the essential capability of protecting itself long enough to determine the real nature of a threat of attack, and making certain *before* we retaliate that we are not plunging the world to destruction as the result of some mistake, accident, or misunderstanding. Both these weapons can, by reason of high mobility and effective concealment, be free of the dangerous requirement that these missiles be launched in retaliation *before the supposed incoming attack has actually hit.*

Combined with the Nike-Zeus (of which more later) in defense of our unarmed cities, a modest number of missiles—Polaris, ALBM, ICBM—would in my opinion provide a quite adequate posture of deterrence, with the added assurance of permitting *restraint.* Those who play the numbers racket by advocating more and more ICBM's without regard to the limited nature of the requirement, and with an apparent total disregard of the cost in time, labor, material and money, are rendering a disservice to the nation.

At the same time, our geographic situation cries out for a self-contained, globally mobile, lightweight force which could deal promptly with any localized threat to our security or that of our allies. The nation should assign the highest priority to the provision of a sufficient airlift to move, in one single motion, a highly trained force, fully equipped with its own weapons support, that could stand alone until more power could be brought to bear if necessary. Strategic mobility, not inflexibility, and precision forces rather than massive and heavyweight equipment are the logical backbone for our future defense structure.

The alternative is to man heavily all the frontiers of the free world. Even with the assistance of our allies, we cannot achieve that objective in sufficient force to meet whatever threat could be marshaled against us at a single time and place of an enemy's choice.

Central reserves with global mobility are the only practical solution to meet our present commitments. If that kind of protective force cannot be provided, the alternative is to reduce our international commitments. If we must take that course, we must forsake some of our allies and automatically reduce our international influence. Where would the withdrawal stop? In Fortress America? That was an empty dream of the past and is completely unattainable at a time when fast action, world-wide communications and transportation, and long-range striking power are not a monopoly of the Free World. We cannot live alone when the initiative and unmistakable means to impose their will upon less powerful states are in the hands of those who would destroy freedom.

As I turn now to assess our defensive measures as opposed to the counterstrike and the requirement for mobile, self-contained and self-sufficient forces to carry the fight to the enemy, I would like to paraphrase an old cliché. When offensive capabilities are equal, the best offense is a good defense. Certainly our most urgent requirement today is adequate defense against the nuclear-tipped ICBM.

The long-range missile has assumed fearsome proportions because it has not been intelligently evaluated for what it is, a man-made device capable of being defeated by a superior technology. Because we have allowed fear to dominate our reaction, our civil defense planning is thoroughly unrealistic, impractical and entirely contradictory to our national philosophy. The concept of mass evacuation of high-density population centers and the burial of our citizenry in deep shelters would negate any kind of positive reaction to attack. It would convert our people into a horde of rabbits scurrying for warrens where they would cower helplessly while waiting the coming of a conqueror.

Desperately we need a positive civil defense program that will teach the people how to react in emergency, how to fight panic, how to prevent chaos. They want to know how to do those things which are essential to national survival. That is the kind of positive action that would appeal to the American people. But in addition to this, why not plan boldly to defeat the menace itself? It may not be technically possible to construct an *absolute* defense against ballistic missile attacks, but I insist that we can develop a weapon of sufficient capability to tip the balance of power. When we can do something the aggressor cannot do, we shall have a positive deterrent.

As I have indicated several times in this book, in my opinion we have only one present answer to the more formidable ballistic missile threat. This is the Nike-Zeus, the antimissile system now in advanced development. It is the only conceivable and positive defense for the next decade. The lead time which must be expended in the genesis of any such complex weapon system compels me to conclude that no really new approach could be available for deployment prior to 1970. Meantime the inhabitants of our concentrated industrial centers are living under the dread shadow of the nuclear bomb, suspended only by the thin thread of an enemy's rationality.

Technically speaking, based upon my personal knowledge, I can assure the reader that the immediate and discernible problem of straightforward defense against ordinary ballistic missiles is fully in hand. I am likewise convinced that additional defense against more sophisticated weapons that may be developed can and will be solved at least as fast as they can be brought against us.

Too much time has been wasted in arguing the need for demonstrating the full effectiveness of the Zeus system before initiating the production of scarce components. The fundamental issue has been submerged in a controversy between military and civilian judgment. It can be stated in the simplest terms. Are we to make any effort to defend the major cities of the country against ballistic missiles during the next ten years? I say that we cannot afford to delay any longer in ordering Zeus into production and deployment. I certainly would not care to have on my conscience the responsibility for withholding affirmative decision.

Another area where we are lagging badly is the field of advanced research. The philosophy of rushing blindly ahead on the basis of "not knowing it can't be done" will only work once in a millennium in the missile field, and the price in time and money of trying things that way is higher than we can afford. For that reason, if we are wise, we will devote ample resources to forward-looking theoretical and small-scale research. We are doing far too little of that today, and as a result the future is not being penetrated in advance of the need for new solutions. As von Braun so aptly puts it, "We are not collecting seed corn for next year's crop."

It often seems to me that this preoccupation of the entire government with specific hardware development projects is the inevitable result of a system of budgetary management that puts final decisions in the hands of the accountants of the Bureau of the Budget. What they cannot understand, they will not allow funds to accomplish. They do understand the description of a definite missile or space development, to be accomplished in a definite number of years, and to accomplish a specific thing when finished. They do not understand research and component development that has for its purpose finding a solution to a foreseeable problem, unless the problem is as specific and recognizable as cancer of the lung.

Yet failure to devote a substantial part of our resources to just such research leaves the Armed Services with a real dilemma. They cannot get budgetary funds unless they can describe a product. But if they can in fact describe the product, and know all the answers to the technical problems before they start, it is an odds-on probability that the resulting weapon will be obsolete, or at least obsolescent, before it is available.

If, as is often done, the military men confidently describe a proposed weapon or system, knowing all the time that success depends upon finding some presently unknown and unproven solutions to foreseeable problems, the results can be disastrous. If the hoped for solution is found *not* to work, the project is delayed, costs soar, and eventually the nation finds itself once again with a weapon that is obsolete before it is ready.

Such was the fate of the Navajo, which finally had to be scrapped after hundreds of millions had been spent. If the weapon could have come out on the original time scale, it would have been timely and effective. But to be successful, the Navajo required the solution of difficult problems to which the answers were unknown or only dimly calculated when development started. The answers could not be found nearly so fast as had been anticipated. By the time these essential research problems neared solution it was too late, and by the time the weapon could have been made ready it would have been vulnerable to the missile defenses of a nation far less advanced than the Russians.

To hedge this problem, many advanced projects must resort to duplication in the development of essential parts of the system. Two or more different approaches to solution of the problem must be pursued, so that if either is successful the project can proceed on schedule. This too is expensive, since the experiments to find a solution must be carried on with costly full-scale hardware

—there is no time for exhaustive laboratory investigation—and finally the attempts to find a solution are themselves limited in scope, for the result must fit into a missile or weapon system already being set into the concrete of tooling and hardware.

It is a fact, but apparently totally incomprehensible to the nontechnical administrator, that *in the long run* we could get better weapons, sooner, at less cost, if we devoted major research effort to finding and solving the included problems before we ever started to describe, much less develop, a new weapon system. Instead, the funds available for supporting research within the Defense budget have steadily gone downhill. Given the small Army budget to begin with, they have almost disappeared in the weapon portion of Army Research and Development.

I apologize for hammering so hard on this point, but I think it is impossible to overemphasize the critical importance of this type of research. Unless we collect more seed corn, as Wernher said, our harvest is likely to be a very disappointing one. We had better start collecting it soon.

As I said at the beginning of this book, I believe the one best way to assure success, to eliminate duplication and waste, is to unify the entire missile and space effort. It is the only guarantee against failure and the only protection against the possibility of bankrupting the country as the proportions of current and projected spending in the enormously costly retaliatory capability portend. If they are to be truly unified, the missile and space programs, military and civilian, should be placed within the framework of the Department of Defense. It should be entirely logical to establish a Joint Command to which should be entrusted the undivided responsibility for directing the major missile and space activities. This would permit maximum utilization of the expert talent and the unique facilities administered by the three Services. The scientific community could be represented at the command level. Thus we could align individual and national objectives, and the over-all program would benefit from a joint and co-ordinated approach.

In summary, then, let me restate my conclusions concerning the state of our national defense:

We already possess or have committed to production more than adequate retaliatory capability to inflict unacceptable damage upon a potential enemy.

We are needlessly wasting resources in the duplication and enlargement of that capability at the expense of more useful and therefore more important objectives.

We have abjectly failed to recognize the urgency of providing the only visible means by which to protect our major centers of population, and our counter-strike power, against the threat of nuclear missile attack.

We have largely ignored the immediate requirement to provide self-sufficient forces with adequate mobility to deal with the likelier threats of less-than-total aggression.

We are earmarking insufficient funds for advanced research.

Excesses in the massive retaliatory capability, and shortcomings in other forms of military power instantly available for use, have endangered the nation's security and vitiated the Free World's collective strength.

Compromise and expediency dictated by pressure groups have adversely affected our defense posture.

The splintering of the missile and space programs has delayed progress at enormous cost and lowered our international prestige.

None of these problems is incurable. Timely, intelligent and forceful decisions still can undo much of the mischief, though they cannot recover lost time or squandered resources. The cure lies within us and it can be applied through the normal processes of democratic government.

But to bring this cure about, our people must awaken to the obligations and duties of citizenship at this time when other free men look to them for leadership. They must recognize that they are citizens of America first, and that selfish or local interests, or the special requirements of any one group, must take second place. They must fully understand the nature of the total threat to their security and to their freedom, and recognize that this threat is by no means limited to the military sphere. Selfishness, softness, and disinterest can be just as deadly to America's future as any lack of military power.

The crises of these times demand patriotism of the highest order. If our people understand this, I have no doubt that they will rise fully to the occasion and demonstrate—as they have in the past—that the strength of free men is far superior to that of any system of slavery.

CHAPTER XXIII

The Summing Up

As everyone knows, old soldiers never die, they just fade away—sometimes into industry, sometimes between the covers of a book. Before I disappear from these pages altogether, I should like to summarize some of my basic personal convictions about the troubled but fascinating world in which we live.

As I said in the beginning, I believe the broadest and most important question facing us today is simply this: Can mankind learn to control, and direct to constructive purposes, the tremendous forces that science and technology have made available? This question is first and most important for the simple reason that if it cannot be affirmatively answered, the other tormenting problems of our age will be of no consequence. Mankind will go down to destruction at worst, or slavery at best, and there will be few if any problems at all.

Politically, we live in a rapidly shrinking world. The technological advances of the last fifty years, particularly in transportation and communication, have so compressed space and time that watertight political compartments are becoming impossible. To paraphrase Abraham Lincoln slightly, "This planet cannot endure half slave and half free." It will become all one thing, or all the other.

This great contest of our time is really a religious struggle. It is a clash between the concept of man as born in the image of God and therefore having individual dignity and individual responsibility, and the concept of man as the servant and slave of a monolithic state where his personal welfare may be sacrificed as the leader of the moment may consider necessary.

This contest is so widespread that elements of the battle appear in all fields—military, economic, psychological, diplomatic and ethical. For the same reason—the all-encompassing nature of the contest—the battle cannot be won by military means alone. But military power is one vital element of a nation's strength, and we neglect it at our peril.

As I have indicated, I am afraid that in our preoccupation with "massive retaliation" as the best shield against attack, we may have gotten ourselves into a position where we have only the butcher's axe available to us while the surgeon's scalpel is not in our kit of tools. As things stand today we have no shield, only a flaming sword. We cannot delay and evaluate, we can only strike. We have shoved all the poker chips of human civilization into the middle of the table, but if our bet is called and we must show our hand, there can be no winners—only losers.

I believe it is far past time for a complete, basic, and searching re-examination of our military policy, and for the application of the best brains available to the task of determining by what means this nation's military strength can be brought to a type and a quantity consistent with our national morality and our Christian heritage. I trust we will be granted the time to do so.

In the international economic area we face another and equally serious challenge—the challenge of the underprivileged peoples of the world. Here we are in danger of being deluded by our own good intentions and our satisfaction with our own way of life. We seem to want to wave a wand and *make* people better off, rather than help them to *become* better off, preserving their dignity and enhancing their sense of accomplishment and responsibility. Yet the final victory in this great conflict must depend upon bringing to all people a sense of personal dignity, the education essential to future progress, and the personal independence that can only come through personal productivity.

It seems to me that in this global struggle ethics, international morality, and religion are all so closely interrelated as to be the warp and woof of the same cloth. Without religion there can be no real sense of morality and no compulsion to ethical conduct. Thus it is impossible to conceive of a sound and stable international society, based on universal acceptance of government under stable law, without the fullest acceptance by the majority in all nations of faith in a Divine Power upon whose authority the laws of man are based. Called by whatever name, a belief in God is the only possible foundation for a world at peace. The alternative is the division of the peoples of the earth into strong armed encampments, threatened by destruction at every tick of the clock.

Since we have no intention of ramming our beliefs down the throats of the world by force, we can only convey the knowledge of the benefits and virtues of the free way of life to the uninformed through creating the strong impression in their minds that we are friends worth having, and leaders worth following. This emphasizes, among other things, that we must win the space race.

Outstanding feats in outer space are today the greatest advertising medium the world has ever known. If we are to sell our product, our system of freely organized society, to the rest of the world and most particularly to the uncommitted nations, we *must* advertise our competence and our ability to protect our friends by demonstrated superiority in the penetration of this new and challenging environment. We cannot afford *not* to compete. We must put our energies into the competition determined to win, and we must admit that we are competing. So far I do not see either that admission or that determination. We seem to have been far more the "reluctant dragon," dragged in by our heels, and with only half our heart in our work. There are some signs, like the first faint harbingers of spring, that this attitude is changing, but the change is all too slow in making itself felt.

A concentrated and successful American effort in the space field—or the lack of one—will have far-reaching effects in almost every area of human concern. We can be constantly and reliably informed of any developing threats against our security or the peace of the world, or we can be totally blinded. We can command the means for certain and continuous communication with our resources and our friends all over the world, or be hampered and delayed by restricted and vulnerable channels. We can spearhead the conquest of new frontiers and the penetration of the farther reaches of the solar system, guiding those energies along the paths of peaceful progress, or we can sit by and see the skies dominated by the instruments of a godless and destructive philosophy of human slavery. We can capitalize on the inevitable by-products of advancing science, using them to the benefits of the free peoples of the world, or we can watch those by-products and that new knowledge rigidly disciplined to support the destructive aims of the communist ideology. All of these choices are inherent in our decision to regain and maintain supremacy in space, or to pursue a casual and purely theoretical program just to keep our hand in.

This much is certain. We can avoid disaster and assure success only if we develop and maintain the discipline and determination domestically that will strengthen the hand and harden the will of those engaged on the international field of battle. There are tough problems to be solved, and in our form of society they can only be handled if the great majority of our people recognize the need, and have the intelligence, the will, and the spirit of sacrifice for the common good without which a government by the directly expressed will of a majority of the people must weaken and eventually die.

We can begin with education—and I do not mean training. I mean rather the type of broad and thoroughly grounded educational experience that alone fits the individual to handle the wholly new problems of society and government in an age when change is the order of the day.

Any change is a threat to someone, or some group of individuals. Society cannot be all things to all people. If the rights of a minority are overprotected, the rights of the majority are impaired. If technology and automation increase the potential production of material things and thus raise the over-all standard of living, they also threaten the immediate economic security of those who are face to face with their own technological obsolescence.

These conflicts mean that at least a majority of our citizens must have a sufficiently broad education, and a full enough understanding of the roots and foundations upon which the whole thesis of government by the people and for the people has been erected, and a strong enough feeling that liberty is worth the price it costs, that they will set aside their personal and individual selfish ends and aims to insist upon governmental decisions that are best for the *whole* of our society. It is not in terms of hard daily toil, or of higher taxes, or of any other direct sacrifice that America demands the best of her people. It is rather in the understanding willingness to set aside personal considerations and stand up for that which represents the greatest good for our nation taken as a whole society. It is, in other words, the opposite of pressure-group government.

Time is running out. The dominant position of technology demands that our youth be educated at least to a rudimentary understanding of science and technology. Yet to answer the first great question posed at the beginning of this chapter, there must be a growth of real and broad education. Our people, young and old, must relearn the values of the old virtues: that self-discipline is the first element of character; that what is given is without value, and that only what is earned is worth while; that leisure is not an objective in itself, but only a means to allow for broader and more productive activities in partnership with our fellows; that virtue is an asset and not a liability; that principle is more important than expediency; and finally, that this nation was conceived under God, and will continue to prosper only with His favor.

We must have an end to special favors for the few at the expense of the many. We must realize that the "hand-out" costs us all. We must know that there is no miracle by which money or resources are created without cost, that no matter how the pie is cut, there will never be any more to divide among us than the total production of our people. And finally, there must be full realization of the basic fact that there is no evil in nature or the intricate devices of man's creation, except as man himself may use them to evil purpose.

What are the problems of the space age? I believe they are the problems of humanity itself, in the age-old struggle between good and evil, made more important and more demanding by the accelerating progress of science and technology.

Can a democratic form of government survive? That was the question, asked me that February day in Washington, that brought purpose and focus to my decision to write this book. Can democracy compete with the single-minded and autocratically directed forces of evil that would turn back the clock of human progress? I firmly believe that we can survive, and that we can compete, but only if we can revive and rejuvenate the spirit of unity and of dedication to Christian principles that upheld our forefathers through the privations of the revolution, the Gethsemane of Valley Forge, and the conquest of the wilderness.

To acquire the wisdom demanded if man is to control the machines he has devised, to set the welfare of the nation ahead of self-interest and to inspire others to do likewise, to rededicate one's self to the principles and to the faith of our founding fathers and lead others to unite in the common effort . . . these are the *direct* and *immediate personal obligations* of every man and woman who has prospered under this system of government.

So long as we face up to these responsibilities, freedom will not perish from the earth.

Epilogue

August, 1960

The clock is still ticking—insistently. Six months have passed since I laid aside my uniform, and the tempo of events seems to increase steadily. Interspersed with a few scattered bright spots, the pattern seems to turn steadily darker. Almost every day brings some symbol of the fact that the task of seizing the initiative from the forces of evil, discord, and destruction becomes steadily more difficult.

A few days ago I had lunch with Wernher von Braun and Dr. Bill Pickering. The talk, naturally, centered on the space race. After many months the problem of the upper stages for Saturn has again been "finally resolved." Almost exactly one year after the first solution was approved by Mr. Roy Johnson of ARPA, and our round of difficulties really began, there is a new solution, this time backed with money. But the time lost cannot be made up. If we look at the situation only in the light of today, the solution looks good. The upper stages that have been approved will use more advanced power plants, and yield greater performance than could have been achieved with our original plan. *But,* the original plan would have given us a flying multistage Saturn at least a year earlier than can now be achieved. The pursuit of perfection has again proven the truth of the old Russian adage, that "the Perfect is the enemy of the Good," and more time has been lost in the race.

I was particularly amused at Wernher's comments on the static test firings of the Saturn, which began about April 29th and have been repeated numerous times since. Several full-duration, full-power tests of all eight engines have been completed. I asked Wernher how it was going. His answer provides a good insight into the philosophy of an experienced missile-man. "Too good," said Wernher. "We have had no difficulties at all, and I am scared to death that the percentages will catch up with us later." I tried to reassure him, reminding him that accumulated experience was sure to change the "percentage" in his favor.

Bill Pickering's major interest at the Jet Propulsion Lab is directed toward advanced work on payloads for lunar and far-out interplanetary exploration. We noted with great personal interest a recent report from the House Committee on Science and Astronautics dealing with the possibilities of establishing a manned expedition on the moon. The U. S. Army Corps of Engineers had produced detailed plans for such an operation. Sardonically amusing was the fact that these plans carefully avoided any consideration of the vehicles to be used to get the men and materials to and from the lunar outpost, although we knew that the material presented had originally been a carefully co-ordinated part of a complete Army plan for the establishment of a lunar outpost. The plan had been produced over a year ago, but had been shot down in flames by the assignment of all space vehicles to the Air Force. Nevertheless, we were very happy to see some attention being paid to the subject even at this late date.

As we ranged over the whole field of vehicles and payloads—satellites, lunar expeditions, interplanetary probes, advanced propulsion systems and communication with and control of instruments in the far-out reaches of the solar system—I could not avoid the personal notation that not a single item considered was totally devoid of present or future military implications. Yet these great men and their fine organizations are debarred from considering those implications, and carefully fenced off from co-operative work on any military objective! Truly an Alice-in-Wonderland approach.

I am reminded of the events following the successful launching of Tiros, the meteorological satellite. When the first pictures of "cloud cover" were released to the public, the intelligent American press seized on the obvious and asked questions as to the capability of the satellite to take intelligence-type ground pictures. Dr. Glennan was in a very difficult position, and his efforts to justify the division of the indivisible, and to deny either military implications or military capabilities, were certainly amusing. For our nation, the hard fact remains that two separate satellite photographic projects must be pursued which, if operated under single direction, could be accomplished in less time and with less money.

Considering the happenings of the past six months gives me no cause to change any of the conclusions I have expressed earlier. In fact, the central thread of events seems to add emphasis and urgency to the two major problems of streamlining the decision-making process, and seizing the initiative in the field of foreign policy. Russian activities have certainly underlined many of my observations. Following their success in hitting the moon, and then photographing the back side of it, there was a long period of quiet without visible demonstration of progress. Renewal of activity with a satellite carrying (according to the Russian statement) a capsule with a dummy man aboard reaffirms the conclusion that they intend not to repeat successes, but to go forward in a series of major jumps. The statement that there was no intention of attempting recovery of the capsule was an obvious cover plan, and strictly untruthful. It saved them the necessity for explaining failure when attitude control failed, separation was delayed, and rockets intended to check the speed of the capsule and return it to earth worked in reverse and actually pushed their "dummy" further out into space.

Meantime emphasis had been added to the certainty of Russian capability by additional long-range shots into the Pacific—shots called in advance with accuracy as to time and place. While assumedly demonstrating Russian long-range missile capabilities, those shots could well have been confirmation tests for an improved space vehicle.

Certainly we can expect a repetition of the capsule recovery effort, with the probability that the second or third try will succeed, and be followed very shortly by a man (or men) in orbit.

In the field of military weapons there have been many occurrences, some Russian, and some in our own programs, that are deserving of careful and objective evaluation. The U-2 was shot down over Russia. The big noise was in the political field, but underlying implications must not be overlooked. It is vital that we not kid ourselves, and that we avoid the most fatal error in military intelligence—underestimating the enemy. Those who advance the fact of the U-2 penetration deep into Russian territory as proof of Russian vulnerability ignore the probability that it took some time for the Kremlin to decide to attack, and transmit the necessary orders. Those who advance the possibility of engine trouble having caused the vehicle to descend, and only thus make it vulnerable, are kidding themselves and doing the country a disservice. The fact is that our own Hercules has destroyed a target at 100,000 feet, and we have no reason or excuse for assuming that the Russians can do less. There are, in fact, ample indications of the existence of advanced Russian air defense missile systems. In fact, I am personally convinced that the Russians are far along toward the development of an antimissile missile system, which naturally brings up the subject of the Nike-Zeus.

Without regard to the numbers possessed by each, which for reasons expressed earlier I consider to be of lesser importance, there is no question but that both the United States and Russia possess both a medium- and long-range nuclear missile capability, extending to full intercontinental distance. It should be obvious that the first possessor of a defensive capability of any reasonable effectiveness will thoroughly upset this uneasy balance of power in the area of strategic deterrence and retaliatory capability. That such a defense is at least a possibility has been amply proven (to those willing to take note) by Hercules' recent success in defeating a Corporal ballistic missile in a straightforward test of attack and defense. Thus it has been proven that "a bullet *can* hit a bullet." Zeus development proceeds on schedule. In spite of this, and of the vital need of the country for such a defense, and in the face of strong Congressional support for the Nike-Zeus, the program is held back, strangled, and impeded in almost every conceivable fashion. Money repeatedly voted by the Congress for a start toward deployment has not been released for use. Quite a noise was made not long ago about the release of a supposed 25 million dollars for further engineering studies in preparation for production. In fact, added money was *not* released, but the Army was told that it could apply up to that amount *if* it could find the money or divert it from other Army needs! As I write this I have been unable to find any confirmation that any of the amount has yet been made available for actual use.

Meantime even the rules are being rigged to make it more difficult for Zeus to prove its case. The Army's plea for permission to set up intermediate-range missiles as targets for the system during its first tests in the Kwajalein area has been denied, and the system must be tested *only* against full-range IRBM's fired from the West Coast. This is like throwing a promising young heavyweight into the ring against Floyd Patterson for his first fight! No opportunity is allowed for the proper and logical approach of starting with the easier and moving to the more difficult, as the inevitable "bugs" are ironed out. Win the championship on the first fight, in the first round, or back to the bench! Meantime our cities remain undefended, and the possibility exists that successful development of a missile defense by our enemies could free them from the threat of retaliation and open the door to our destruction.

Our own Atlas program has slipped, though perhaps not seriously. The Air Launched Ballistic Missile (ALBM) is on contract for development, but nothing has been reduced or eliminated as a result. Thus we now have at least *six* programs for strategic nuclear weapons not requiring foreign bases—Atlas, Titan, Titan II, Minuteman, Polaris, and the ALBM—but no effective support for a defense against such weapons. There has been considerable publicity about "mobility tests" for the Minuteman system, and these bring to the mind of the professional military logistician a significant question. A mobile weapon system must be supported by a mobile logistic system. When the Air Force abandons its bases and moves into the field of mobile ground-launched weapons, must we now expect to see the development of another system of logistic support, duplicating that already available to the Army?

A new field of inter-project rivalry has developed within the last several months, as Polaris and Pershing meet in competition for the privilege of filling an important NATO need for a mobile missile. Polaris offers to convert a missile designed for submarine launching to a land mobile weapon, as if such a task were utterly simple. It is not simple. In fact, to adapt Polaris to the rough and ready life of a field soldier presents problems almost equivalent to those involved in the development of a whole new system. Pershing offers to extend its range to that required by NATO, a range in excess of Pershing's current capabilities. Extension of the Pershing range is, in fact, a very much easier task. The uniform success of the Pershing test program to date would argue strongly in favor of that solution. But of course we must be very careful not to let the Army get very far out into the long-range field or, who knows, they might suggest turning over the Jupiter and the Thor to Army control! For my part, I feel that the original mission of Polaris is so important that they would do much better to stick to their knitting and assure maximum success and reliability for that mission. The fact that a few missiles have been successfully launched from the first Polaris-class submarine does not mean that there still isn't a lot of work to assure full and uncompromised success.

It is not easy to be a critic, in spite of the platitude to the contrary. All critics are self-appointed, since man by nature does not like to be told that he is wrong. However, I believe strongly with John Erskine that "we have a moral obligation to be intelligent," and I have no desire to be either unintelligent or immoral. My choice, then, has of necessity been to be critical.

All the recent upsetting events in the international field should underline the broad range and unpredictability of possible military challenge. Vital military needs in space and on the ground clamor for attention, while we overspend on mass destruction. There is little apparent relationship between our foreign policy and our military posture, yet the whole military establishment is primarily the handmaiden of foreign policy and the base of support for our efforts in the field in international relations. Time is running out. I pray God our leaders can find the inspiration, the intelligence, and the moral courage to call "Hold," and repair the damage—correct the defects—before we are all engulfed in flames.